REASONING WITH RULES AND PRECEDENTS

A Computational Model of Legal Analysis

Reasoning with Rules and Precedents

A Computational Model of Legal Analysis

by:

L. Karl Branting

Department of Computer Science,
University of Wyoming,
Laramie, Wyoming, U.S.A.

SPRINGER-SCIENCE+BUSINESS MEDIA, B.V.

A C.I.P. Catalogue record for this book is available from the Library of Congress.

DOI 10.1007/978-94-017-2848-5

Printed on acid-free paper

Contents

List of Figures

List of Tables

Acknowledgments

This book has its origin in my 1991 Ph.D. dissertation, which proposed a computational framework for the integration of rules and cases for analytic tasks typified by legal analysis. The current volume updates this framework, sets forth a new model of legal precedent based upon the framework, and shows how this model satisfies key jurisprudential criteria for precedent-based legal reasoning.

Anne Gardner played a pivotal role in the research described in this book. The insights of Anne's seminal work on AI models of legal reasoning (Gardner, 1987) were the starting point of the path that this research has followed. Far down this path, Anne again made a key contribution, providing an extremely cogent, insightful, and constructive critique of the text of this book, particularly the more controversial portions of Chapter 3.

I am indebted to Bruce Porter for his advice, criticism, and encouragement during my years at the University of Texas at Austin Artificial Intelligence Laboratory. I am also indebted to my wife Susan, and to my son Eric, whose curiosity, sense of humor, and companionship have made each day we've shared a fresh joy.

Support for the research described in this book was provided by grants from the Army Research Office (ARO-DAAG29-84-K-0060) and the National Science Foundation (IRI-8620052), and by contributions from Apple Corporation, Texas Instruments, the Cray Foundation, and Hughes Research Laboratories, and from NSF CAREER grant IRI-9502152.

1 INTRODUCTION

A rule qua *rule is detached, it stands as it were alone in its glory; although what gives it importance is the facts of daily experience.*
—Ludwig Wittgenstein (Wittgenstein, 1958).

General propositions do not decide concrete cases.
—Oliver Wendell Holmes (Holmes, 1906).

The goal of this research is to develop a model for problem solving that integrates general rules with specific examples. Developing such a model is important because neither rules nor examples, standing alone, are sufficient for problem solving in many important domains. Few areas of human expertise are so well understood that problem solving is reducible to deduction from general principles. Similarly, there are few domains in which experience is so extensive that every new problem precisely matches a previous problem whose solution is known. When neither rules nor examples are individually sufficient, problem-solving expertise depends on integrating both.

Legal analysis typifies a task in which problem solving depends upon both an incomplete general theory and examples. A lawyer familiar only with the literal text of legal rules but ignorant of any examples of their use would be critically handicapped in the tasks of making, anticipating, and evaluating arguments. Much of the expertise of an experienced lawyer comes not from knowledge of legal rules themselves, but from familiarity with examples of the use of rules for argumentation, planning, and adjudication. The dependence of expert performance in law on both rules and examples makes law an ideal domain for illustrating and evaluating models for integrating general and specific knowledge sources.

1.1 Classification and Explanation in Weak-Theory Domains

A central component of intelligent problem solving is the ability to determine whether a given set of facts is an instance of a category relevant to the goals of the problem solver. For example, planning requires determining whether the result of a sequence of operator applications is an instance of the category of goal states. Medical diagnosis requires determining whether the physiological state of a patient exhibiting certain symptoms is an instance of a given disease category. Legal analysis requires determining whether a given set of facts is an instance of a category of events having legal consequences, such as negligence, breach of contract, or employment-related accidents. Determining whether an entity is an instance of a category is the task of *classification.* Classification can be viewed either as determining whether a set of facts is an instance of a category or as determining whether it satisfies the predicate corresponding to that category. This follows from the duality between categories and predicates: for every category there is a corresponding predicate that is true for a set of facts only if the entity is a member of the category; conversely, for every predicate there is a corresponding category consisting of those sets of facts that satisfy the predicate. These two characterizations of classification, which correspond to intensional and extensional characterizations of a category, respectively, are used interchangeably throughout this book.

In the context of the classification task, an *explanation* or *argument* is a collection of reasoning steps that justifies the classification of a set of facts, or *case.*[1] Explanations are important for several reasons. First, verifying a classification requires evaluating the reasoning that supports it. Thus, a classification is credible only to the extent that its explanation is persuasive. Second, explanations can be used to persuade others to accept a particular classification. Third, past explanations can be used to assist in classifying subsequent cases. Finally, weaknesses in an explanation suggest additional facts whose acquisition could resolve classification uncertainty. In problem-solving contexts

[1]The terms *explanation* and *argument* are treated as synonymous in this book. However, the term "explanation" is preferred when referring to the justification for a single unique conclusion, whereas "argument" is preferred when referring to a justification for one of several inconsistent conclusions.

in which these factors are important, a classification must be accompanied by an explanation to be useful.

Knowledge for problem solving in a domain is called the *theory* of the domain. A domain theory may include both general rules and *exemplars*, specific past cases with known classifications. A conclusion about a case is justified by a rule if all the antecedents of the rule have explanations under the facts of the case. This form of justification has been termed ***rule-based reasoning***. Similarly, a conclusion about a case can be justified by the similarity of the case to an exemplar to which the conclusion applied. This form of justification is termed ***case-based reasoning*** (Aamodt and Plaza, 1994, Kolodner, 1993).[2]

If a domain theory contains sufficient rules to precisely define the conditions for category membership, determining a classification is a deductive process and the explanation of a classification is a proof. For example, in artificial domains such as mathematics and chess, precise definitions can be given for concepts such as "prime number" and "knight fork."

In most areas of human expertise, by contrast, precise conditions for category membership are difficult or impossible to determine. Diagnostic categories, for example, often reflect physiological processes that are only imperfectly understood or in which there is high variability. Membership in functional or goal-oriented categories, such as "chair," "friend," or "things to carry out of the house in the event of a fire," is highly dependent on context and human intentions. The absence of precise conditions for membership in such categories has been termed *polymorphy* (Rosch and Mervis, 1975), *graded category structure* (Lakoff, 1987), or *open texture* (Hart, 1961). Open-textured, graded category structure, and polymorphic categories are characteristic of *weak* domain theories (Porter et al., 1990).

The absence of precise, tractable methods for determining category membership in weak-theory domains can give rise to arguments both for membership of a case in a given category and for membership in the category's *contrast set* or complement. Under these circumstances, the task of classification requires determining the strongest and most persuasive argument. Even if it is impossible to determine with certainty whether the stronger argument is for or against category membership, simply knowing the strongest arguments for each position is nevertheless often very useful.

In weak domain theories that include both rules and cases, the strongest argument that can be made for a classification may draw on both of these knowledge sources, since neither is individually sufficient. Classification in weak-theory domains therefore requires the ability to construct and evaluate explanations involving both rule-based and case-based reasoning. Law exempli-

[2]The term "case-based reasoning" refers to two related but distinct problem-solving methods: reasoning with exemplars; and reuse of sequences of problem-solving operators or configurations. Legal analysis entails the first form of case-based reasoning. For a representative application of case-based reasoning for reuse of operator sequences, see (Veloso, 1992). For a discussion of a number of applications of case-based reasoning to legal problem-solving tasks other than legal analysis, *see* (Ashley, 1993).

fies a domain in which classification requires constructing and evaluating such explanations.

1.2 The Task of Legal Analysis

Attorneys engage in a variety of professional activities, including legal planning, advocacy, and adjudication. Central to all of these activities is the task of determining whether an actual or hypothetical case is an instance of a legal category. For example, legal planning requires anticipating the legal classifications of the situations resulting from each possible course of action (Sanders, 1994). Advocacy consists of propounding arguments in favor of a particular legal consequence and against alternative consequences. Adjudication requires weighing competing arguments for and against particular classifications. The task of determining and explaining the legal classification of a set of facts has been termed *legal analysis* (Meldman, 1975).[3]

Explanations play a central role in legal analysis. In advocacy, explanations are used as arguments in support of a given conclusion. Planning requires evaluating the explanations of the possible legal consequences of various courses of action. Explanations are used in adjudication to justify the resolution of legal disputes.

The principal knowledge sources for legal analysis are legal rules and legal *precedents*, previously decided cases. Precedents can function as exemplars in case-based reasoning.[4] There are several types of legal rules, including *statutory rules*, which are enactments of federal, state, and local legislative bodies, *common-law rules*, which are enunciated by appellate courts, as well as constitutions, treaties, and regulations. *Legal precedents* are past cases in which a court resolved a legal dispute. The binding effect of legal precedents on subsequent cases is embodied in the doctrine of *stare decisis*,[5] which holds that when a point of law has been settled by a judicial decision, it is not ordinarily to be departed from afterward. The propositions set forth in a precedent that are binding as to subsequent cases are termed the *ratio decidendi* of the precedent.[6] The facts and reasoning of precedent cases are recorded in published judicial opinions. Judicial opinions are indexed in various restatements, compendia, and treatises so that other attorneys can use them as a guide for the analysis and adjudication of subsequent cases.

In addition to legal rules and precedents, other factors such as general conceptions of justice and fair play (*e.g.*, "No man may profit from his own wrong") can sometimes play an important role in legal analysis. It has been argued that such general principles differ from legal rules in that contradictory principles

[3] Meldman's definition of legal analysis was "the logical derivation of a legal conclusion from a particular factual situation in the light of some body of legal doctrine."

[4] However, as argued below in Chapters 2 and 3, legal precedents typically have a complex internal structure comprising multiple exemplars.

[5] *Stare decisis* is an abbreviation for *stare decisis et non quieta movere*, meaning "to stand by precedents and not to disturb settled points."

[6] The complexities of determining just what these propositions consist of are explored in Chapter 3.

may simultaneously apply to the same case (Dworkin, 1977). However, there is little consensus as to precisely how the relationship between principles, on the one hand, and legal rules and precedents, on the other, should be modeled.

There is a broad consensus that legal analysis does not consist solely of deduction (McCarty and Sridharan, 1982, Gardner, 1987, Burton, 1985, Moore, 1981). Legal rules typically contain abstract, open-textured antecedents that are not operational in terms of the facts of new cases. For example, the applicability of legal rules for liability or guilt depends on whether abstract, general predicates like "reasonable care," "malice," or "activity in furtherance of employment" are satisfied by the facts of a case. However, the facts of a case are typically expressed as detailed descriptions of specific actions and events. The gap between abstract predicates appearing in rule antecedents and the concrete facts of specific cases gives rise to uncertainty about whether the predicates are satisfied.

Case-based reasoning is a central technique for reasoning about open-textured legal predicates (Ashley, 1993, Rissland, 1990). The applicability of an open-textured predicate to a new case can be analyzed by comparing the facts of the case to those of precedent cases in which the truth value of the predicate was determined by a previous court, or to uncontroversial hypothetical cases (Burton, 1985, Christie, 1969, Feinman, 1989). Case-based reasoning is thus complementary to rule-based reasoning in that it is necessary when the rules "run out" (Gardner, 1987).

While case-based reasoning addresses the uncertainty that arises from the difference in abstraction between open-textured rule antecedents and new-case facts, it is itself subject to a different form of uncertainty. A new case invariably is different in some respects from any given past case. Determining the controlling case requires determining the relevance and significance of the similarities and differences between the new case and past cases (Murray, 1982).

Various factors are important for assessing the degree of match between cases. The significance of similarities and differences between cases is determined in part by the "normative purposes, policies, or principles" underlying the specific area of the law (Burton, 1985). The explanations of past cases also serve as a guide to comparison to future cases (Murray, 1982, Golding, 1980, Stoljar, 1980).

Thus, general knowledge and specific cases are mutually dependent in legal analysis. The primary expression of legal doctrine, in many areas of the law, is in the form of legal rules. However, case-based reasoning is often necessary for determining the applicability of open-textured rule antecedents to specific cases. Case-based reasoning depends, in turn, on general explanatory knowledge for assessing the degree of relevant similarity between cases.

Law is a domain in which the necessity of integrating both rules and cases for problem solving is thoroughly institutionalized and extensively documented (Rissland, 1988). Law libraries contain vast quantities of written legal judgments justified in part by general legal rules and principles and in part by analogy to earlier cases.

1.3 Research Goals

This book demonstrates how rule-based reasoning and case-based reasoning can be used as complementary processes for classification and explanation in legal analysis. The next chapter sets forth a framework for integrating rules and exemplars. Under this framework, rules and exemplars differ primarily in that exemplars are much less abstract than rules. Exemplars can therefore provide a bridge between abstract rule antecedents and specific case descriptions. However, rule-based reasoning is often necessary to determine whether an exemplar matches a new case. Two mechanisms—case elaboration and term reformulation—are described for using rules to improve matching.

Chapter 3 describes a formal model of the *ratio decidendi* of legal precedents based on the framework set forth in Chapter 2 and demonstrates how this model, termed the *reduction-graph* model, satisfies an important set of characteristics of *ratio decidendi* identified in the jurisprudential literature. In particular, the model shows how the theory under which a case is decided controls its precedential effect.

Chapter 4 presents an implementation of the framework for integrating rule-based reasoning and case-based reasoning in GREBE (Generator of Recursive Exemplar-Based Explanations), a system for legal analysis in the domain of Texas workers' compensation law. This implementation includes a semantic-network representation for cases that satisfies two key requirements for legal analysis: First, the representation is *extensible*, that is, expressive enough to express arbitrary sequences of actions. The facts of a case constitute a narrative or story, and a fundamental characteristic of true stories is that their details can never be precisely anticipated. The second criterion of representational adequacy is *expressiveness*, the ability to represent case facts in sufficient detail to express all legally relevant aspects of the case. The most effective legal arguments are those that are grounded in the particular facts of the given cases. Such arguments can be produced only to the extent that the specific case facts on which they are based can be represented.

However, the representational complexity needed to satisfy the extensibility and expressiveness requirements comes at the price of increased retrieval and matching costs.[7] Chapter 4 presents techniques for retrieval and matching that address this increased complexity.

Examples of analysis by GREBE are set forth in Chapter 5. Chapter 6 contains an evaluation in which GREBE's analysis of 18 hypothetical cases was compared to the analysis of the same hypotheticals by law students and an empirical evaluation of several algorithms for structured case retrieval. Chapter 7 sets forth related work, and the contributions of the GREBE project are described in Chapter 8.

Only a few small corners of human knowledge and experience have yielded to axiomization. Surrounding them is a vast jungle of incomplete explanatory and causal theories populated by exception-ridden rules and partially understood examples. Problem solving in this environment requires the ability to improvise the best explanations possible from profuse but weak resources. This book represents an effort to model the process whereby two weak knowledge sources—rules with nonoperational antecedents and partially understood exemplars—can be integrated to produce expert performance in a domain that is challenging even for human experts. It therefore represents an effort to accommodate computational methods to the untidy environment of human problem solving rather than domesticating that environment to fit our formal biases.

1.4 Terminology

In this book the term "relation" refers to any predicate of arity at least 2. Both atomic sentences formed by applying n-ary predicates to n-tuples of terms, and sentences formed by applying truth functional operators to atomic sentences are referred to as "facts," "propositions," or "conclusions." "Fact" is preferred for sentences known or assumed to be true, whereas "proposition" and "conclusion" are preferred for sentences whose truth value may be at issue. Facts of a particular case are sometimes referred to as "attributes" or "features" of the case. The term "legal predicate" denotes a predicate appearing in a proposition that was at issue in a legal dispute or that determines the rights, obligations, or liabilities of one or more persons. A "tuple" is a LISP representation of an atomic sentence. A given collection of facts whose classification is at issue is usually referred to as the "new case," while a previous case used to assist in classifying a new case is referred to as an "exemplar." An exemplar that is a member of a category is termed an "instance exemplar," whereas an exemplar that is instead a member of a category's complement, or "contrast set," is termed a "noninstance exemplar." A legal case that has given rise to

[7] *See* (Branting, 1994b) for a discussion of the tradeoff between representational complexity and the costs of retrieval, matching, and problem formulation.

a judicial decision is termed a "precedent." A precedent is therefore a special form of exemplar, *i.e.*, an exemplar that arises from the resolution of a legal dispute. However, as discussed below, a legal precedent can often be viewed as comprising multiple exemplars.

The symbol $\Rightarrow$ is used in two distinct ways in this book:

1. To represent the relationship between the antecedents and consequent of a warrant, such as a rule, *e.g.*,

   duty $\wedge$ breach of that duty $\wedge$ injury $\Rightarrow$ negligence liability

2. To represent a *mapping*. A mapping from C_1 to C_2, denoted $M : C_1 \Rightarrow C_2$, is a set of ordered pairs $\{(s,t)|s \in O(C_1) \wedge t \in O(C_2)\}$, where $O(C_i)$ consists of the objects in case C_i.

2 A FRAMEWORK FOR INTEGRATING RULES AND EXEMPLARS

This chapter presents a framework for expressing the relationship between rules and exemplars. This framework permits weak-theory domains to be characterized as domains lacking a particular kind of abstraction knowledge. Exemplars compensate for this deficiency in abstraction knowledge by providing a bridge between abstract features and case descriptions. However, matching new cases with exemplars usually requires general domain rules. Thus, rules and exemplars are mutually supporting in weak-theory domains.

2.1 The Relationship between Rules and Exemplars

A rule is an expression of the connection between a set of conditions, or *antecedents*, and a conclusion, or *consequent*, justified by those conditions. For example, legal rules express the connection between legal predicates and conditions that can satisfy those predicates. In the following legal rule, the consequent is the legal predicate *negligence liability* and the three numbered antecedents are the conditions under which the negligence liability predicate is satisfied:

> A person is liable to another person for damages under negligence if (1) the first person owed a duty of reasonable care to the second, (2) the first person breached that duty, and (3) the breach was the proximate cause of the damages suffered by the second person.

An exemplar is a collection of facts to which a conclusion is known to apply. Thus, an exemplar also expresses a connection between a set of conditions and a conclusion justified by those conditions. For example, an exemplar of negligence might be the following:

> Dr. Jones failed to exercise reasonable medical care by counting sponges during surgery on Brown. As a result, a sponge was left in Brown, who developed peritonitis and required a second operation to remove the sponge.

The essential difference between rules and exemplars lies in the degree of generality of the antecedent conditions that justify the conclusion. In rules, these conditions are typically abstract, *e.g.,* "proximate cause," "duty of reasonable care," whereas in exemplars the conditions are very specific, *e.g.,* "Jones left a sponge in Brown's surgical incision." The language in which the concrete, specific, observable facts of a particular case are expressed is termed the ***case-description*** language. By contrast, the abstract terms that appear in rule antecedents but that do not appear in the case-description language are termed ***abstract features*** (Porter et al., 1990).

Although they differ in the generality of their conditions, rules and exemplars are alike in that each can be used to justify a conclusion in a new case that matches the conditions. If the connection between the conditions and the conclusion reflects a regularity within the domain, the same conclusion is justified in any new case that matches the same conditions. Thus, both rules and exemplars can act as ***warrants*** (Toulmin, 1958) for conclusions about new cases.

Warrants can be expressed at a variety of levels of abstraction. For example, warrants for negligence include the following:

- General rules (*e.g.*, an action is negligent if the actor fails to use reasonable care and the failure is the proximate cause of damages)
- Specific exemplars (*e.g.*, Dr. Jones was negligent because he left a sponge in Brown during surgery)
- Warrants at intermediate levels of abstraction (*e.g.*, a medical procedure is negligent if it fails to conform to the standard of reasonable care of the medical community and thereby injures a patient)

The relationship between warrants at different levels of generality can be expressed by ***reduction operators***. Each reduction operator expresses a taxonomic relationship between the antecedents of different warrants for the same conclusion (*e.g.,* breach of the standard of reasonable care of a medical community is a kind of failure to use reasonable care). In general, a reduction operator is a rule that connects a pair of descriptions at different levels of abstraction. A hierarchy of warrants for a given conclusion and the reduction operators that connect them is a problem-reduction graph termed a *warrant-reduction graph.*[1] Figure 2.1 illustrates a portion of a warrant-reduction graph for negligence. The least abstract warrants in such a graph are exemplars.

Reduction operators are themselves warrants, since they express the connection between an abstract feature and a set of conditions under which the abstract feature is satisfied. In particular, reduction operators that justify conclusions in terms of facts expressed in the case-description language (*e.g.,* failure to count sponges is a failure to conform to the standard of reasonable care of a medical community) are exemplars.

Establishing a conclusion about a new case requires matching the facts of the new case with the facts of some authoritative warrant for that conclusion. For example, if the authoritative pronouncements on negligence in a given jurisdiction were just those warrants shown in Figure 2.1, establishing negligence in a new case would require matching the antecedents of one of the warrants for negligence to the facts of the new case.

2.2 Exemplars Strengthen Weak Theories

Classification in Warrant-Reduction Graphs

In practice, reasoning systems explicitly represent only a small proportion of the warrants that could appear in each warrant-reduction graph. As a result, a path of inference steps often must be constructed from the facts of the new case to an explicit warrant. Such an inference chain constitutes an explanation for the conclusion.

For example, Figure 2.2 shows an explanation for conclusion C in new case NC given domain rules $AF \Rightarrow C$ and $NC \Rightarrow AF$. $AF \Rightarrow C$ permits conclusion C to be reduced to abstract feature AF. $NC \Rightarrow AF$, in turn, permits AF to be reduced to NC, which is given.

Inadequate Reduction Operators Lead to Weak Theories

A domain theory for classification is strong if for every category and new case there is a chain of sound inferences connecting the facts of the new case to an explicitly represented warrant for the category or for its complement, but not

[1] As explained in (Amarel, 1968) and (Barr and Feigenbaum, 1982), every reduction graph is isomorphic to a state-space graph.

Figure 2.1. A warrant-reduction graph consisting of four levels of warrants for negligence. Vertical arrows represent reduction operators expressing a taxonomic relationship between facts of warrants on different levels, *e.g.*, failing to count sponges during an operation is a kind of breach of reasonable medical care; the connection between failing to count sponges and peritonitis caused by an uncounted sponge is a kind of proximate cause.

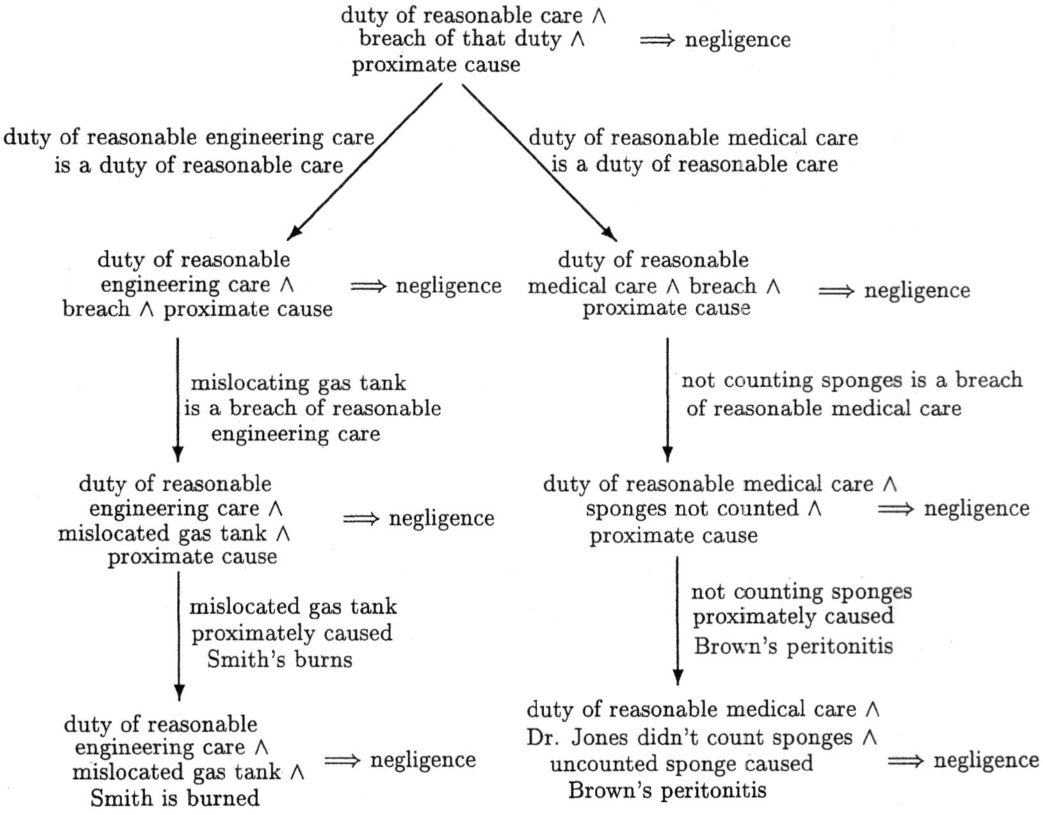

Figure 2.2. An inference path explaining conclusion C in new case NC. AF is an abstract feature.

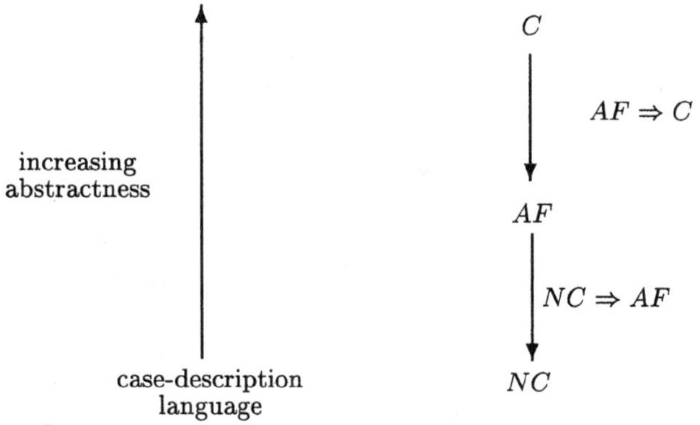

both, *i.e.*, if a sound explanation exists either for or against membership in the category. By contrast, a domain theory is weak if no such inference chain can be constructed (or if multiple inconsistent inference chains can be constructed) for some new cases and categories.

If the antecedents of rules for a given category contain abstract features, any inference path from a new case to the category must include reduction operators connecting the case-description language to those abstract features. If such reduction operators are inadequate or missing, no inference path can be constructed, and the theory is therefore weak.

For example, physiological states are abstract features of patients that determine diagnostic categories. However, the mechanisms connecting observable patient symptoms to physiological states are often only partially understood. The incompleteness of abstraction knowledge connecting patient symptoms to physiological states makes medicine a weak-theory domain.

A second form of inadequacy in reduction operators is intractability. For example, there are sufficient reduction operators to connect the abstract feature "white mates in 20 moves" to descriptions of board positions in chess, but the computational expense of applying these rules is usually prohibitive. A third form of inadequacy is overgeneral rules, the antecedents of which match cases to which the rule consequent is inapplicable (Golding and Rosenbloom, 1996). A

Figure 2.3. An exemplar, Ex, operationalizes the abstract feature AF by acting as an reduction operator that connects AF to the case description language in which the facts of the new case NC are expressed.

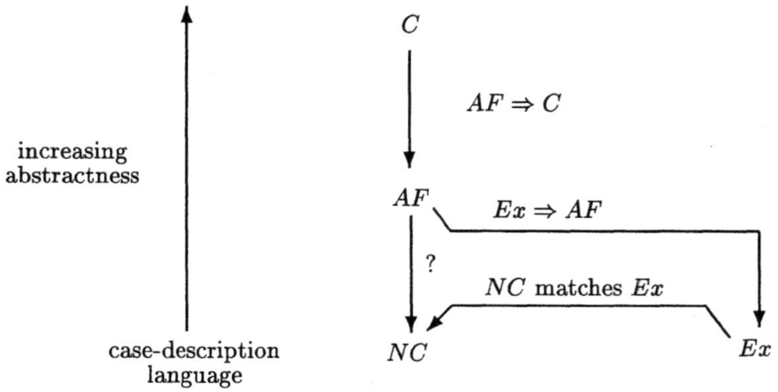

related form of inadequacy is "promiscuity," a superfluity of reduction operators that leads to multiple, conflicting inferences (Dietterich, 1990).

Exemplars Can Compensate for Inadequate Abstraction Knowledge

The facts of exemplars and those of new cases are at the same level of abstraction, since both are expressed in the case-description language. As a result, an exemplar of an abstract feature (*i.e.*, a past case to which the abstract feature applied) can substitute for inadequate reduction operators by serving as a bridge between the abstract feature and the case-description language. The problem of constructing an inference chain between a new case and an abstract feature can therefore be reduced to the problem of constructing a match between the new case and some exemplar of the abstract feature.

Figure 2.3 illustrates a domain theory consisting of $AF \Rightarrow C$ and $Ex \Rightarrow AF$. This theory lacks reduction operators connecting the facts of new case NC to abstract feature AF. However, a match between the new case and Ex permits an inference path to be constructed from the new case NC to category C.

Precedents can convert a weak domain theory into a strong theory only if there are sufficient precedents, or sufficient matching knowledge, that a high certainty match can be made between every otherwise unclassifiable new case and some precedent. These conditions are seldom met. However, precedents often make it possible to construct explanations that could not otherwise be constructed. Precedents can also compensate for overgeneral rules by representing exceptions. This approach to using cases to compensate for an inadequate set of rules was used in Anapron, a system for surname pronunciation (Golding and Rosenbloom, 1991, Golding and Rosenbloom, 1996). In summary, precedents can be an important knowledge source in weak-theory domains.

2.3 Accurate Case Matching Requires Rules

Precedents can compensate for inadequate reduction operators by bridging the gap between abstract features and the case-description language in which new cases are expressed. However, the specificity and detail of case descriptions means that few pairs of distinct cases ever have identical facts. Matching a new case to a precedent therefore typically requires inference to establish the equivalence of nonidentical cases.

Three distinct forms of case-matching inference can be distinguished:

- Case elaboration
- Goal reformulation
- Attribute dropping

Only the first two methods are, in general, sound, and both of these usually require general domain rules. Thus, there is a mutual dependence between rules and precedents in weak-theory domains.

Case Elaboration

Inferring facts that are not explicitly stated in cases can often improve their match. For example, a new case can match a precedent even if it lacks some of the precedent's attributes, provided that the missing attributes can be inferred. Similarly, differing case features can be matched if both are manifestations of the same abstract feature, *e.g.,* if both are symptoms caused by the same underlying physiological state or both have the same generalization. The sequence of inference steps that justify an inferred case fact is an explanation of the fact. Constructing explanations of new case facts to assist in matching is termed *case elaboration.*

Protos (Bareiss et al., 1990) and Casey (Koton, 1988) typify the use of case elaboration to improve match accuracy. Both used rule-based reasoning in this process.

In Protos, causal, associational, and definitional rules acquired from teacher-provided explanations of case classifications were used to construct explanations

Figure 2.4. Two explained attribute matches in Protos.

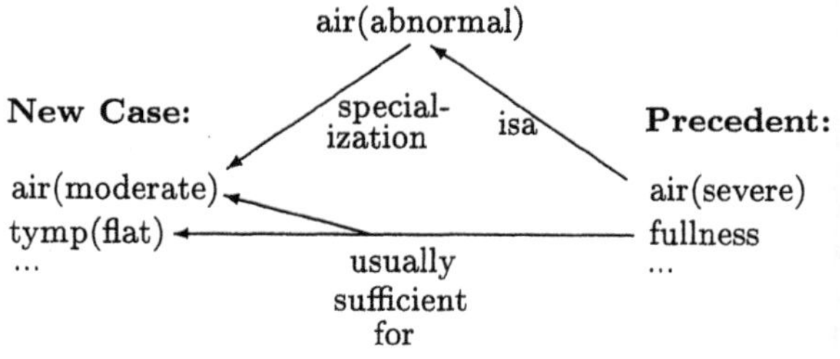

of the match between case features. Figure 2.4 illustrates two explanations used by Protos to match attributes of a precedent case to a new case. The first precedent attribute, *air(severe)*, was matched to a new case attribute, *air(moderate)*, through a common abstraction, *air(abnormal)*. The second precedent attribute, *fullness*, was matched to the new case using the rule that *tymp(flat)* and *air(moderate)* is usually sufficient for *fullness*. An ablation study of Protos demonstrated that explanations for matching such as these made a significant contribution to Protos' problem-solving ability (Mallory, 1989).

In Casey (Koton, 1988), an observable new case feature was considered equivalent to an observable feature of a precedent if the new case feature could be caused by the physiological or diagnostic state that was known to have caused the precedent feature. Causal rules connecting observable features to states was provided by the Heart Failure program, a model-based expert system for cardiac disorder diagnosis. Figure 2.5 illustrates how the new case feature *pulse has slow rise* is matched with the feature *sustained apex impulse* by Casey. Part of the causal explanation of the precedent is that *sustained apex impulse* was caused by *slow ejection*. The Heart Failure program provided a rule that *pulse has slow rise* can also be caused by *slow ejection*. Accordingly, the two features are consistent with the same causal model.

Case matching by finding shared ancestors of corresponding features in a taxonomic hierarchy has been used in a number of projects in the analogy community, including Meldman's legal analysis system (Meldman, 1975), Winston's ARCH program (Winston, 1980), and ACME (Holyoak and Thagard, 1989b). Finding shared ancestors of corresponding features in a taxonomic hierarchy can be viewed as case elaboration because it uses general knowledge in

Figure 2.5. Sustained apex impulse and pulse has slow rise are treated as equivalent by Casey because slow ejection was known to be the cause of sustained apex impulse in the precedent, and slow ejection can also cause pulse has slow rise.

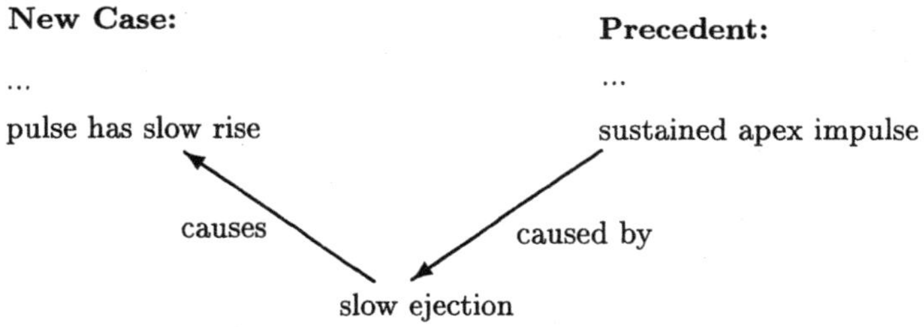

the form of isa links in a taxonomic hierarchy to infer abstract features of the cases being matched.[2]

The source of rules for matching can be either the *a priori* domain theory, *e.g.*, the causal model provided by the Heart Failure program and isa links in a taxonomic hierarchy, or explanations of precedents, *e.g.*, teacher-provided explanations in Protos. Knowledge for case elaboration is not necessarily limited to general warrants. Case-based reasoning can itself be used for case matching and adaptation (Leake et al., 1997). However, rule-based reasoning is often essential for case elaboration.

Goal Reformulation

A second way in which rule-based reasoning can improve case matching is by permitting a goal to be reformulated as a new goal for which there are exemplars that more closely match the new case. Suppose, for example, that a domain theory consists of the rule $AF_1 \Rightarrow C$, precedent Ex_1 of AF_1, and precedent Ex_2 of AF_2. Suppose that new case NC matches Ex_1 weakly but Ex_2 strongly. The only inference path that can be constructed to establish conclusion C involves a weak match between NC and Ex_1. However, adding the rule $AF_2 \Rightarrow AF_1$ to the domain theory permits the goal AF_1 to be refined as AF_2. As shown in Figure 2.6, this leads to a stronger alternative inference path involving a strong match between NC and Ex_2.

---

[2]The process of determining "implicit shared properties" of cases from differing explicit representations was termed ***reformulation*** in (Russell, 1986). A related notion in machine learning is ***constructive induction,*** which has been defined as "any form of induction that generates new descriptors not present in the input data" (Dietterich and Michalski, 1983).

Figure 2.6. The rule $AF_2 \Rightarrow AF_1$ permits a reformulation step between AF_1 and AF_2. This leads to a stronger explanation of C because NC matches Ex_2 more strongly than Ex_1.

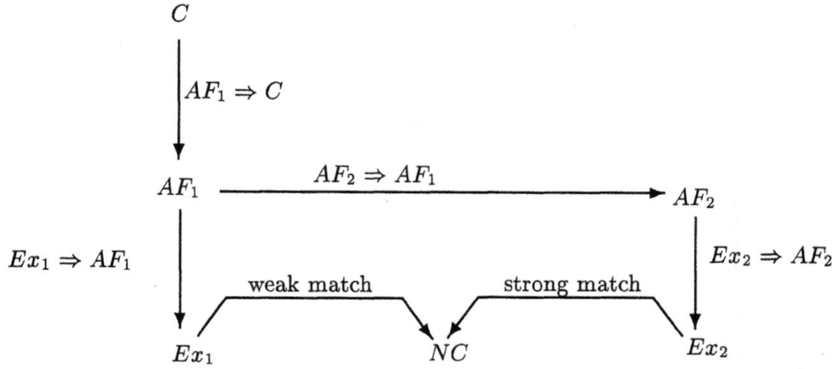

In general, goal reformulation can be used to replace an open-textured predicate with a *combination* of predicates. If some exemplar of each of the new predicate matches the new case, the system can explain the classification by combining the individual reasoning steps into a single explanation.

A particularly important use of goal reformulation is in refining the granularity of the exemplars to which a new case is compared. The price of using exemplars to bridge the gap in abstraction between abstract features and case descriptions is the necessity of matching exemplars that potentially contain a very large number of facts. If the facts of an exemplar can be partitioned into smaller meaningful collections, these collections can more easily be matched. This can lead to stronger explanations because a new case may match portions of the facts of several exemplars more strongly than it matches the entire set of facts of any single exemplar.

The source of knowledge of the meaningful collections into which a exemplar can be partitioned is the explanation of the exemplar. Specifically, explanations of exemplars often contain reasoning steps that connect portions of case facts to intermediate conclusions justified by those facts. When the exemplar is a legal precedent, these reasoning steps will be referred to as *precedent constituents*. Precedent constituents are a particular form of case "snippets" (Redmond, 1990, Kolodner, 1993), inferences internal to a case constituting a portion of the case's solution. The case facts constituting the antecedent of a precedent constituent are termed the *material facts* of the case with respect

Table 2.1. A coarse-granularity view of $Prec_1$ and $Prec_2$. B and $\neg B$ represent *battery* and *no battery*, respectively.

Precedent	Classification	Material facts
$Prec_1$	$\neg B$	F_1 = hitting hockey stick $\wedge$ F_2 = hockey game
$Prec_2$	B	F_3 = punching chin $\wedge$ F_4 = family argument

to the conclusion (generally shortened to "the material facts of the precedent constituent").

The utility of goal reformulation can be illustrated with a simplified legal example. Suppose that a domain theory for the legal category *battery* consists of two precedents:

- Precedent 1. During a hockey game, John intentionally hit a hockey stick held by Bill. John was not liable to Bill for battery.

- Precedent 2. Sam intentionally hit Jim in the chin during a heated family argument. Sam was liable to Jim for battery.

The precedents are summarized in Table 2.1.

Consider the task of determining whether the following two new cases are instances of battery:

- New case 1. Fred punched Roger in the nose during a boxing match.

- New case 2. Arthur shoved an umbrella held by Mary during an argument over some items on sale at a department store.

The new cases are summarized in Table 2.2.

Directly comparing the facts of NC_1 and NC_2 with those of the precedents is insufficient to determine whether the new cases are instances of battery because each case partially matches both $Prec_1$ and $Prec_2$. NC_1 matches $Prec_1$ in that boxing and hockey are both types of games. However, NC_1 matches $Prec_2$ in that a punch to the nose and a punch to the chin are both involve direct contact with the body. Similarly, NC_2 matches $Prec_1$ in that a hockey stick and an umbrella are both objects in contact with the body. However, NC_2 matches $Prec_2$ in that a family argument and an argument at a store are both types of

Table 2.2. Two new cases to be classified.

New Case	Facts
NC_1	$F_3' =$ punching nose $\wedge$ $F_2' =$ boxing match
NC_2	$F_1' =$ shoving umbrella $\wedge$ $F_4' =$ argument at store

arguments. Thus, there are conflicting weak arguments for both classifications for each case.

This indeterminacy can be resolved by using the explanations of the precedents to refine their granularity. Suppose that the domain theory includes the rule that battery (B) is satisfied if there is an intentional touching (T) and no consent ($\neg C$), *i.e.*, $T \wedge \neg C \Rightarrow B$, where intentional touching and consent are abstract features. Suppose further that $Prec_1$ and $Prec_2$ have the following explanations (illustrated in Figure 2.7): Battery is not satisfied in $Prec_1$ because a participant in hockey has implicitly consented to the physical contacts that are part of the game (*i.e.*, $F_2 \Rightarrow C$). Thus, even though intentionally hitting a player's hockey stick is sufficient to satisfy the requirement of intentional touching (*i.e.*, $F_1 \Rightarrow T$), the requirements for battery are not met. The plaintiff's burden of proof is a form of closed-world assumption under which the failure to establish either of the prerequisites for battery implies that the absence of battery, *i.e.*, , $T \vee C \Rightarrow \neg B$.[3]

On the other hand, battery is satisfied in $Prec_2$ because a blow to the chin satisfies the touching requirement (*i.e.*, $F_3 \Rightarrow T$) and there is no consent to being hit in a family argument (*i.e.*, $F_4 \Rightarrow \neg C$). The inferences connecting the specific facts of the precedents to the abstract features are precedent constituents. Table 2.3 summarizes the precedent constituents in the explanations of $Prec_1$ and $Prec_2$.

NC_1 and NC_2 match individual precedent constituents more strongly than they match the entire facts of either $Prec_1$ or $Prec_2$. The rule relating abstract features T and C to the category B permits matches to individual precedent constituents to be combined to create strong explanations of the classifications of both new cases. These explanations, illustrated in Figure 2.8, are as follows:

[3]For a formal model of burden of proof in legal argumentation, see (Freeman and Farley, 1996).

Figure 2.7. Explanations of precedents $Prec_1$ and $Prec_2$.

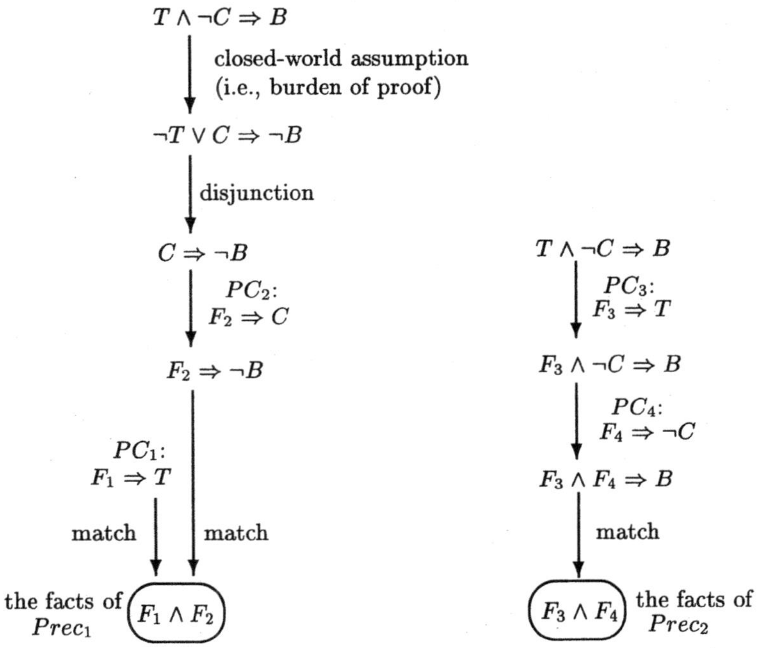

Table 2.3. A fine-granularity view of the precedent constituents of $Prec_1$ and $Prec_2$ revealed by their explanations.

Precedent constituent	Classification	Material facts
PC_1	T	F_1 = hitting hockey stick
PC_2	C	F_2 = hockey game
PC_3	T	F_3 = punching chin
PC_4	$\neg C$	F_4 = family argument

- NC_1. An intentional touching does not constitute battery if there is consent to the touching. Part of the explanation of $Prec_1$ is that a participant in hockey has implicitly consented to the physical contacts that are part of the game (*i.e.*, $F_2 \Rightarrow C$). Boxing is similar to hockey in that both involve physical contact (*i.e.*, F_2' matches F_2).[4] Thus, there is implicit consent to being punched in the nose during boxing, and such punches therefore do not constitute battery.

- NC_2. Battery requires intentional touching and no consent. A second part of the explanation of $Prec_1$ is that intentionally hitting a player's hockey stick is sufficient to satisfy the requirement of intentional touching (*i.e.*, $F_1 \Rightarrow T$). Intentionally shoving someone's umbrella is similar to intentionally hitting their hockey stick in that both involve contact with something that is contact with the person (*i.e.*, F_1' matches F_1). Thus, the element of intentional touching, (*i.e.*, T), was satisfied by Arthur shoving Mary's umbrella. Part of the explanation of $Prec_2$ is that there is no consent to being hit in a family argument (*i.e.*, $F_4 \Rightarrow \neg C$). An argument over sale items is similar to a family argument (*i.e.*, F_4' matches F_4). Accordingly, there was no consent to the intentional touching (*i.e.*, $\neg C$). Since the elements of battery—intentional touching and no consent—are satisfied, NC_2 is an instance of battery.

The explanations of the classifications of NC_1 and NC_2 illustrate how refining the granularity of precedents by identifying precedent constituents permits multiple partial matches to be leveraged into strong explanations. Precedent-granularity refinement requires two types of knowledge. The first is knowledge of precedent constituents, that is, the collections of specific case facts that warranted conclusions about abstract case features. The second is knowledge of reduction rules, that is, rules relating abstract features to classifications. Knowledge of precedent constituents derives from the explanations of precedents. Reduction rules may come either from precedent explanations or from *a priori* domain theory (such as the rule that battery requires an intentional touching and no consent).

Case-Matching by Attribute Dropping

The weakest method of case matching is to form a common abstraction by dropping unshared attributes. For example, new case $NC = F_1 \wedge F_2$ and exemplar $Ex = F_2 \wedge F_3$ can be matched by dropping the attributes on which they differ, F_1 and F_3, and retaining the attribute that they share, F_2. As shown in Figure 2.9, one way to view this process is as a pair of problem-reduction steps by which the goal, $F_1 \wedge F_2 \Rightarrow C$, is reduced to $F_2 \wedge F_3 \Rightarrow C$,

[4]Note that this and the other matching steps in the explanations of NC_1 and NC_2 require case elaboration, since they involve matching nonidentical case facts. For simplicity of presentation, these case elaboration steps are omitted.

Figure 2.8. Explanations of two new cases, NC_1 and NC_2, using precedent constituents from $Prec_1$ and $Prec_2$ together with the rule that $T \land \neg C \Rightarrow B$.

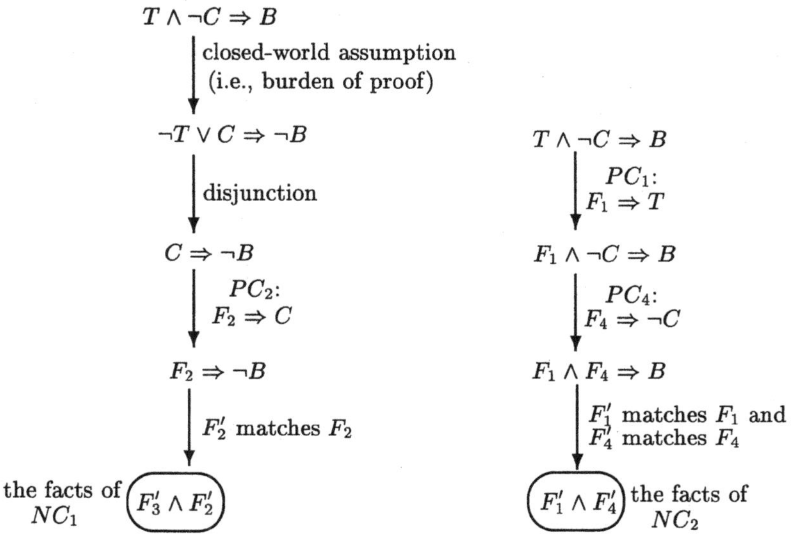

Figure 2.9. A common abstraction of NC and Ex is formed by dropping nonmatching case attributes.

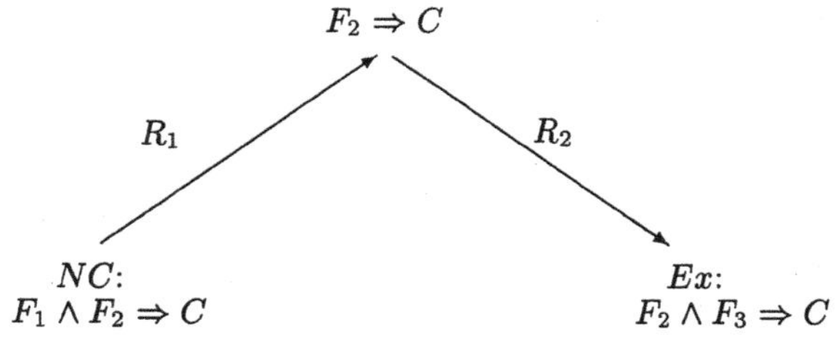

an explicit warrant. The reduction step R_2 is sound, since $F_1 \wedge F_2 \Rightarrow C$ follows from $F_2 \Rightarrow C$. Reduction step R_1 is not in general valid, however, since $F_2 \Rightarrow C$ does not follow from $F_2 \wedge F_3 \Rightarrow C$. R_1 is only valid if F_1 is irrelevant to the conclusion C. Accordingly, attribute matching is sound only if the exemplar attributes unmatched in the new case are irrelevant to the category of which the exemplar is a member.

The relevance of an exemplar attribute to a category of which the exemplar is a member is determined by the exemplar's explanation. Any exemplar fact that does not appear in any inference step in the explanation of the exemplar can be validly dropped without doing violence to the explanation. If exemplar explanations are unavailable, then heuristic estimates of attribute importance, such as the weighted feature matching schemes discussed in Section 7.2, must be used instead.

In summary, attribute dropping is a method of case matching by finding a shared abstraction between a new case and an exemplar. Attribute dropping is sound only if the exemplar attributes dropped are irrelevant to the category. Unless explanatory knowledge is available to distinguish irrelevant from relevant exemplar attributes, attribute dropping is a weak, heuristic method.

2.4 Rules and Precedents as Search Operators

This chapter has presented a model of explanations as inference paths from a new case to a category or its contrast set through a warrant-reduction graph. Since individual steps in such an inference path can be justified by either rules or exemplars, the process of constructing an explanation is a search problem in which the available operators include both rules and exemplars.

This chapter has argued that rules and exemplars are similar in that each expresses a regularity connecting a collection of facts to some conclusion. Moreover, rules and cases are complementary in that exemplars can operationalize abstract rule antecedents, while rules assist in case matching. The similar form and complementary function of rules and exemplars suggests that they can be treated identically as operators in the search for a solution path. However, this appealing model of uniform treatment must be qualified in weak-theory domains. In such domains, the facts of a new case may fail to match the facts of any exemplar even after goal reformulation, case elaboration, and dropping attributes known to be irrelevant. In these circumstances, the new case can be matched to an exemplar only by dropping possibly relevant exemplar attributes.

Since attribute dropping is not, in general, a sound inference technique, an explanation that contains a case-based inference step involving attribute dropping is weaker than one that does not. In general, if multiple explanations can be formed, the strongest explanations are those that minimize, under some criteria, the attributes that are dropped during any case-based reasoning step occurring in the explanation.[5]

Exemplars may also impose different requirements for indexing and retrieval than rules. Exemplars are typically much more numerous than rules because there can be many different instances of a single generalization. As a result, finding an exemplar that minimizes the attributes that must be dropped in order to match a new case may entail comparing the new case to a large number of exemplars. Moreover, each such comparison may be relatively expensive because of the detail and complexity of exemplar facts. As a result, specialized techniques for indexing and retrieval are often more important for exemplars than for rules.

Apart from these qualifications concerning attribute dropping and retrieval, however, exemplars and rules can be treated in a uniform fashion as operators in the search for a solution path through a warrant-reduction graph. This general framework for classification in weak-theory domains leaves a number of implementation details unspecified. Any particular implementation must specify the following:

- A search control strategy, such as back-chaining, forward-chaining, or mean-ends analysis.
- A knowledge-base consisting of a set of exemplars and rules.
- Case-representation and generalization languages for expressing exemplars, new cases, and rules.
- Indexing and retrieval mechanisms for warrants, particularly exemplars.

To perform case elaboration and goal reformulation, a control strategy must be *impartial* (Branting and Porter, 1991, Branting, 1991), that is, it must not impose arbitrary ordering restrictions on the use of rules and precedents. This is because case elaboration requires rule-based reasoning **after** case selection, whereas goal reformulation requires rule-based reasoning **before** case selection. Any *a priori* ordering constraint on the use of rules and cases will therefore preclude either case elaboration or goal reformulation. Chapter 5 sets forth several examples showing how impartiality is necessary to produce the strongest explanations based on rules and precedents.

The next chapter sets forth a formal model of legal precedent based on the framework, and Chapter 4 describes GREBE, an implementation that applies this framework to the task of legal analysis.

[5]The exact criteria for determining the effect on explanation strength of particular missing attributes may depend on the particular domain and problem-solving context (Murphy and Medin, 1985).

3 A FORMAL MODEL OF RATIO DECIDENDI

Any complete account of legal analysis using precedents must include a model of *ratio decidendi*, the content of a precedent that is authoritative as to subsequent cases. Predicting, advocating, and justifying the binding effect of a precedent on subsequent cases all require identifying the authoritative elements of the precedent and showing how they can apply to subsequent cases involving different facts. Although the very existence of *ratio decidendi* is a disputed question among legal scholars, a functioning system of precedent rests on the assumption that some consensus can be reached concerning the the authoritative content of precedents (MacCormick, 1987) p. 157.

In general, development of an adequate computer model entails three distinct tasks. First, the phenomenon to be modeled must be precisely specified. Second, an appropriate computational model must be described. Finally, the ability of the computational model to account for the phenomenon must be demonstrated.

Section 3.1 addresses the the first of these tasks—describing the phenomenon to be modeled—arguing that the jurisprudential literature on legal precedent provides a set of minimal criteria for the adequacy of computational models of *ratio decidendi*. Section 3.2 describes a *reduction-graph* model of *ratio deci-*

dendi, under which the *ratio decidendi* of a precedent is a justification structure consisting of a series of reasoning steps, some of which relate abstract predicates to other abstract predicates and some of which relate abstract predicates to specific facts. Section 3.3 argues that the reduction-graph model satisfies most of the adequacy criteria set forth in Section 3.1. Section 3.4 argues that a purely exemplar-based model of legal precedent consisting of representations of the material facts of each precedent case together with a global relevance metric fails to satisfy an important criterion: representing how the theory under which a case is decided controls its precedential effect. Three pragmatic issues in the implementation of the reduction-graph model are discussed in the Section 3.5: the difficulty of exemplar matching; the role of the justification of warrants; and the problem that the written justifications for judicial decisions are often incomplete.

The reduction-graph model is intended as a *knowledge level* (Newell, 1982) description of precedent-based reasoning, that is, a "specification of what a reasoning system should be able to do" independent of any particular "symbol-level" implementation of this process. The emphasis of this chapter is therefore on identifying the knowledge required for precedent-based reasoning and showing how this knowledge is used in the resolution of new cases.[1]

3.1 Evaluation Criteria for Models of Ratio Decidendi

The first step in developing a computational model of *ratio decidendi* is specifying the characteristics of *ratio decidendi* that the model should account for. Several knowledge sources for describing the phenomenon of precedent-based legal reasoning can be distinguished. One possible source of information would be detailed empirical studies of what elements of precedent are actually treated as authoritative by judges' and attorneys in problem solving. Unfortunately, few such empirical studies exist.

An alternative source of information is introspection on one's own use of precedents. Unfortunately, introspection is notoriously unreliable (Gardner, 1985) pp. 105–107. However, the law's "tradition of examining its processes and assumptions" (Rissland, 1990) as embodied in jurisprudential literature provides another alternative. While jurisprudential writings are often contradictory and frequently serve a prescriptive rather than a descriptive agenda, jurisprudential ideas that survive prolonged critical scrutiny are likely to contain at least an element of truth.

There is little dispute that within the Anglo-American system of law, judicial precedents are a primary source of legal authority (Bodenheimer, 1974). Unfor-

[1]This chapter includes material originally appearing in (Branting, 1994a).

tunately, there is less unanimity about precisely how "the point of law settled by a judicial decision," *i.e.*, the *ratio decidendi* of the decision, is to be determined. A number of different characterizations of *ratio decidendi* have been proposed. These characterizations tend to fall into two general approaches, differing primarily in the degree of generality or abstractness attributed to the *ratio decidendi.*[2] One approach views the *ratio decidendi* of a precedent as a general rule or principle, typically contained in the language of the judge's decision. The emphasis of advocates of this approach is usually on isolating the *ratio decidendi* from surrounding nonauthoritative language, or *dictum.* The alternative approach focuses on the specific facts of precedents. This approach tends to be associated with skepticism about the ostensible justifications advanced by judges for their decisions. An important issue under this approach is determining precisely which facts of a case were material to the judge's decision.

The remainder of this section sets forth five widely recognized characteristics of *ratio decidendi* that can be discerned from among the diversity of jurisprudential proposals. Collectively, these characteristics describe what has been termed the *orthodox* view of precedent (Llewellyn, 1960). Many legal scholars, including Llewellyn himself, would argue that the orthodox view is a drastic simplification of the actual use of precedents in legal discourse and problem solving. However, even if these characteristics do not constitute sufficient conditions for an complete model of precedent, they are arguably a core set of conditions necessary for any adequate computational model of precedent.

1. The *ratio decidendi* of a precedent consists of propositions of law, explicit or implicit in the opinion, that are necessary to the decision. This characterization of ratio is rooted in two observations. The first is that appellate judicial decisions almost invariably contain a written justification. Appellate opinions typically contain a summary of the facts of the case, identification of the issues of law raised in arguments by counsel for each of the parties, pronouncement of the legal propositions supported by the controlling authorities, and declaration of a decision that resolves the issues by applying the legal propositions to the facts of the case. Predictability, judicial economy, and the principle that like cases should be treated alike all suggest that the legal propositions under which a case is resolved should apply equally to similar future cases.

The second observation is that not every part of the written justification is authoritative. As early as 1673,[3] it was recognized that written decisions frequently contain language unnecessary for the resolution of the issues before

[2] *See* (Collier, 1988) for a detailed comparison of these two approaches.
[3] *Bole v. Horton*, Vaughn 360.

the court and that this unnecessary language is not part of the *ratio decidendi* of the case.[4]

These two observations together suggest that the *ratio decidendi* of a case consists of just those pronouncements of legal propositions by the judge that are necessary to the resolution of the issue before the court. The numerous advocates of this characterization of *ratio decidendi* include Neil MacCormick:

> A ratio decidendi is a ruling expressly or impliedly given by a judge which is sufficient to settle a point of law put in issue by the parties' arguments in a case, being a point on which a ruling was necessary to his justification (or one of his alternative justifications) of the decisions in the case. (MacCormick, 1987) at p. 170.

Other typical statements of this position include those of Edmund Morgan,who argued that the *ratio decidendi* of a case consists of "those portions of the opinion setting forth the rules of law applied by the court, the application of which was required for the determination of the issues presented ..." (Morgan, 1948) and of Sir John Salmond, who stated that courts should limit themselves to formulation of principles that are "required for the due decision of the particular case" (Salmond, 1900).

Another proponent of this view, Eugene Wambaugh, proposed a widely accepted test for determining whether a given proposition is the *ratio decidendi* of a precedent: if the deciding court could have believed the negation of the proposition without changing the outcome of the case, the proposition is *dictum* rather than *ratio decidendi* (Wambaugh, 1894). Wambaugh's formulation differs somewhat from that of Morgan and Salmond in holding that the proposition representing the *ratio decidendi* of a case might not actually be articulated by the court. However, Wambaugh asserted that it can be discovered by anyone who "diligently studies the problem and the result" (Wambaugh, 1894).

2. A unique proposition of law necessary to a decision can seldom be determined. Instead, a gradation of propositions ranging in abstraction from the specific facts of the case to abstract rules can satisfy this condition. A widespread but naive view of *ratio decidendi* is that the *ratio decidendi* of a precedent consists of a single, unique proposition of law "without which the case must have been decided otherwise."

Rupert Cross in "Precedent in English Law" (Cross, 1991) illustrated the untenability of this view with the example of *Donoghue v. Stevenson*,[5] a case holding the manufacturer of a bottle of ginger beer containing a decomposed snail liable to the ultimate consumer. Lord Atkin's opinion contained two propositions of law justifying the decision. The first was very general:

[4]The United States Supreme Court in *Carroll v. Carroll's Lessee*, 57 U.S. 128, 136, 16 How. 275, 286–287 (1853) similarly observed that "if [statements] go beyond the case, they may be respected, but ought not to control the judgment in a subsequent suit."
[5]A.C. 562 (1932).

> A party must take reasonable care to avoid acts or omissions which he can reasonably foresee would be likely to injure persons ... closely and directly affected by his act ....

The second was much more specific:

> A manufacturer of products, which he sells in such a form as to show that he intends them to reach the ultimate consumer in the form in which they left him with no reasonably possibility of intermediate examination ... owes a duty to the consumer to take ... reasonable care.

Cross observes that both of these propositions satisfy Wambaugh's test: the negation of either proposition would require a different decision.

Similarly, Herman Oliphant in *A Return to Stare Decisis* (Oliphant, 1928) (as paraphrased in (Collier, 1988)) analogized the process of viewing a precedent to that of a spectator entering a stadium:

> The spectator has a choice not only of where around the field to sit (angle of view, or legal subject area), but also of how far up the rows of bleachers to go (level of generalization). No internal logic dictates a resting place in either dimension.

Oliphant gave the example of a decision holding that a father was privileged to induce his daughter to break a promise to marry. Oliphant argued that the decision was consistent with any of six distinct holdings, ranging in generality from "1. Fathers are privileged to induce daughters to break promises to marry" to "6. All persons are so privileged as to all promises made by anyone."[6]

3. The *ratio decidendi* of a precedent must be grounded in the specific facts of the case. An important source of uncertainty in legal reasoning is the "gap" in generality between abstract legal concepts and the specific facts of new cases (Gardner, 1987, Branting and Porter, 1991). Precedents are useful in deciding new cases because they provide examples of specific facts that satisfy such concepts. Accordingly, a model of *ratio decidendi* that omits specific case facts cannot fully account for the precedential effect of past cases.

Typical expressions of the centrality of precedents' specific facts include:

- "[I]t is the facts, and not the general rules of law found in precedents ... which serve as the foundation of the decisional process." (Cueto-Rua, 1981) at 56.
- "Judgments must be read in light of the facts of the case in which they are delivered" (Cross, 1991).

---

[6]For further discussion of the multiple levels of abstraction at which the holding of a case can be expressed, see (Stone, 1947) and (Stone, 1959).

- "It is clear that the most important part of a representation for cases is the representation of the facts and the outcome." (Gardner, 1987) at 47. Gardner quotes with approval Corbin's admonition that cases should be studied "not so much for their doctrinal statements as for ... their operative facts" and Gilmore's statement that one should "never quote general language from an opinion, divorced from the factual context in which the language was delivered."

Some legal scholars have taken the extreme position that the specific facts of precedents are not just *necessary*, but are also *sufficient* representations of *ratio decidendi*. Early proponents of this view included adherents of the *legal realist* movement. Legal realists adopted an empirical approach to *ratio decidendi* because they were skeptical about the importance of judges' ostensible justifications in judicial decision making. For example, Oliphant opined that:

> the predictable element ... is what courts have done in response to the stimuli of the facts of the concrete cases before them. Not the judges' opinions, but which way they decide cases, will be the dominant subject matter of any truly scientific study of law (Oliphant, 1928).

In its most extreme form, the realist position held that judges' written explanations have no bearing whatever on the outcome of cases and that cases represent only judges' disposition to behavior in response to stimuli (Collier, 1988). This position has few adherents today.[7]

A more tenable formulation of this position was put forth by Arthur Goodhart. Goodhart argued that "the *ratio decidendi* of a case ... must not be sought in the reasons on which the judge has based his decision" but must be sought instead in "the material facts on which the judge has based his conclusion" (Goodhart, 1930). Goodhart asserted that a judge:

> founds his conclusions upon a group of facts selected by him as material from among a larger mass of facts, some of which might seem significant to a layman, but which, to a lawyer, are irrelevant. ... It follows that our task in analyzing a case is ... to state the material facts as seen by the judge and his conclusion based on them. It is by his choice of the material facts that the judge creates law (Goodhart, 1930).

Goodhart shared the skepticism of Oliphant and the other realists that the *ratio decidendi* of a precedent is to be found in judges' enunciation of legal rules, but differed from the realists in believing that it nevertheless is possible to determine the *ratio decidendi* of a case from the judge's written opinion:

> [T]he reasons given by the judge in his opinion, or his statement of the rule of law which he is following, are of peculiar importance, for they may furnish us with a guide for determining which facts he considered material and which

---

[7]However, *jurimetrics* (Loevinger, 1963, Baade, 1963) represents an attempt to derive useful empirical information concerning judges' behavior without reference to their written justifications.

> immaterial. His reason may be incorrect and his statement of the law too wide, but they will indicate to us on what facts he reached his conclusion. (Goodhart, 1930) pp. 175–176.

4. The *ratio decidendi* of a precedent includes not only the precedent's material facts and decision, but also the theory under which the decision follows from the material facts. Goodhart's model of *ratio decidendi* as material facts plus decision thereon has now been largely rejected. The most important reason for this rejection is that:

> [sometimes] it is quite impossible to formulate the *ratio decidendi* merely by reference to the facts, regarded as material by the court, and the decision based on those facts. It is often essential to know why certain facts were regarded as material and for this purpose it may be necessary to know what portions of the law were in the mind of the court when the selection was made (Cross, 1991).

Cross (Cross, 1991) illustrates the importance of knowing the theory under which a case was decided with the example of *Bourhill v. Young*,[8] in which the following facts were found to be material:

> Young, a motorcyclist, was killed because of his own negligence when he passed a tram at excessive speed and collided with a car about 50 feet beyond the tram. At the time of the accident, the tram was stopped and Mrs. Bourhill was alighting. Mrs. Bourhill heard the collision and saw blood on the road after the accident and as a result suffered a nervous shock. Mrs. Bourhill was outside what Young ought to have contemplated as the area of potential danger that would arise from his careless driving, since she was alighting on the side of the tram opposite the side on which Young passed.

The decision was that Mrs. Bourhill's action against Young's estate was dismissed. From the material facts and the decision alone it is impossible to determine which of the following two rationales underlies the decision: (1) a driver owes no duty of care in respect of his driving to persons outside the area of reasonably foreseeable danger, or (2) although the driver owes a duty of care to such persons, damages flowing from nervous shock are too remote a consequence of the breach of duty to be recoverable.

Without knowledge of the controlling rationale, it is impossible to determine from the material facts and the decision alone how either of the following hypotheticals should be decided:

- **H1.** The same facts as *Bourhill* except that the motorcycle driven by Young collides with a fireworks truck instead of a car, and Mrs. Bourhill is burned by a fragment from the resultant explosion of fireworks.

---

[8] A.C. 92 (1943).

- **H2.** The same facts as *Bourhill* except that Young passes the tram on the same side as the alighting Mrs. Bourhill, missing her by inches and causing a severe emotional shock.

Under the first rationale, Mrs. Bourhill could recover in *H2* but not *H1*. Under the second rationale, the results would be reversed.

To summarize, in some cases, such as *Bourhill v. Young,* there may be alternative theories under which the material facts could have led to the decision. A representation of *ratio decidendi* that includes only the material facts but excludes the operative theory is insufficient to distinguish among these theories.

5. Subsequent decisions can limit, extend, or overturn earlier precedents. The effect of later decisions on earlier decisions has led many scholars to argue that the *ratio decidendi* of a case is determined, at least in part, by subsequent cases. According to Sidney Post Simpson and Julius Stone (as summarized in (Bodenheimer, 1974)):

> [E]ach case has implicit in it a whole congeries of possible principles of decision. When a case is decided, no one can be certain which of the possible principles of decision is destined eventually to become the controlling one .... Only a study of a whole series of decisions on a particular problem of law will to some extent reveal what the fate of a particular precedent has been in the dynamic process of restricting, expanding, interpreting, reinterpreting, and reformulating a prior body of doctrine ....

There are innumerable instances in which the exact scope of a precedent is gradually defined by subsequent cases. Most commonly this occurs when the language of an earlier opinion is narrowed and circumscribed by subsequent cases. Goodhart (Goodhart, 1930) discusses the example of *Rex v. Fenton,*[9] which contained the following language: "If death ensues as the consequence of a wrongful act, an act which the party who commits it can neither justify nor excuse, it is not accidental death, but manslaughter." Fifty-three years later, *Regina v. Franklin*[10] held that "a civil wrong ... is immaterial to this charge of manslaughter." *Franklin* thus narrowed the scope of *Fenton* by restricting the wrongful acts that can give rise to manslaughter to criminal, as opposed to merely civil, wrongs.

Similarly, the scope of a precedent can be expanded by subsequent opinions. For example, in *Barwick v. English Joint Stock Bank*[11] Willes, J. ruled that "The general rule is, that the master is answerable for every such wrong of the servant or agent as is committed in the course of the service and for the master's benefit, though no express command or privity be proved." Forty-five years after this decision, the English House of Lords ruled in *Lloyd v. Grace,*

[9] 1 Lew. C. C. 179 (1830).
[10] 15 Cox C. C. 163 (1883).
[11] L. R. 2 Ex. 259 (1867).

Smith & Co.[12] that the words "and for the master's benefit" were merely descriptive of the facts in the *Barwick* case, and not a necessary part of the principle involved.

Much of the law concerning the compensability under workers' compensation law for injuries occurring while traveling consists of accumulated exceptions to the common-law rule that commuting is not an activity within the scope of employment (Larsen, 1989). Similarly, much of the law of products liability consists of incremental extensions to an initially narrow common-law rule (Levi, 1949).

In consonance with these examples, Goodhart observed that:

> [F]urther decisions are frequently required before the scope of a principle is finally determined ... Paton's metaphor is a sound one: 'One case, so to speak, plots a point on the graph of tort, but to draw the curve of the law we need a series of points.' (Goodhart, 1959) p. 124.

A more subtle form of retroactive modification of past cases occurs when later decisions erode the justification for earlier decisions without explicitly rejecting their holding. Don Berman and Carole Hafner (Berman and Hafner, 1995) use as an example of this phenomenon the evolution of conflict of laws doctrine in New York state concerning whether the law of the situs (place of accident) or the law of the forum control liability of drivers to passengers. In *Smith v. Clute*[13] and *Kerfoot v. Kelley*[14] the New York courts adopted a "territorial" doctrine of choice of law under which the law of the situs applies. In 1963, however, the New York's highest court held in *Babcock v. Jackson*[15] rejected the territorial doctrine and adopted instead a "center of gravity" approach that weighed the relative interests and contacts in the two forums.

Berman and Hafner show how this result could have been predicted after *Auten v. Auten*[16] and *Haag v. Barnes,*[17] which rejected the territorial rule as to contracts, and *Kilberg v. Northeast Airlines,*[18] which, while not rejecting the territorial rule as to torts, avoided its application by invoking a public policy exception. Although none of these three decisions explicitly overruled *Smith* or *Kerfoot*, collectively they indicated that key portions of the justifications of these decisions had been rejected.

An adequate model of precedent should, at a minimum, account for these five recognized characteristics of *ratio decidendi*. Accordingly, these characteristics can provide a set of evaluation criteria for models of precedent-based reasoning.

---

[12] A. C. 716 (1912).
[13] 277 N.Y. 407, 14 N.E.2d 455 (1938).
[14] 294 N.Y. 288, 62 N.E.2d 74 (1945).
[15] 12 N.Y.2d 473, 473 N.Y.S. 743, 191 N.E.2d 279 (1963).
[16] 308 N.Y. 155, 124 N.E.2d 99 (1954).
[17] 9 N.Y.2d 554, 175 N.E.2d 441, 216 N.Y.S.2d 65 (1961).
[18] 9 N.Y.2d 34, 172 N.E.2d 526, 211 N.Y.D.2d 133 (1961).

3.2 The Reduction Graph Model of Ratio Decidendi

This section proposes a model of *ratio decidendi* intended to satisfy the criteria set forth in the previous section. The central tenet of this model is that the *ratio decidendi* of a precedent is best modeled as a justification structure consisting of a series of reasoning steps, some of which relate abstract predicates to other abstract predicates and some of which relate abstract predicates to specific facts. Inference steps of the first type are warranted by rules; those of the second type are warranted by exemplars. The authoritative elements of the precedent are the rules and exemplars constituting the justification for the decision.

Rules and Exemplars as Warrants

A justification for the conclusion that a predicate applies to a case consists of a warrant for the predicate together with all inferences necessary to match the antecedents of the warrant to the facts of the case. Various representations of such a justification are possible. Figure 3.1 represents a justification in terms of the subgoals that arise in the process of constructing an inference path from the predicate to be established to the facts of a case. The predicate to be established, negligence, is at the top. The rule that duty of reasonable care, breach of that duty, and proximately caused harm imply negligence permits this goal to be reduced to the subgoals of establishing a duty of reasonable care, breach of that duty, and proximately caused harm. These subgoals can in turn be reduced by reduction operators to the facts of the case: that Jones was a doctor rendering professional services in operating on Brown, that Jones failed to count sponges during the operation, and that Brown developed peritonitis from the sponge left during the operation. This representation is termed a *goal-reduction graph.*[19]

Figure 3.2 shows an equivalent alternative representation of this justification in which reduction operators are used to repeatedly rewrite the antecedents of a warrant for negligence until it matches the facts of the case. This representation is the *warrant-reduction graph* representation introduced in Chapter 2.[20] Goal-reduction graphs and warrant-reduction graphs are equivalent alternative ways to represent a series of reduction steps (Amarel, 1968). The two representations differ only in that the order of reduction operator application and the resulting warrants for the ultimate result are made explicit in a warrant-reduction graph, whereas the subgoals addressed by each reduction operator are made explicit in the goal-reduction graph.

---

[19]This representation is also referred to as an *AND/OR graph* (Barr and Feigenbaum, 1982). In this particular graph, there are no OR branches, just AND branches.

[20]Figure 3.2 is, in fact, a more detailed version of the right branch of the warrant-reduction graph shown in Figure 2.1.

Figure 3.1. The justification, represented as a goal-reduction graph, for Jones' liability to Brown under negligence for the injuries that resulted from a sponge left by Jones in Brown's abdominal cavity during an operation.

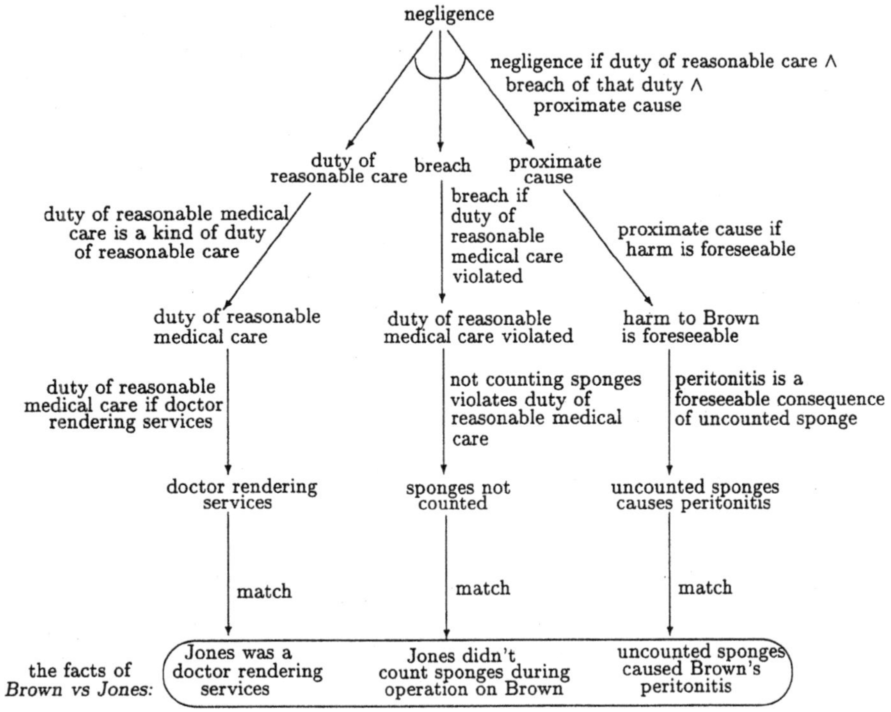

Figure 3.2. The justification for Jones' liability to Brown represented as a warrant-reduction graph.

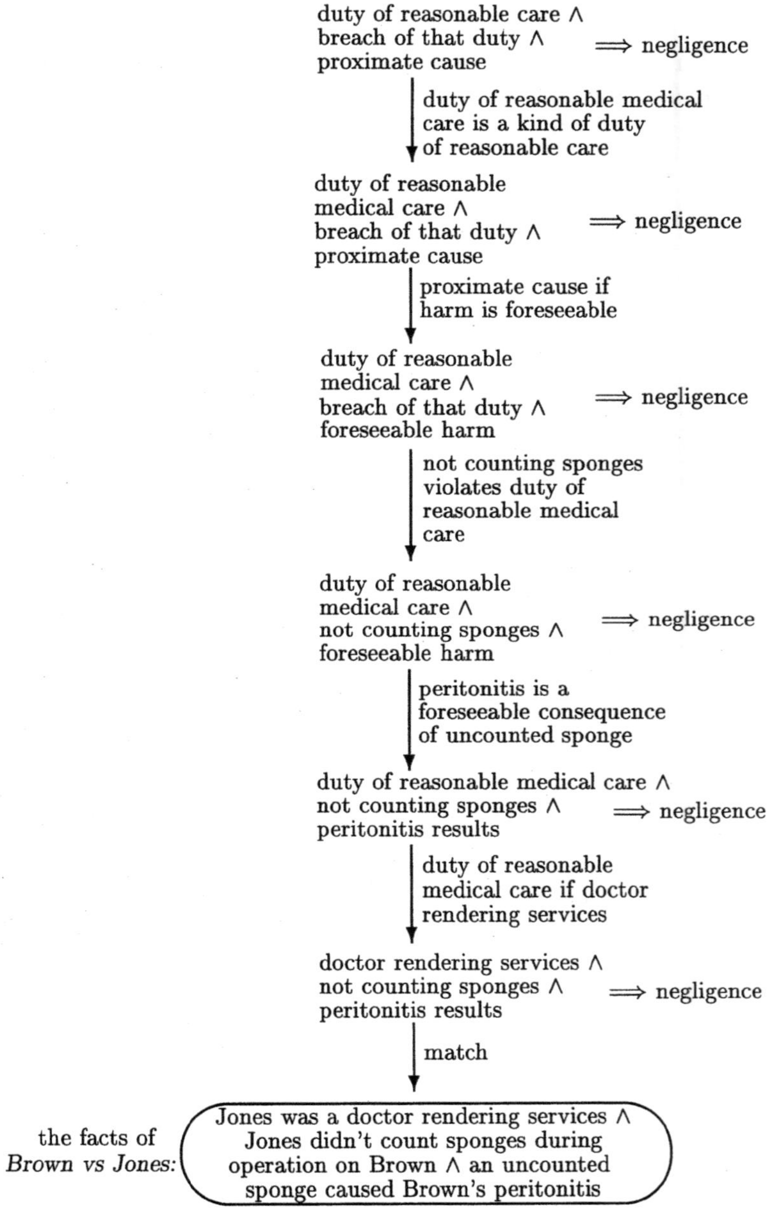

The Elements of Ratio Decidendi

A judicial decision consists of a determination that some legal predicate, *e.g.*, negligence liability, is satisfied by the facts of a case as determined by the trier of fact. If the decision has a justification in terms of these facts, this justification must necessarily include a warrant for the predicate together with all inferences necessary to match the antecedents of the warrant to the facts. Predictability, judicial economy, and the principle that like cases should be treated alike all argue that each warrant in this justification should apply equally to similar future cases.

In Figure 3.2, for example, the warrants necessary for the ultimate conclusion that negligence liability applies to Jones include (1) each warrant for negligence appearing in the reduction graph and (2) each reduction operation connecting successive warrants for negligence. Thus, the authoritative elements of the justification include not only the general rule "negligence follows from a duty of reasonable care and a breach of that duty that proximately causes harm," but also more specific warrants, including "negligence follows from a duty of reasonable medical care and a breach of that duty that proximately causes harm," and "not counting sponges violates the duty of reasonable medical care." If the Jones case were a precedent having the justification shown in Figure 3.2, then it could legitimately be cited for any of these propositions, for each is necessary to the ultimate decision under this justification.

The reduction-graph model of *ratio decidendi* is therefore as follows: if the justification for the decision in a precedent is represented as a warrant-reduction graph, the authoritative elements of the justification include (1) each warrant for the ultimate result appearing in the reduction graph and (2) each warrant used as a reduction operator to connect successive warrants for the ultimate result. Warrants of both types meet Wambaugh's test: if the warrant were false, the decision would no longer follow from the material facts of the case and the remaining warrants. For example, if failing to count sponges were not a violation of reasonable medical care, then one of the elements of negligence would not be met. In terms of the goal-reduction graph shown in Figure 3.1, there would be a gap between the goal of showing that a "duty of reasonable medical care was violated" and the facts of *Brown v. Jones*.

3.3 Adequacy of the Reduction-Graph Model

The previous sections identified five characteristics of *ratio decidendi* described in jurisprudential literature and set forth a computational model of *ratio decidendi*, the reduction-graph model. This section argues that the reduction-graph accounts for the most important of the characteristics identified in Section 3.1.

The first characteristic that an adequate model of *ratio decidendi* should account for is that the *ratio decidendi* of a case include the propositions of law, explicit or implicit in the opinion, that are necessary to the decision. As discussed above, the warrants constituting a reduction-graph representation of the justification for a decision each satisfy Wambaugh's criterion in that the negation of any such warrant would prevent the decision from following from the facts of the case and the remaining warrants in the justification. Each such warrant is therefore part of the *ratio decidendi*; conversely, the opinion's *dictum* is not represented in the reduction graph. The reduction-graph model therefore provides a criterion for distinguishing *ratio decidendi* from *dictum* and accounts for the logical relationship among the legal propositions constituting the *ratio decidendi*. Thus, the reduction-graph model satisfies the first criterion (provided that the justification for a judicial decision is accurately characterized as consisting of a warrant for the ultimate issue in the case together with all inferences necessary to match the antecedents of the warrant to the facts).

The second characteristic of *ratio decidendi* is that a gradation of warrants for the ultimate result in the case can usually be found in a single precedent, as typified by *Donoghue v. Stevenson.* As illustrated in Figure 3.2, the warrant-reduction representation of a precedent's justification makes explicit the manner in which successive reduction steps give rise to warrants at a range of levels of abstraction. The reduction-graph model therefore accounts for the existence of multiple warrants at different levels of abstraction in a single case.

The third characteristic of *ratio decidendi* is that the *ratio decidendi* of a precedent must be grounded in the specific facts of the case. This criterion is satisfied because the lowest abstraction warrants in a reduction graph are exemplars, *i.e.*, warrants that express the connection between concrete case facts and abstract predicates. For example, the lowest abstraction warrants in the goal-reduction graph shown in Figure 3.1 (which are equivalent to the last three reduction steps in the warrant-reduction graph shown in Figure 3.2) are (1) a duty of reasonably medical care arises when a doctor renders medical services (2) not counting sponges during an operation violates the duty of reasonable medical care, and (3) peritonitis is a foreseeable consequence of failing to count sponges during an operation. These warrants relate specific case facts (*e.g.*, failing to count sponges during an operation) to abstract legal predicates (*e.g.*, foreseeable harm).

Moreover, the antecedent of the lowest abstraction warrant in a warrant-reduction graph directly matches the material facts of the case. Thus, this warrant is an exemplar. Indeed, the lowest abstraction warrant in a warrant-reduction graph is very similar to Goodhart's model of *ratio decidendi*, consisting of the material facts of the case plus the decision justified by those facts.

Fourth, the reduction-graph model addresses the phenomenon that the precedential effect of a case depends not just on its material facts and the outcome justified by those facts, but also upon the theory under which the facts justified the outcome. This can be illustrated with Cross's example of *Bourhill v. Young*.

The two alternative justifications for the decision in *Bourhill v. Young* can be represented (in simplified form) by the warrant-reduction graphs shown in Figures 3.3 and 3.4.[21] Figure 3.3 represents the justification of *Bourhill* under the rationale that a driver owes no duty of care in respect of his driving to persons outside the area of reasonably foreseeable danger. At the top of Figure 3.3 is the rule that duty of reasonable care, breach of that duty, and harm proximately caused by the breach together imply negligence liability. The closed-world assumption (*i.e.,* the plaintiff's burden of proof) permits the converse of the contrapositive of this rule to be inferred, *i.e.*, if any of the conditions of the rule is false, there is no negligence liability.[22] The reduction operators necessary to match this rule to the facts of *Bourhill* under the first theory are the following:

- If a person is outside the area of foreseeable danger from an activity, then no duty of reasonable care is owed to that person by the actor.
- If a driver passes on the opposite side of a tram from which the plaintiff is alighting and has a collision 50 feet beyond the plaintiff, then the plaintiff is outside of the area of foreseeable danger.

Figure 3.4 represents the justification of *Bourhill* under the rationale that damages flowing from nervous shock are too remote a consequence of the breach of duty to be recoverable. The reduction operators necessary to match the rule under this theory are the following:

- If the harm complained of is a remote consequence of the breach of duty of reasonable care, then there is no proximate cause.
- Nervous shock suffered by an observer of an accident is a remote consequence of any breach of duty of reasonable care by the driver.

Recall the two hypothetical cases discussed above illustrating the inadequacy of material facts plus the decision thereon to represent *ratio decidendi*:

[21] These justifications are represented as warrant-reduction graphs, rather than by the equivalent goal-reduction graphs, because it is less convenient to represent the application of the closed-world assumption in a goal-reduction graph.

[22] Alternatively, the top-most warrant of the justification could be formulated as a biconditional, *e.g.*, duty & breach & proximate cause IFF negligence. The warrant IF (no duty) or (no breach) or (no proximate cause) THEN negligence would follow directly from this biconditional. I believe that this approach is less satisfactory than an appeal to the closed-world assumption because there is often ambiguity concerning whether a rule is actually intended to be a conditional or a biconditional (Allen and Saxon, 1991). However, it should be noted that the use of the closed-world assumption in Figure 3.3 and in subsequent justifications in this chapter applies to rules rather than to domain propositions, as in more typical models of legal burden of proof, *e.g.*, (Farley and Freeman, 1995).

- **H1.** The same facts as *Bourhill* except that the motorcycle driven by Young collides with a fireworks truck instead of a car, and Mrs. Bourhill is burned by a fragment from the resultant explosion of fireworks.

Figure 3.3. The first theory of *Bourhill v. Young*.

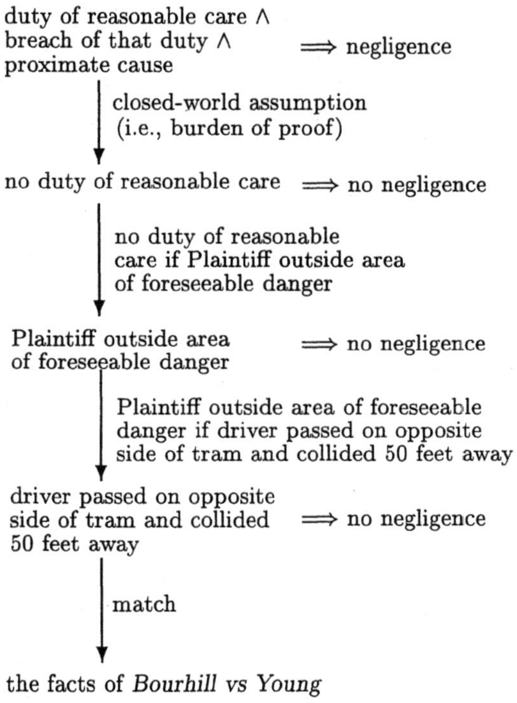

Figure 3.4. The second theory of *Bourhill v. Young*.

duty of reasonable care $\wedge$
breach of that duty $\wedge$ $\Longrightarrow$ negligence
proximate cause

↓ closed-world assumption (i.e., burden of proof)

no proximate cause $\Longrightarrow$ no negligence

↓ no proximate cause if harm is a remote consequence of breach

the harm is a remote consequence of breach $\Longrightarrow$ no negligence

↓ nervous shock resulting from observing accident is a remote consequence of breach

the harm suffered by Plaintiff is nervous shock resulting from observing accident $\Longrightarrow$ no negligence

↓ match

the facts of *Bourhill vs Young*

- **H2.** The same facts as ***Bourhill*** except that Young passes the tram on the same side as the alighting Mrs. Bourhill, missing her by inches and causing a severe emotional shock.

Suppose that the first theory of ***Bourhill*** was intended by the House of Lords (as speeches make clear was indeed the case). The lowest generality warrant in Figure 3.3 matches the facts of *H1* just as well as it matches as the facts of ***Bourhill*** itself. Thus, the justification for ***Bourhill*** under Theory 1, which is represented in Figure 3.3, would apply equally to *H1:* Young would not be liable because Mrs. Bourhill was outside the area of foreseeable danger, notwithstanding that an unforeseeable causal chain led to her injury.

If the House of Lords had instead intended the Theory 2, the lowest generality warrant represented in Figure 3.4 would match the facts of *H2*. Thus, the justification for ***Bourhill*** under Theory 2, which is represented in Figure 3.4, would apply equally to *H2*: nervous shock is a remote consequence of Young's breach of duty of reasonable care, notwithstanding that Mrs. Bourhill was within the area of foreseeable harm.

The antecedents of the lowest generality warrant in each reduction graph omit some facts that are arguably "material" to the cases. For example, the fact that Young was not exercising reasonable care in driving is surely a material fact, unlike, *e.g.*, Young's hair color. If the accident had been caused by a meteor striking the ground while Young was waiting at an intersection, it would have been unnecessary to address the issues of the scope of foreseeable danger or remoteness of Bourhill's injuries. However, Young's lack of reasonable care is not part of the *ratio decidendi* under either interpretation because it plays no role in the justification of the case under either interpretation, notwithstanding that there was in fact a determination that Young failed to exercise reasonable care. This is consistent with Wambaugh's criterion: the decision in the case would have been no different had the court believed that Young had exercised reasonable care in driving (although the case might have been decided on different grounds). The reduction-graph model therefore embodies a more restrictive criterion for relevance than Goodhart's criterion of materiality: only those facts appearing in the antecedents of a warrant in a precedent's justification are in the *ratio decidendi.*

Showing how negligence liability would follow in *H2* under Theory 1 and in *H1* under Theory 2 requires an additional precedent.[23] For purposes of illustration, let *P2* be a precedent in which a carelessly driven motorcyclist passes on the same side as a passenger who has just alighted and is stepping across the street to the sidewalk. Jumping from the path of the motorcycle,

[23]Note that "theory" in this context means more than just the *ratio decidendi* of a particular case. Instead, a theory of a legal predicate like "negligence" consists of a set of secondary predicates relevant to that legal predicate (e.g., "duty," "breach," "proximate cause," "foreseeability") together with a consistent set of warrants that relate these secondary predicates to the legal predicate.

Figure 3.5. The justification for *P2* under Theory 1.

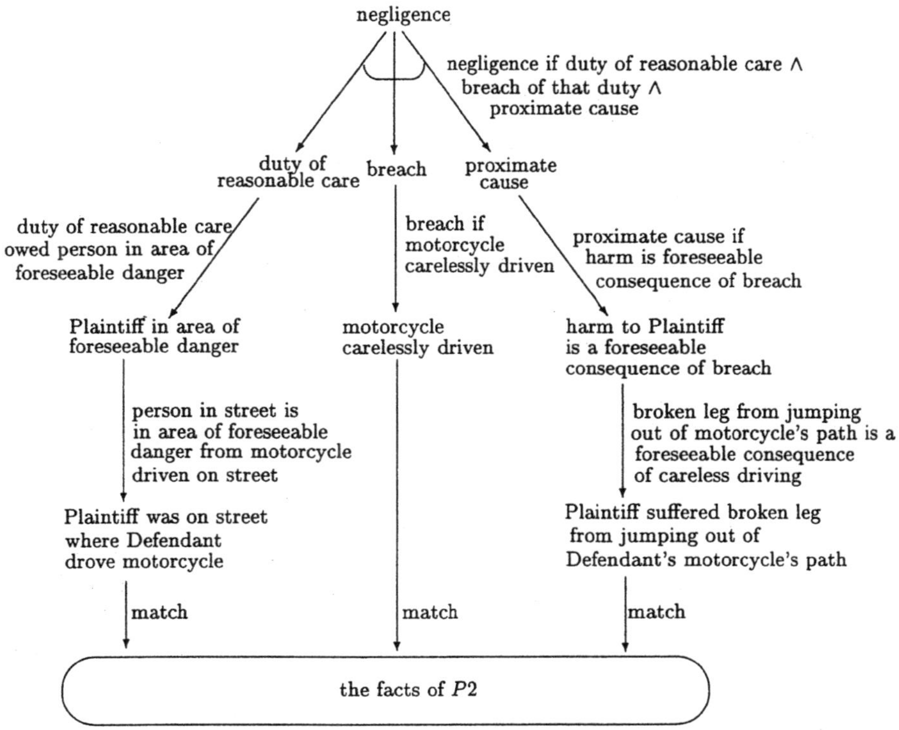

the passenger trips and suffers a broken leg. The motorcyclist is held liable to the passenger for her injuries.

Figure 3.5 shows a justification for *P2* under Theory 1 as a goal-reduction graph.[24] The reduction steps are as follows:

- A duty of reasonable care is owed persons within the area of foreseeable danger from an activity.

[24]The goal-reduction representation is used in Figures 3.5–3.8 because it is somewhat more compact than the equivalent warrant-reduction representation.

Figure 3.6. The justification for $P2$ under Theory 2.

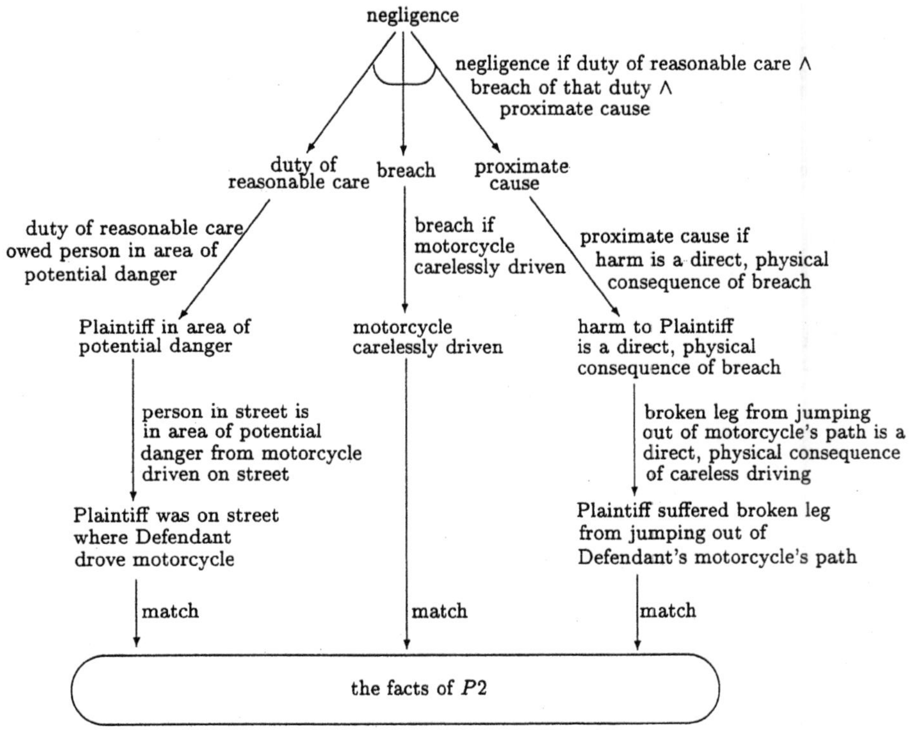

- A person on a street is within the area of foreseeable danger from a motorcycle driven on the street.
- Carelessly driving a motorcycle is a breach of the duty of reasonable care.
- An action is the proximate cause of harm if the harm is a foreseeable consequence of the action.
- A broken leg suffered from when jumping from the path of a carelessly driven motorcycle is a foreseeable consequence of careless driving.

A justification for *P2* under Theory 2 is shown in Figure 3.6. The reduction steps are as follows (steps differing from the justification under Theory 1 are shown in bold):

- A duty of care is owed persons **within the area of potential (though not necessarily foreseeable)** danger from an activity.[25]
- A person on a street is within the area of **potential danger** from a motorcycle driven on the street.
- Carelessly driving a motorcycle is a breach of the duty of reasonable care.
- An action is the proximate cause of harm if the harm is a **direct, physical** consequence of the action.
- A broken leg suffered from when jumping from the path of a carelessly driven motorcycle is a **direct, physical** consequence of the carelessness.

Assume that it is undisputed in *H1* that a burn resulting from the collision between the carelessly driven motorcycle and a fireworks truck is an unforeseeable, but direct, physical consequence of the carelessness. Assume, in addition, that it is undisputed in *H2* that nervous shock from nearly being hit by a carelessly driven motorcycle is a foreseeable consequence of careless driving.

As with *Bourhill*, the precedential effect of *P2* depends on the particular theory under which it was decided. If *P2* were decided under Theory 1, the justification for negligence liability shown in Figure 3.7 could be constructed for *H2*. Warrants that are identical to those in *P2* are annotated with "[*P2*]," indicating that the *backing* (Toulmin, 1958)—that is, the reason for believing that the warrant's conclusion follows from its antecedent—is the authority of the court in *P2* to enunciate the warrant. The only warrant in this justification not present in *P2* is that nervous shock from nearly being hit by a carelessly driven motorcycle is a foreseeable consequence of the carelessness, which is

[25]This warrant was expressed by the dissent in *Palsgraf v. Long Island R.R. Co.*, 248 N.Y. 399, 162 N.E. 99 (1928).

Figure 3.7. The justification for negligence in $H2$ given that $P2$ was decided under Theory 1.

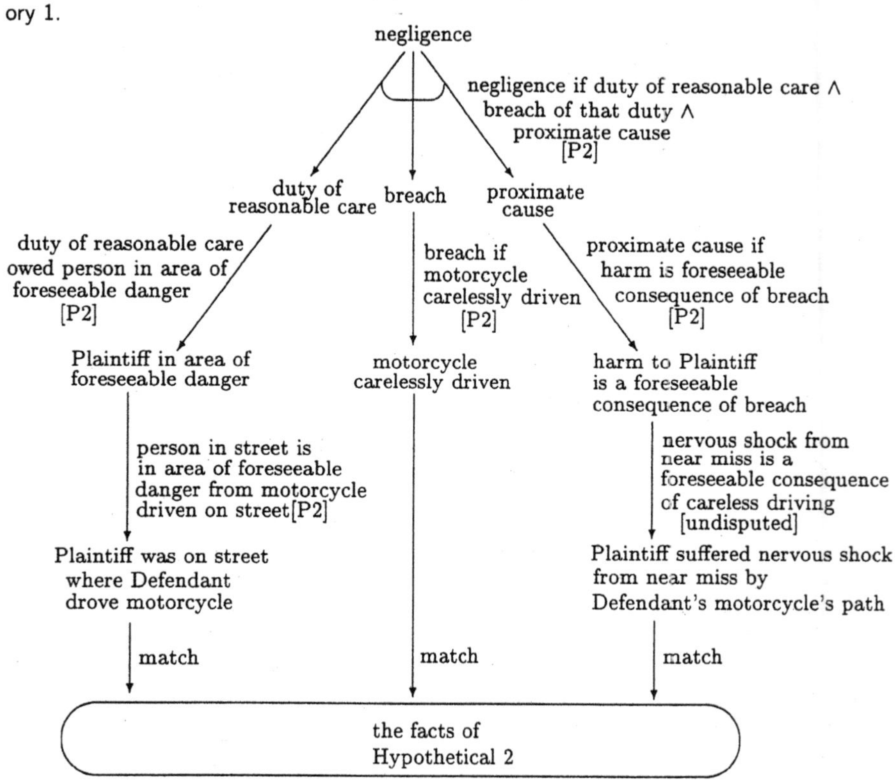

Figure 3.8. The justification for negligence in $H1$ given that $P2$ was decided under Theory 2.

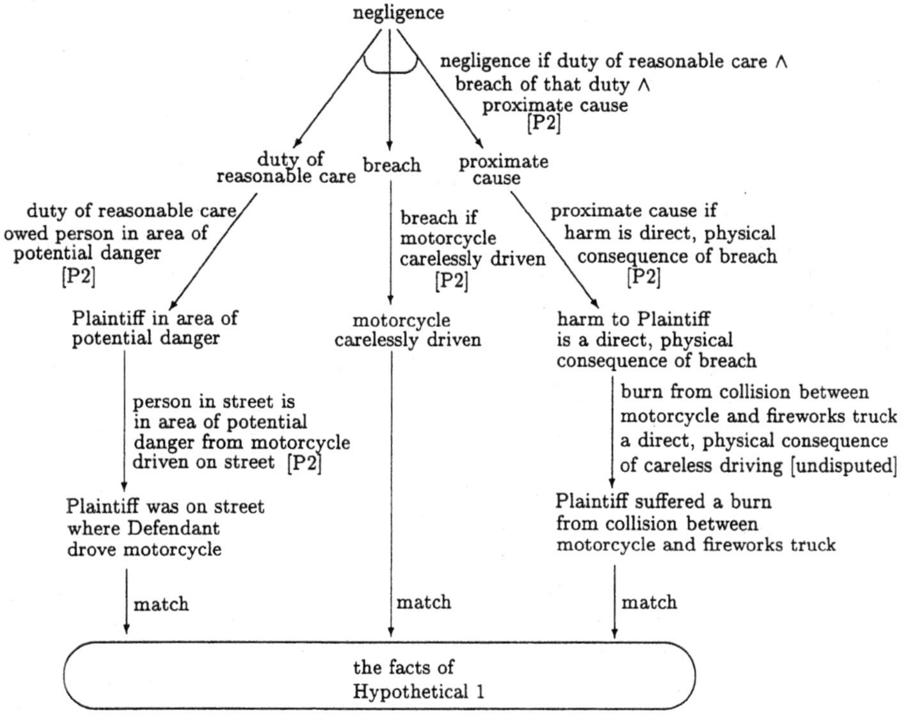

undisputed. *P2* would not apply to *H1* because the injury in *H1* was not foreseeable, as required under this theory of decision.

If *P2* were instead decided under Theory 2, the justification for negligence liability shown in Figure 3.8 could be constructed for *H1*. The only warrant in this justification not present in Figure 3.6 is that a burn resulting from a collision between the carelessly driven motorcycle and a fireworks truck is a direct, physical consequence of the carelessness, which is undisputed. *P2* would not apply to *H2* under this theory because nervous shock is not a physical consequence of the defendant's carelessness. Thus, the outcome in the hypotheticals under Theory 2 is the reverse of the outcome under Theory 1.

In summary, the reduction-graph model permits the theory of decision to control the case's precedential effect by explicitly representing the connection between the material facts of a case and the theory under which it was decided.

The fifth characteristic of *ratio decidendi* is that subsequent decisions can limit, extend, or overturn existing precedents. Three distinct forms of retroactive effect of precedents on the *ratio decidendi* of earlier precedents can be distinguished. One form of retroactive modification occurs when later cases incrementally extend or restrict the scope of an earlier precedent. Goodhart's reference to the metaphor that "the curve of law [requires] a series of points" (Goodhart, 1959) p. 124, is a recognition of the phenomenon that the precise scope of a precedent is determined in part by other precedents.

A second form of retroactive modification occurs when a later court explicitly modifies or rejects the holding of an earlier precedent or precedents. For example, the U.S. Supreme Court in *Brown v. Board of Education*[26] explicitly rejected the "separate but equal" doctrine of *Plessy v. Ferguson*[27] as it applied to education. The third form of retroactive modification occurs when later decisions erode the justification of earlier decisions without explicitly rejecting their holding.

Retroactive modifications of the first type arise from the nature of arguments based on exemplars. The persuasiveness of an argument based on the similarity between a new case and an exemplar of a predicate depends not just on the degree of relevant similarity between the new case and the exemplar, but also on the degree of relevant similarity between the new case and members of the predicate's *contrast set*, that is, exemplars of the predicate's negation. The scope of an exemplar therefore depends not only on the knowledge available for determining relevant similarity, but also on the propinquity of other exemplars. The boundaries of a legal concept in instance space, ill-defined when there are

[26]347 U.S. 483 (1954).
[27]163 U.S. 537 (1896).

few exemplars, are gradually delineated as additional exemplars are successively added.[28]

Modeling this form of retroactive modification requires explicit representation of the exemplars corresponding to each precedent. The reduction-graph model satisfies this requirement, as do the exemplar-based based models discussed below in Section 3.4.

Two distinct aspects of retroactive modifications of the second type must be modeled: the effect of the adoption or rejection on the *ratio decidendi* of the earlier precedent; and the warrant in the later case expressing the adoption or rejection. Modeling the effect on the earlier case is trivial. If a warrant such as the "separate but equal" doctrine has been rejected, it should simply be removed from the knowledge base. No change need be made to a *ratio decidendi* that is adopted by in subsequent decision.

Modeling the warrant in a later case expressing the adoption or rejection of an earlier warrant is somewhat more problematical. The reduction-graph representation includes all warrants necessary for the decision to follow from the material facts of the case under a particular rationale. The decision to reject one warrant in favor or another is, however, a meta-level decision that has no obvious place in the reduction graph *per se*. In effect, it represents instead a choice among possible reduction graphs rather than a step within a single reduction graph.

However, the rejection by a higher court of a given warrant, such as the "separate but equal" doctrine, is unquestionably binding on lower courts, notwithstanding that the rejection might not have been absolutely necessary for the decision in the higher court, *e.g.*, even if the earlier warrant could have been merely narrowed rather than outright rejected. This suggests that Wambaugh's criterion—that a proposition is part of the *ratio decidendi* of a decision only if the deciding court could not have believed the negation of the proposition without changing the outcome of the case—is too narrow to account for this aspect of *ratio decidendi*. The institutional obligation of courts to enunciate clear rules for the guidance of lower courts and potential litigants sometimes leads courts to explicitly alter prior decisions or mediate between competing lines of decision even when doing so is not strictly necessary for a decision in the case before the court. Because they are not strictly necessary for the outcome of the case, these explicit choices among rationales are not elements of a reduction graph, notwithstanding that they are binding on subsequent decisions.[29]

Accounting for the third form of retroactive effect on precedents, in which later cases erode the justifications for earlier cases without explicitly reversing their outcome, requires a model of precedent in which the intermediate rea-

---

[28]It has been noted that exemplar-based categories tend to be "hyper-polygons whose edges maintain equal 'distance' from nearest examples of different classes, where distance is measured by the system's similarity metric. These boundaries are somewhat analogous to contours of zero potential between positive and negative electric charges in physical space" (Clark, 1988a).

[29]A model of explicit choices among competing rules of decision is proposed in (Prakken and Sartor, 1998).

soning steps, as well as the case facts and outcome, are represented. Berman and Hafner (Berman and Hafner, 1995) set forth a *red-flag algorithm* that uses an explicit representation of the warrants constituting the *ratio decidendi* of precedents to recognize ("red-flag") precedents whose precedential effect has been weakened by subsequent decisions. By making these warrants explicit, the reduction-graph model provides the information required by the red-flag algorithm.

In summary, the reduction-graph model can model the phenomenon that later cases incrementally extend or restrict the scope of earlier precedents because reduction graphs explicitly represent the exemplars in precedents' justifications. Moreover, the reduction-graph model makes explicit the warrants whose erosion can weaken precedents that have not yet been explicitly overruled. However, the reduction-graph model is not adequate to represent a court's choice among competing rationales.

3.4 Limitations of Purely Exemplar-Based Models of Ratio Decidendi

The previous sections have argued that exemplars are an essential component of the *ratio decidendi* of a case. This section argues that exemplar-based reasoning is not *per se* sufficient as a model of *ratio decidendi.* Specifically, a model of precedent consisting of representations of the material facts and outcome of precedents together with a single global measure of similarity is equivalent to Goodhart's model of precedent. Such a model is therefore subject to Cross's critique of Goodhart's models. The applicability of Cross's critique to purely exemplar-based models of *ratio decidendi* can be illustrated with the example *Bourhill v. Young.*

At least four different approaches to exemplar-based reasoning have been investigated. The first and simplest approach treats precedents as points in a feature space. The legal classification of a new case is determined by finding the new case's nearest neighbor in the feature space and applying the legal classification of that neighbor to the new case. The nearest neighbor is determined by a metric that typically consists of a weighted sum of featural differences, where the weight of a feature is intended to represent its relevance or "salience." Typical instances of this approach include PANNDA (Tyree, 1989) and the nearest-neighbor approach described in (MacKaay and Robillard, 1974). This approach is a legal application of nearest-neighbor instance-based classification algorithms, which have been used for classification in a wide variety of domains. *See generally* (Aha, 1990).[30]

[30] A more detailed description of the weighted nearest-neighbor and dimensional approaches is presented in Chapter 7.

A second approach also involves nearest-neighbor classification, but employs a structural representation of case facts and uses ***structural similarity*** between case facts as a similarity metric. Two cases are structurally similar if "objects in ... two analogs can be placed into correspondence so that relations also correspond" (Holyoak and Thagard, 1989a). This approach, which was originally suggested as a model of precedential legal reasoning in (Winston, 1980), was used in BRAMBLE (Bellairs, 1989). The motivation for use of structural similarity as a similarity metric is the hypothesis that relevant similarity between cases is a function of "relational commonalities independent of the objects in which those relations are embedded." (Gentner, 1989b).

A third approach, ***dimensional analysis*** (Ashley, 1990), uses knowledge of the factors that tend to establish or negate a predicate and the magnitude of these factors in precedents and new cases. These factors, or ***dimensions***, provide criteria for determining the "most on-point" precedents and a mechanism for generating arguments based on a comparison between a new case and precedents. Specifically, a precedent is similar to a new case ("on-point") if the two cases share one or more dimensions. One precedent is more similar to a new case than a second precedent if the dimensions shared by the first precedent and the new case are a superset of those shared by the second precedent and the new case. The most similar ("most-on point") precedents are those that are similar and for which there is no more similar case. Arguments for a classification of a new case can be based on a comparison between a new case and the most similar precedents.

The final approach is the "prototype-plus-deformation" model used in TAXMAN II and described in (McCarty and Sridharan, 1982). Under this model, a legal concept has three components. First, there is an optional invariant component that provides necessary, but not sufficient, conditions for satisfying the concept. Second is a set of exemplars providing sufficient conditions. Third, there is a set of transformations expressing various relationships among the exemplars. The result is an "ordered space of exemplars" in which a partial ordering is imposed on the exemplars by the transformations. Such a space can sometimes be represented by a single prototype together with a series of transformations, which act as "deformations." A legal argument for a particular classification is modeled as a set of transformations that includes all the exemplars and the given case. A counter-argument consists of a set of transformations that includes the exemplars but excludes the given case. The most persuasive argument is the one that "imposes the greatest degree of coherence on the set of exemplars."

Consider first the structural similarity approach. Whether *Bourhill* or *P2* has a higher degree of structural similarity to *H1* or to *H2* depends only on the representation used for the cases and not at all on the theory under which *Bourhill* and *P2* were decided. A representation that leads to the correct matches under one theory will necessarily lead to incorrect matches under the other theory. Therefore, the structural similarity approach is inadequate to distinguish among the possible *rationes* of *Bourhill.*

Under the dimensional approach, the precedents and hypotheticals might be represented as shown in Figure 3.9. There are two dimensions: foreseeability of harm, which ranges from none to high; and directness of consequences, which ranges from none to direct. Greater values along each of the dimensions tends to strengthen the plaintiff's claim for negligence. *Bourhill* and *P2* share all the same dimensions as *H1* and *H2* and are therefore "most on point" cases.

The most that can be said about *H1* and *H2* under this approach is simply to compare the magnitudes of the two dimensions in the hypotheticals with those in *Bourhill* and *P2.* There is no way to represent either of the alternative theories under which either precedent has greater relevant similarity to one hypothetical than to the other.

A featural representation of the cases might be that each case consists of two features (foreseeability and directness) each with three possible values (the same as under the dimensional approach). The featural approach would differ from the dimensional approach in two respects. First, under the featural approach there would be no notion that changing a value feature in a particular direction would tend to establish or negate a given recovery by the claimant. Second, the featural approach would have explicit feature weighting.[31]

At first glance it appears that if such a weighting scheme could be devised, it would provide a mechanism for expressing the precedential effect of individual precedents under each possible theory. For example, suppose that *Bourhill* and *P2* were decided under the first theory, under which *H1* should be controlled by *Bourhill* and *H2* should be controlled by *P2.* This could be modeled by placing a higher weight on the foreseeability feature than on the directness feature. Given a standard weighted Euclidean distance function, $\sqrt{a(F_1 - F_2)^2 + b(D_1 - D_2)^2}$ (where F_n and D_n are the values (1–3) of foreseeability and directness of consequences respectively for case n, a and b are nonnegative weights of foreseeability and directness respectively, and adjacent feature values are separated by a unit distance) setting $a > b$ would cause *H2*'s strongest match to be to *P2* and *H1*'s strongest match to be to *Bourhill.*

However, suppose that there is a third hypothetical, *H3*, in which the motorcyclist speeds on a path directly towards Mrs. Bourhill, who is unable to get out of the way. However, just as the motorcycle is about to hit Mrs. Bourhill an IRA bomb blows up the motorcyclist, injuring Mrs. Bourhill. *H3*, shown in Figure 3.9, differs from *P2* by a distance of 1 in the foreseeability feature

[31] An argument for the infeasibility of devising such a weighting scheme is made in (Ashley and Rissland, 1988).

Figure 3.9. Featural and dimensional representations of precedents and hypotheticals.

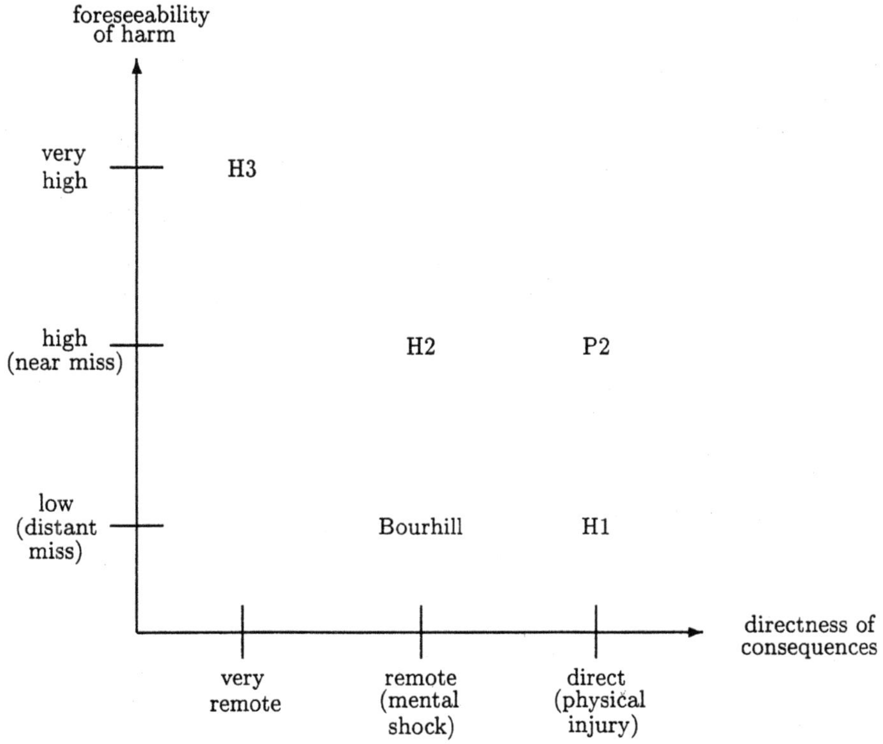

and 2 in its directness feature. *H3* differs from *Bourhill* by a distance of 2 in the foreseeability feature, but 1 in the directness feature. Thus, *H3*'s difference from *P2* is $\sqrt{a1^2 + b2^2} = \sqrt{a + 4b}$, and *H3*'s difference from *Bourhill* is $\sqrt{a2^2 + b1^2} = \sqrt{4a + b}$. *H3* clearly should have the same result as *Bourhill*, since there is no direct connection between the motorcyclist's wrongdoing and the Plaintiff's injury. Thus, it must be the case that the distance from *P2*, $\sqrt{a + 4b}$, is greater than the distance from *Bourhill*, $\sqrt{4a + b}$. However, $\sqrt{a + 4b} > \sqrt{4a + b}$ implies (assuming, in consonance with the assumption that the roots represent positive distances, that only positive roots are considered) that $b > a$, which contradicts the assumption that $a > b$. Thus, no global feature weighting scheme based on a Euclidean distance function can adequately model the precedential effect of the justifications of *Bourhill* and *P2* on these hypotheticals.

Finally, the transformation coherence approach suffers from the same inadequacy as the other approaches. Whether the transformations from *Bourhill* to *H1* and *P2* to *H2* are more or less coherent than the transformations from *Bourhill* to *H2* and *P2* to *H1* depends only on the facts being transformed and not at all on the theory under which *Bourhill* and *P2* were decided.[32] Thus, this approach is also inadequate, standing alone, to model the effects of different possible *rationes* of the precedents.

In summary, exemplar-based reasoning is essential for any adequate model of *ratio decidendi*, but a model of *ratio decidendi* that consists only of exemplar-based reasoning implicitly subscribes to Goodhart's view and is therefore subject to Cross's critique.

3.5 The Pragmatics of the Reduction-Graph Model

The reduction-graph model is a theory about the form of knowledge necessary to represent the *ratio decidendi* of legal precedents. Any implementation of this model must address several issues beyond the model itself, including the problem of exemplar matching, the role to be played by the backing of warrants, and phenomenon that judicial opinions typically fail to articulate all the reasoning steps necessary to justify the case decision.

The Problem of Exemplar Matching

Establishing a conclusion about a new case requires reduction operators to bridge the gap between abstract legal predicates and the specific facts of the new case. Exemplars play a central role in constructing justifications for conclusions about new cases because they connect specific facts to abstract features.

[32]One description of the prototypes-and-deformations model suggests that it may be intended to apply to the explanations, as well as the facts, of precedents (McCarty, 1991). This refinement would represent a departure from the simple exemplar-based approach and therefore from the applicability of Cross's critique.

However, it is rare for the facts of any exemplar to precisely match the facts of a new case.[33] As a result, determining which abstract features are satisfied by a new case typically requires determining which exemplar or exemplars have the highest degree of relevant similarity to the new case. This determination requires a reliable criterion for the degree of "relevant similarity" between pairs of cases.

Unfortunately, an appropriate criterion for relevant similarity between legal exemplars and new cases is difficult to devise. Typical formulations among legal scholars are that two cases share relevant similarity with respect to a legal category if the "principle of policy" (Bodenheimer, 1974), "rationale" (Murray, 1982), or "justification" (Raz, 1979) for membership in the category by the first applies as well to the second. An alternative formulation by Frederick Schauer focuses on the *category of assimilation* formed by equating two cases. Schauer views the task of a theory of precedent to be to explain how and why "in a world in which a single event may fit into many different categories ... some assimilations are plausible and others are not." (Schauer, 1987) p. 581.

Precedents vary in the extent to which they articulate reasons that the facts of an exemplar satisfy a legal category. Often, precedents set forth no reasons why the facts of exemplars satisfy the legal categories of which they are members. Determining the degree of relevant similarity between the facts of an unjustified exemplar and a given case requires determining the most plausible justification that can be constructed to apply to both the exemplar and the new case. A number of sources of knowledge for constructing and evaluating such justifications have been identified, including social custom, historical development of legal doctrine, and models of social justice (Cardozo, 1921). However, these knowledge sources are external to the precedents themselves. Often, these knowledge sources permit conflicting arguments to be constructed, but provide no firm ground for choosing among these arguments. A judge faced with such a case must engage in "interstitial" law making, imposing, rather than discovering or inferring, a justification common to the exemplar and the new case.

Sometimes a precedent sets forth a justification for an exemplar, but the justification is too general to be directly applicable. For example, knowing that the justification of an exemplar is that "no one should be permitted to profit from his own wrongdoing" may be of little help in resolving a subsequent case involving a lesser degree of wrongdoing, because the determinative issue—what degree of wrongdoing is sufficient to foreclose recovery—is not resolved by this general statement of policy. Just as under the first possibility, a more specific justification must be constructed and evaluated using knowledge of custom, history, and social justice. However, the possible justifications that such

[33]The hypotheticals posed in the context of *Bourhill* were contrived to minimize problems of exemplar matching.

a precedent can share with any other case are restricted under these circumstances to justifications consistent with this policy. Thus, a general statement of policy constrains, but doesn't obviate, the construction of new justifications.

Even if a precedent provides specific reasons why the facts of an exemplar satisfy a legal predicate, it may be problematical to determine whether these reasons apply strongly enough to a new case that the legal predicate should apply to the new case as well. The variety of complex factors that affect whether an entity satisfies a given category are explored in (Murphy and Medin, 1985) and (Lakoff, 1987).

Each of the four computational approaches discussed above in Section 3.4—nearest-neighbor, dimensional analysis, structure matching, and prototypes-and-deformations—accounts for certain aspects of the phenomenon of exemplar matching. However, none provides an complete model of the manner in which knowledge of social custom, historical development of legal doctrine, or models of social justice can guide decisions about the equivalence of cases with respect to a legal category.

Any implementation of the reduction-graph model must provide some mechanism for exemplar matching. However, the reduction-graph model itself is not tied to any position on the issue of which of the four existing computational methods best models the process of matching unexplained exemplars, or whether instead some alternative approach might be superior.

Regardless of the particular mechanism for exemplar matching or model of case similarity adopted, knowledge of the *ratio decidendi* of a precedent—that is, of a warrant for the ultimate conclusion in the case together with all reduction steps necessary to match the antecedents of the warrant to the facts—can simplify the task of exemplar matching by permitting the precedent to be viewed as consisting of multiple exemplars rather than as a single exemplar (as illustrated in Section 2.3). Exemplar matching should therefore be applied to the smallest collections of case facts that justify legal conclusions in a precedent. Any coarser granularity matching compromises the ability to express and use the *ratio decidendi* of the precedent.

Justifications for Warrants

Under the reduction-graph model, the warrants in the explanation of a judicial decision that are authoritative as to subsequent cases include a warrant for the ultimate result and all reduction operators necessary to match the antecedent of this warrant to the facts of the case. These warrants each satisfy Wambaugh's criterion because if any were negated the decision would no longer follow from the remaining warrants.

However, the warrants constituting the *ratio decidendi* of a precedent may themselves have justifications. Two forms of such justifications for warrants can be distinguished. The *backing* for a warrant consists of the institutional justification for believing that the warrant's consequent follows from its antecedents. For example, the backing of a statutory rule consists of the authority under which the statute was enacted. Similarly, the backing at the appellate level for an exemplar that resolves a question concerning whether a given set of facts satisfies a particular legal predicate is the institutional deference of the appellate court to findings by triers of fact. Thus, the backing for a warrant is related to its "pedigree or the manner in which [it] was adopted or developed" (Dworkin, 1977) p. 17, rather than to its content.

The *rationale* for a warrant, by contrast, consists of the purposes, motivations, or reasoning that underlying the content of the warrant. The rationale for warrants representing the resolution of legal issues can include social custom, historical development, and models of social justice—the factors discussed above in the context of exemplar matching.

The rationale for a warrant that constitutes an element of the *ratio decidendi* of a case is not itself part of the *ratio decidendi.* This is because the decision in a precedent would still follow from the warrants and facts of the case even if the rationale were absent or negated. In practice, subsequent courts may attempt to narrow or distinguish a warrant whose rationale is unsound or unpersuasive. However, the authoritative character of a precedent's warrants is not determined by the soundness of the rationale for those warrants. Law is at best only a partially deductive system. Judges must engage in interstitial law making because existing authoritative warrants are typically insufficient to deductively entail the resolution of new disputes.

The distinction between warrants and their rationales is illustrated by Goodhart's observation that many of the most influential precedents were decided on the basis of specious arguments. Among other examples, Goodhart discusses the case of *Hochster v. Delatour*,[34] in which it was held that suit for breach of contract could be brought after renunciation of the contract by the defendant but before the date on which the contract was to be performed. Lord Campbell, C.J., stated that "It is surely much more rational ... that, after the renunciation of the agreement by the defendant, the plaintiff should be at liberty to consider himself absolved from any future performance of it, retaining his right to sue." Goodhart quotes with approval Corbin's statement that "it does not follow therefrom that the plaintiff should be allowed to sue before the date fixed for performance by the defendant." Notwithstanding Campbell's *non sequitur*, *Hochster v. Delatour* became a leading case in contracts.

[34] 2 E. & B. 678 (1853).

The rule that suit for breach of contract can be brought any time after renunciation is a warrant necessary for the decision in *Hochster v. Delatour*, *i.e.*, the decision in *Hochster* would no longer follow from facts of the case and the remaining warrants if this rule were absent or negated. Accordingly, the rule is authoritative as to subsequent cases. Lord Campbell's rationale for this rule, by contrast, is a not essential for the outcome of the case. If the rationale for the rule had been entirely different, the rule would nevertheless have been valid because Lord Campbell was empowered to enunciate whatever propositions of law were necessary to resolve the dispute before him.

Even if Lord Campbell had ruled instead that a plaintiff must wait until the date on which a contract was to be performed before suing for breach, the rationale for the ruling would still not have been a sound deduction, because the law of contract at the time of the decision in *Hochster v. Delatour* was insufficient to deductively resolve this issue.[35]

In summary, the authoritative character of warrants enunciated in precedents comes from the institutional obligation of courts to resolve the disputes that come before them, even if doing so requires use of warrants that cannot be justified by sound deductions. Therefore, it is the warrants necessary for the resolution of a case and not the rationale for those warrants that are authoritative as to subsequent cases.

Although not part of the *ratio decidendi* of precedents, the rationale underlying decisions play an essential role in actual legal discourse (Berman and Hafner, 1993). Accordingly, a complete theory of legal precedent must account for the teleological elements of precedents as well as their *ratio decidendi.*

Explanation Incompleteness

Even the most complete model of *ratio decidendi* is only useful to the extent that the *ratio decidendi* of precedents can in practice be determined. Unfortunately, judicial opinions seldom make explicit all inference steps necessary to justify a decision:

> Incompleteness is the rule, not the exception; even a brief examination of cases makes this apparent ... Legal decisions contain obvious gaps .... (Warner, 1989) pp. 1532-1533.

Explanation indeterminacy is therefore a problem for any theory of *ratio decidendi.*

Richard Warner in *Three Theories of Legal Reasoning* (Warner, 1989) suggests that gaps in the reasoning of precedents can occur when there are several alternative rationales leading to the same conclusion. "[S]ince the court could decide the case without choosing any one alternative, the court may simply not

---

[35] For example, a possible rationale for the opposite ruling would be that a contract can only be breached after the date on which the contract was to be performed. However, this reasoning simply begs the question whether renunciation of a contract itself constitutes a breach.

have chosen any." Regardless of their source, such gaps can only be bridged by constructing a plausible inference step: "[C]ompleting incomplete legal reasoning is typically a matter of constructing premises, not of divining what unstated premises were in the mind of the court."

Three distinct approaches to the problem of explanation incompleteness in modeling *ratio decidendi* are possible. One approach is to adopt the most plausible completion of the missing reasoning steps. The result of this approach is a representation of the *ratio decidendi* under one construction of the decision.[36] This construction, and therefore the corresponding representation of the *ratio decidendi* might have to be revised in light of subsequent decisions interpreting the precedent. In the meanwhile, however, a plausible and complete representation of the *ratio decidendi* would exist.

A second approach is to represent all plausible completions of the justification of a decision, suitably annotating the alternative reasoning steps. This amounts to representing a precedent as a set of plausible *rationes*. The benefit of this approach is that it provides a mechanism for modeling the ability of skillful attorneys to base a variety of plausible arguments on a single precedent by exploiting the ambiguities in the precedent's justification.

The most conservative approach is to omit any implicit reasoning steps, retaining only those warrants stated explicitly. This approach has the benefit of precluding spurious warrants at the cost of making it impossible to model an attorney's ability to generate the plausible constructions of a precedent.

Some choice among the these approaches to explanation incompleteness must be made in any implemented model of *ratio decidendi.* Criteria for making this choice include the purposes for which the precedents are being modeled and the manner in which the representations of *rationes* will be used.

In summary, explanation incompleteness is a problem for any model of *ratio decidendi* and indeed for any model of precedent-based legal reasoning. The representation of the *ratio decidendi* of a precedent that best models attorneys' use of precedents is one in which "gaps" in the justification of the precedent have been bridged by one or more plausible constructions of the precedent.[37]

3.6 Summary

This chapter has described a model of *ratio decidendi* under which the authoritative elements of a precedent include (1) each warrant for the ultimate result appearing in the warrant-reduction graph of the precedent's justification and (2) each reduction operator connecting successive warrants in this reduction graph. This collection comprises those warrants in the precedent's justification

[36] As discussed in Section 4.3, this approach was used in the development of GREBE's case library.

[37] The task of automatically generating plausible justifications to bridge gaps in the reasoning of precedents is a form of *abduction* (Pople, 1973).

that satisfy Wambaugh's criterion: if any such warrant were false, then the outcome of the case would no longer follow from the remaining warrants. The reduction-graph model accounts for most of the important characteristics of *ratio decidendi* identified in the jurisprudential literature. In particular, the reduction-graph model shows how the theory under which a case is decided controls its precedential effect. However, the reduction-graph model is not *per se* adequate to represent a choice among competing theories of decision, since this is equivalent to a choice among reduction graphs.

A purely exemplar-based model of precedent implicitly adheres to Goodhart's view of *ratio decidendi* and therefore suffer from its critical weakness: failure to represent the reasoning under which a decision follows from the material facts of the case. By contrast, the reduction-graph model explicitly represents this reasoning. This permits a new case to be matched against the smallest collections of case facts that justified a legal conclusion in a precedent rather than requiring a new case to match the entire facts of any one precedent.

A complete computational theory of legal precedent must address several issues beyond the scope of the reduction-graph model of *ratio decidendi*. One of the most critical is the nature of the processes of generating and evaluating plausible justifications for (1) exemplar matching and (2) bridging gaps in the reasoning of precedents. These processes depend on sources of knowledge external to precedents themselves, such as custom, historical development, models of social justice, and the purposes underlying legal warrants. An adequate model of plausible justification probably requires, in addition, a cognitive model of legal categories accounting for their formation, development, and variations in plausibility.

The effectiveness of any computational model of precedent is limited by the representational power of the case-description language in which the facts of precedents and new cases are expressed. This case-description language must be capable of expressing any legally significant distinctions among the facts of cases. There is a growing recognition that no representation less expressive than first-order predicate calculus is likely to be sufficient for this purpose (McCarty, 1989). Finally, a complete computational theory of legal precedent must specify a control strategy under which the warrants in the justifications of precedents are used to solve legal problems. Any such control strategy must at a minimum be capable of integrating warrants at various levels of abstraction.

The next chapter presents GREBE, a system for legal analysis based on the reduction-graph model of legal precedent. GREBE uses a relational case representation language capable of expressing an unlimited range of legally significant factual distinctions among the case facts. GREBE implements a control strategy capable of integrating warrants of various levels of abstraction, and GREBE's case library consists of precedents represented as reduction graphs.

4 GREBE: INTEGRATING RULES AND PRECEDENTS FOR LEGAL ANALYSIS

GREBE (Generator of Recursive Exemplar-Based Explanations) is a Common Lisp implementation of the framework for integrating rules and precedents described in Chapters 2 and the model of *ratio decidendi* described in Chapter 3. Figure 4.1 depicts GREBE's architecture schematically. The top-level components of GREBE consist of an explanation generator, a memo generator, and a knowledge base of rules and cases. When the explanation generator receives a new case and a proposition about that case, it attempts to construct an explanation for the proposition (and for the negation of the proposition) by back-chaining using any combination of rules and precedent constituents. If successful, the explanation generator outputs one or more explanations of the proposition (and its negation). The memorandum generator orders these explanations by a heuristic estimate of their strength. It then generates a natural-language equivalent of the explanations using a library of templates.

This chapter begins by setting forth the components of GREBE's knowledge base for worker's compensation. The control strategy for constructing explanations is described in Section 4.2. Section 4.3 sets forth GREBE's case-representation conventions. Mechanisms for case-based reasoning are described

Figure 4.1. A schematic representation of GREBE's architecture.

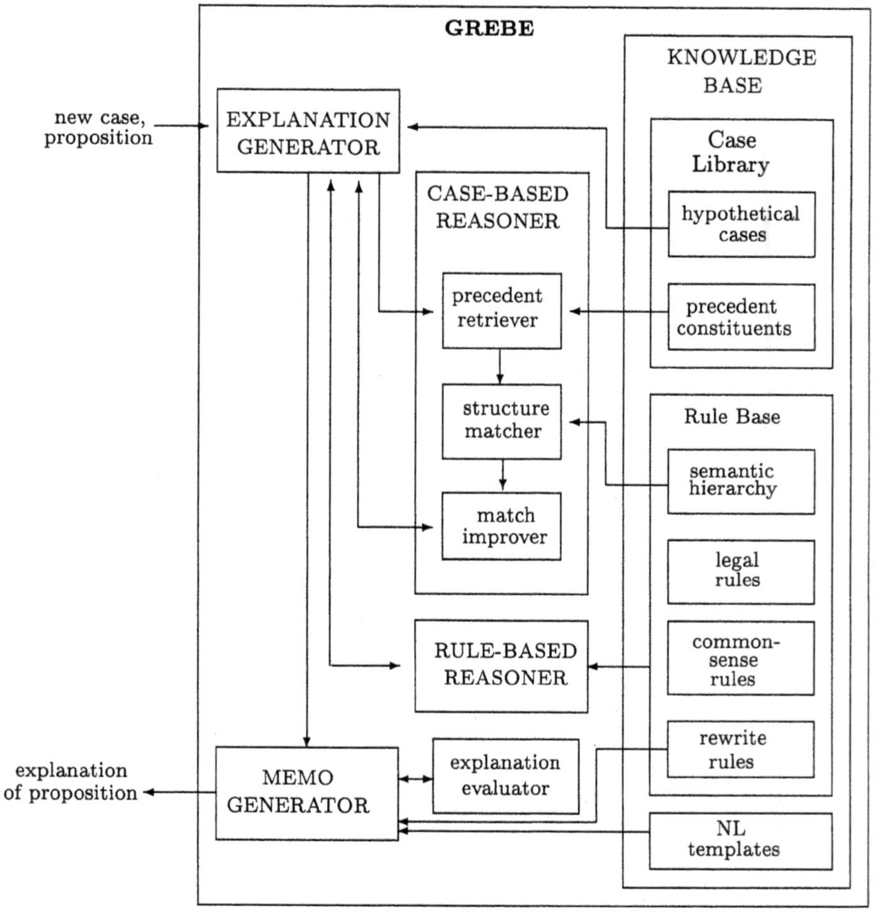

in Section 4.4. The last section describes the operation of the memorandum generator.

4.1 A Knowledge Base for Worker's Compensation

The worker's compensation knowledge base contains legal authorities together with common-sense knowledge useful for applying those authorities. This knowledge is expressed as rules and as precedent constituents.

Rules

There are four distinct types of rules in the worker's compensation knowledge base. The first two are types of legal authorities, while the last two are types of common-sense rules.

Legal Rules. Two types of legal rules can be distinguished on the basis of their source. The first are statutory rules, which are contained in statutes enacted by legislative bodies. An example is the basic rule for worker's compensation liability in Texas, Vernon's Tex. Rev. Civ. Stat. Ann. art. 8309 §1, under which an employer is liable to his employee for worker's compensation if the injury is "sustained in the course of employment."

The second type of legal rules are common-law rules, which are set forth in judicial opinions. An example is the rule, enunciated by the Texas Supreme Court in *Janak v. Texas Employer's Ins. Co.*, 381 S.W.2d 176 (1964), that a passenger in a business car pool is in the course of employment whenever the driver is in the course of his employment, provided that they have the same employer.

Common-Sense Rules. The worker's compensation knowledge base contains two types of common-sense rules. The first, which are derived from judicial opinions, represent reasoning in opinions that is implicit because it is too obvious (to humans) to need pointing out. An example is the inference that if an activity is a duty of employment, then each necessary step of that activity is a duty of employment as well.

The second type of common-sense rules are *semantic rules*, taxonomic relations among individual predicates. Semantic rules can be concisely represented in a hierarchy, as illustrated in Figure 4.2. The traversal distance between two predicates across such a hierarchy is a crude measure of semantic similarity.

Semantic rules differ from the other rules in the worker's compensation knowledge base in that they are not derived from legal authorities, but represent domain-independent semantic information. As discussed in the next section, semantic rules are treated in a somewhat different fashion than the other types of rules. The worker's compensation knowledge base contains approximately 57 legal and nonsemantic common-sense rules and 132 semantic rules.

Figure 4.2. A portion of a semantic hierarchy for relations. The arrows represent specialization relations.

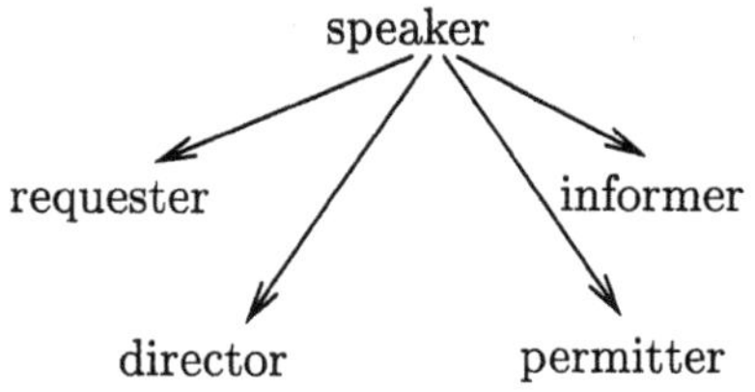

Precedent Constituents

Each precedent constituent is an exemplar from the *ratio decidendi* of a precedent and is therefore a warrant connecting a collection of case facts to an abstract case feature. The explanation of a single precedent case typically contains multiple precedent constituents. Each precedent constituent represents the justification for an intermediate conclusion in the precedent's explanation. As described in Section 4.3, precedent constituents are derived from explanations of legal precedents by identifying the specific case facts relevant to each given intermediate conclusion in the precedent's explanation.

The worker's compensation case library contains 16 published legal precedents concerning the compensability under Texas worker's compensation law of injuries sustained while a worker is traveling. Legal case-based reasoning draws not only on actual decided cases, but on paradigm cases (Christie, 1969, Feinman, 1989, Burton, 1985). Such cases correspond to what H. L. A. Hart referred to as the "standard case[s]" occupying the "core of settled meaning" of legal predicates (Hart, 1958). These often represent cases whose legal classification is so undisputable that they are never appealed and therefore never give rise to published opinions. For example, the reasoning of the worker's compensation cases in GREBE's knowledge base often involves comparing or contrasting a new case with such stereotyped situations as working at a job site, commuting to or from work, or transporting goods for hire. Accordingly, the knowledge base includes four paradigm cases representing these stereotypical situations. The 16 published opinions and 4 paradigm cases are listed in Appendix B.

The *rationes* of the 20 precedents in the worker's compensation knowledge base are represented as 35 distinct precedent constituents. The predicates for which some precedent constituent is a warrant are set forth in Appendix C.

In addition to precedents, the knowledge base contains 21 hypothetical cases for testing GREBE's classification accuracy. These hypotheticals represent variations on five basic fact patterns. Summaries of the hypothetical cases are set forth in Appendix D.

GREBE's entire knowledge base of precedent constituents, hypothetical cases, and rules comprises approximately 870 frames.

4.2 A Control Strategy for Building Legal Explanations

GREBE's explanation generator is intended to produce inference chains that can be mapped directly to an output that is useful and persuasive to attorneys. The explanation generator uses back-chaining as its search-control strategy. Under this strategy, the system attempts to use both rules and precedent constituents as warrants to explain each goal proposition. The control strategy is therefore impartial. Antecedents of the rule or unmatched precedent facts then constitute new subgoals. An explanation is complete when every subgoal has been either matched to the facts of the new case or explained. If multiple rules or both rules and precedent constituents are applicable to some subgoal, multiple explanations are constructed.

The choice of back-chaining as search control strategy in GREBE reflects the nature of the legal analysis task defined in the introduction. In this task, a proposition about a case is given, and the problem is to justify the proposition (and its negation) in terms of the new case facts. This task is exemplified by advocacy and adjudication, where the objective typically is to determine the strongest arguments in favor of (and against) a given conclusion. If the objective were instead to determine all possible legal consequences that might flow from a certain set of facts, a more bottom-up approach, such as forward-chaining, might be more appropriate.

GREBE's explanation generator is similar to horn-clause resolution theorem-provers like PROLOG. It differs in three important ways: (1) GREBE returns an explanation structure as well as a binding list; (2) it uses case-based reasoning in parallel with rules to explain goals; and (3) GREBE can return conflicting explanations. The explanation structure produced by the explanation generator sets forth, for each inference step, the warrant (*i.e.*, rule or precedent constituent) that justifies that inference step, and the *grounds* for the warrant (*i.e.*, the justification for the warrant's application). For example, the grounds for a rule consists of explanations of the rule's antecedents. This model of explanation is based on (Toulmin, 1958).[1]

When the explanation generator receives a proposition as a goal, it attempts to construct an explanation of any of the following types:

---

[1] *See* (Freeman and Farley, 1996) and (Marshall, 1989) for alternative models of legal argumentation based on Toulmin argument structures.

- **Trivial.** The explanation of a proposition is trivial if the proposition is given in the facts of the new case.

- **Rule-based.** In a rule-based explanation, a proposition unifies with the consequent of a general domain rule under a given set of variable bindings, and all of the rule antecedents can themselves be explained under those bindings. The warrant for a rule-based explanation is the rule itself, and the grounds consist of explanations for the rule's antecedents.

- **Case-based.** In a case-based explanation, a conclusion is justified by the similarity between the new case and the facts of a precedent constituent that is a warrant for the conclusion. The grounds for a case-based explanation consists of the mapping between the precedent and new case objects and any explained matchings. The explanation is qualified by any facts of the precedent constituent that were unmatched in the new case.

GREBE's case-based reasoner consists of three modules: a precedent retriever, a structure mapper, and a match improver. The precedent retriever attempts to find the instance and noninstance precedent constituents (*i.e.,* precedent constituents of the current goal's category and contrast set, respectively) that most closely match the new case. The facts of the retrieved precedent constituents then are compared with those of the new case using the mechanism of structure matching (Gentner, 1989a, Holyoak and Thagard, 1989a). As discussed below in Section 4.4, structure matching (as opposed to simple feature matching) is necessitated by GREBE's semantic network representation of case facts. If there are mismatches between a precedent constituent and a new case, the match improver attempts to infer conclusions about the new case that would improve the match.

In addition to these three basic explanation types, two specialized forms of case-based and rule-based explanations are given special treatment by the explanation generator:

- **Conflicting.** A conflicting explanation is a special form of case-based explanation in which a new case matches both an instance of a category and a member of its contrast set. A conflicting explanation is, in effect, short-hand for two case-based explanations: one for a proposition, and the other for its negation.

- **Semantic.** A semantic explanation is a special form of a rule-based explanation in which a proposition is justified by a semantically related proposition given in the facts of the case. For example, the proposition that John was a passenger can be justified by the semantic similarity between "passenger"

Table 4.1. Forms of explanation in GREBE.

Expl. type	Warrant	Grounds
trivial	given in case	none
rule-based	a rule	explained rule antecedents
case-based	a precedent constituent	mapping and supporting explanations
conflicting	instance and noninstance precedent constituents	mappings and supporting explanations
semantic	a semantic rule or rules	similar fact given in case

and "driver" and the proposition that John was a driver. This justification is short-hand for two rule-based steps: "passenger" has generalization "traveler," and "traveler" has specialization "driver."

Semantic explanations receive special treatment for two reasons. First, intractable branching would result if subgoaling were permitted from every semantic variant of a given goal. As a result, only direct matches with semantically related propositions are permitted. This contrasts to other rule-based explanations, in which rule antecedents are treated as subgoals. Second, since semantic rules, unlike legal rules, have no independent authority, explicitly stating the semantic rules that support a semantic explanation adds nothing to the explanation's credibility. As a result, the explanation generator replaces any sequence of semantic rules with a single "semantic similarity" warrant. The grounds of this warrant consist of the semantically similar proposition given in the new case. For example, the explanation above is represented as:

```
((passenger-in John John's-traveling)
     similar-to (driver-in John John's-traveling))
```

Table 4.1 summarizes GREBE's explanation types in terms of the warrant and grounds of each.

The algorithm of the explanation generator is as follows:

GIVEN:

a proposition, $(Pred\ Arg_1 \ldots Arg_n)$, and
a new case NC

DO:

If ($Pred\ Arg_1 \ldots Arg_n$) unifies with a proposition in NC **then** return a trivial explanation
else if ($Pred'\ Arg_1 \ldots Arg_n$) unifies with a proposition in NC, where $Pred'$ is semantically similar to $Pred$, **then** return a semantic explanation with grounds ($Pred'\ Arg_1 \ldots Arg_n$)
else

1. {rule-based reasoning}
   For every rule R whose consequent unifies with ($Pred\ Arg_1 \ldots Arg_n$)
   if the antecedents $A_1 \ldots A_m$ of R have explanations $E(A_1) \ldots E(A_m)$
   then return a rule-based explanation with warrant R and grounds $E(A_1) \ldots E(A_m)$

2. {case-based reasoning}
   If ($Pred\ Arg_1 \ldots Arg_n$) is a ground atomic sentence **then**

   (a) {precedent retrieval}
   Find $PC+$ and $PC-$, the instance and noninstance precedent constituents of $Pred$ most similar to NC

   (b) {structure matching}
   For every $PC \in \{PC+\ PC-\}$ find the best mapping, $M : PC \Rightarrow NC$, from the material facts of PC onto NC

   (c) {match improvement}
   For every $PC \in \{PC+\ PC-\}$:

      i. **If** the match between PC and NC would be improved if facts $f_1 \ldots f_m$ were true in NC **then** attempt to find explanations for $f_1 \ldots f_m$. Let $E(f_i) \ldots E(f_j)$ be the successful explanations and $f_k \ldots f_l$ be the facts that could not be explained.

      ii. **If** the match between NC and PC meets the acceptability threshold after match improvement **then** return a case-based explanation for ($Pred\ Arg_1 \ldots Arg_n$) (or $\neg$($Pred\ Arg_1 \ldots Arg_n$) if PC was a noninstance of $Pred$) with grounds $M : PC \Rightarrow NC$ and $E(f_i) \ldots E(f_j)$ and qualification $f_k \ldots f_l$.

   (d) **If** there are two case-based explanations **then** return a conflicting explanation
   else if there is one case-based explanation **then** return it

   else {($Pred\ Arg_1 \ldots Arg_n$) is not a ground atomic sentence }
   fail

4.3 A Representation for Legal Cases

Accurate assessment of similarity between cases is critical to case-based reasoning, both for determining the most similar precedent constituents and because the relevant similarities and differences between cases are an important part of explanations. Assessment of similarity between cases depends, in turn, on the accuracy and completeness of the representation of the facts of cases and, in the case of precedents, their explanations. This section sets forth GREBE's conventions for representing case facts and precedent explanations.

Complex Domains Require Relational Representations

In most early case-based reasoning systems, case facts were represented propositionally. Examples include the feature-vector representations of Mediator (Simpson, 1985), Casey (Koton, 1988), and Protos (Bareiss, 1988), and the "legal case frames" of HYPO (Ashley, 1990). A propositional representation for case facts enforces representational consistency and simplifies case entry and matching. However, it gives rise to the possibility that relevant aspects of new cases may not be expressible within the available set of propositions, particularly in domains such as law in which the relevant aspects of cases include causal, temporal, and intentional relations among case entities. This is because it is difficult to predetermine a collection of propositions that can accommodate every configuration of causal, temporal, and intentional relations that could arise in some future case (Branting, 1994b, McCarty, 1989). By contrast, the analogical reasoning community has generally used relational case representations. Indeed, structure matching, discussed below, presupposes a relational representation. *See* (Winston, 1980, Gentner, 1989a, Falkenhainer et al., 1989, Holyoak and Thagard, 1989a).

To obviate the representational limitations of propositional case representations, GREBE uses a semantic network representation in which arbitrary orderings of causal, temporal, and intentional relations can be stated explicitly. Because configurations of relations among entities are explicit in semantic network representations, they are sometimes referred to as ***structured*** or ***relational*** representations. In GREBE's representation, objects are represented by frames arranged in a taxonomic hierarchy, and binary relations between objects are represented as slots on the frames.

The top two levels of GREBE's object taxonomy, shown in Figure 4.3, includes frames for events, tangible and intangible entities, places, legal concepts, and relations. Events include activities, such as working, paying wages, traveling, consuming food or drink, and speech-acts; states, such as knowing something, being at a place, being injured, and having a need; and intervals, such as work hours and commuting time. Legal concepts include legal relations, such as employment and worker's compensation liability, legal explanations, and cases. Tangible entities include persons, vehicles, food and drink, and commodities.

Figure 4.3. The top two levels of GREBE's object taxonomy.

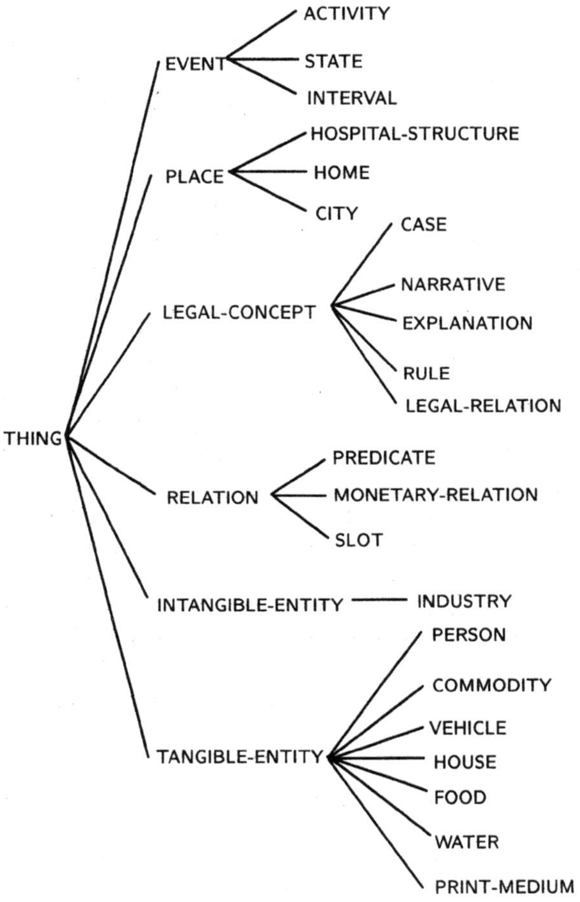

GREBE's vocabulary includes 147 binary relations, which are set forth in Appendix E. To conform to the conventions of semantic networks, relations having more than two arguments are *reified*, *i.e.*, reformulated as a collection of binary relations in the manner suggested in (Nilsson, 1980). For example, the relations employment in:

```
(employment employer.007 employee.23 activity.32 salary.18)
```

is represented as a collection of triples expressing the relationship between each of the arguments of the relation and its reification, *e.g.:*

```
(employer employment.92 employer.007)
(employee employment.92 employee.23)
(had-duties employment.92 activity.32)
(pay employment.92 salary.18)
```

where employment.92 is the reification of the employment relation. In addition to conforming to a graphical representation, this reformulation makes it possible to reason independently about each argument of a given higher-order relation, *e.g.*, an employee's rate of pay might be in dispute, even though there is agreement about the other details of his employment. It also avoids restricting all instances of higher-order relations to having exactly the same number of arguments, *e.g.*, it may be desirable to recognize two instances of employment as the same relation even if a work location is specified in one but not in the other.

Permissible arguments for relations in GREBE include not only objects, but slots and triples (*i.e.*, functions and propositions) as well. For example, the dependency of a worker's need for water on the temperature of the place where he or she works can be expressed by a relation having as arguments the temperature slot of the workplace object and the intensity slot of the worker's-water-need object, *e.g.*,

```
(increases
      (temperature drill-site)
      (intensity worker's-water-need))
```

Similarly, the fact that an unmet need for water impedes the ability of an employee to work can be expressed by a relation having as arguments a triple and an activity, *e.g.*,

```
(impedes
      (intensity worker's-water-need high)
      oil-drilling-activity)
```

These conventions of fact representation can be illustrated with the facts of the case of *Vaughn v. Highland Underwriters Ins. Co.*, 445 S.W.2d 234 (1969). The facts of *Vaughn*[2] can be briefly summarized as follows:

---

[2]Italicized names refer to the case involving the person named, *e.g.*, the *Vaughn* case, whereas unitalicized names refer to the claimant in the case, *e.g.*, Vaughn.

> Vaughn worked as a truck driver hauling three loads of sulfur per night from a mine to a factory. Each round trip from the factory to the sulphur mine and back again took approximately 4 hours. Vaughn normally stopped to eat each night at a roadside restaurant during his second return trip to the factory. On the night of the accident, a technical problem at the factory delayed unloading the first load of sulfur. Vaughn's boss told him that to get back on schedule, he would not be able to stop to eat on his second trip, but should instead eat during the delay in unloading the truck. Vaughn therefore set out on his motorcycle toward a nearby restaurant, but was injured in an accident that occurred on the way to the restaurant.

Figure 4.4 shows a portion of GREBE's representation of the facts of the *Vaughn* case. The object at the top of Figure 4.4 is the employment relation applying to Vaughn, his employer (APF Co.) and his job duties (sulphur conveyance). The high intensity of Vaughn's hunger would have impeded Vaughn's job duties. Eating lunch would have decreased the intensity of Vaughn's hunger. However, having food was a prerequisite for eating, and Vaughn being at a restaurant was a prerequisite for buying food.

There are two specializations of Vaughn being at a restaurant. The first is Vaughn being at restaurant1, the roadside restaurant. This state is achieved by Vaughn's customary traveling back to the factory. However, in APF Co.'s direction not to stop to eat on return trip, Vaughn was directed not to perform his customary traveling back (*i.e.*, it was the replaced activity) but to instead perform a modified conveyance back that would not achieve the state of Vaughn being at restaurant1. However, APF Co. also issued a direction to go get food in which the directed activity was Vaughn's attempted lunch trip. A step of this trip was traveling to restaurant2, which would have achieved the state of Vaughn being at restaurant2, the second specialization of Vaughn being at a restaurant.

The Source of Precedent Explanations

Chapters 2 and 3 argued that the explanation of a precedent as well as its facts must be represented if the precedent is to be useful for reasoning about new cases. The most important source of explanatory information about a legal precedent is the written opinion of the court that determined legal consequences of the precedent's facts. Such opinions constitute the official justification for those legal consequences.[3] However, as discussed in Chapter 3, there is often considerable imprecision in written opinions. Inevitably, some reasoning steps are left implicit, and the precise logical connection between individual reasoning steps is frequently not spelled out. As discussed in Chapter 3, determining the explanation of a precedent is an exercise in legal scholarship. Any particular

[3]Appellate courts are sometimes unable to agree on a single opinion and issue, instead, a collection of concurrences. Such cases, lacking an official explanation, are of virtually no precedential value.

Figure 4.4. A partial representation of the facts of *Vaughn v. Highland Underwriters Ins. Co.*, 445 S.W.2d 234 (1969).

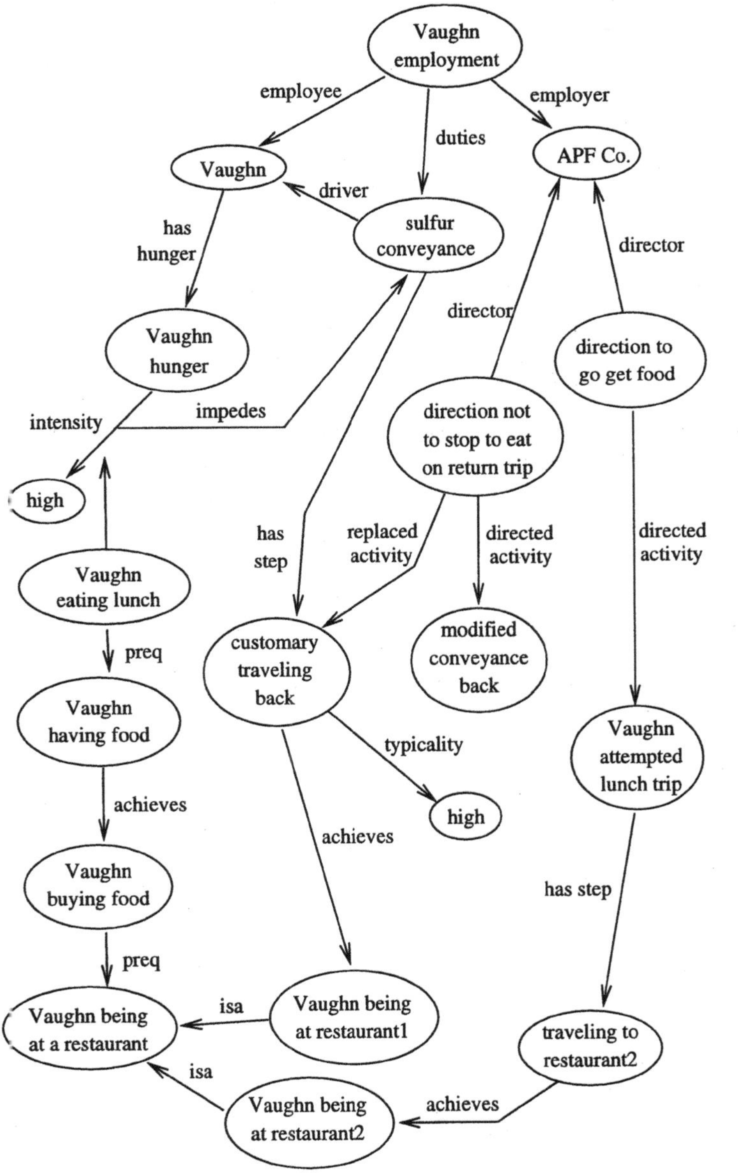

explanation of a precedent therefore represents a construction of the precedent with which other scholars might disagree.

However, there is often a general consensus among scholars as to the explanation of a precedent. Indeed, a precedent is a useful source of legal doctrine only to the extent that some particular explanation can be attributed to it. Thus, a defensible, detailed explanation of a precedent case can usually be determined, even if alternative constructions might also be possible.

Paradigm cases as well as actual decided precedents are often used in reasoning about a new case. Unlike other precedent cases, paradigm cases have no official written opinions setting forth their explanations. Thus, the facts of a paradigm case of a given legal category are purely a scholarly construct.

Representing Precedent Explanations

The explanation of each precedent in GREBE's case library was represented as a goal-reduction graph. Rules were represented as objects with consequent, antecedent, and authority slots. Similarly, precedent constituents were represented as objects with slots for material facts and for the proposition being explained. The representation of precedent explanations can be illustrated with the *Vaughn* case.[4]

The issue in *Vaughn* was whether Vaughn was entitled to worker's compensation benefits for the injuries he suffered from his accident while driving to a restaurant. One construction of the case is as follows:

> Under Vernon's Tex. Rev. Civ. Stat. Ann. art. 8309 §1, an employer is liable to his employee for worker's compensation if the injury is "sustained in the course" of the employee's employment. The same statute provides that an injury is sustained in the course of employment if the injury occurred while the employee was "engaged in or about the furtherance of his employer's affairs or business" and the injury "was of a kind and character that had to do with and originated in" the employment.
>
> The court stated that normally "an injury received while using the public streets in going to or returning from the place of employment is not compensable because not incurred in the course of employment." However, the court noted that exceptions exist when the traveling is "a special mission at the direction of the employer or is ... a service in furtherance of the employer's business." The court identified the central issue as "whether the action of [Vaughn] in making what was to him an unnecessary trip to get food, at the direction of his employer, constituted the performance of a service in furtherance of the employer's business."
>
> The court analogized the facts of the case to an earlier case, *Janak v. Texas Employer's Ins. Assoc.*, 381 S.W.2d 176 (1964), in which an employee was

[4]For brevity, the representation set forth below omits the *Vaughn* court's analysis of the statutory traveling exception and the dual-purpose rule.

injured during a deviation from a direct route to an oil-drilling site to buy ice. The court in *Janak* had reasoned that given the torrid environment of a southern Texas drill site, ice water was "reasonably essential" for the continuation of the drilling operation. Buying ice was therefore more like "picking up tools essential to the drilling operation," an activity in furtherance of employment, than buying "a particular kind of hamburger," a clearly personal activity.

The court in *Vaughn* reasoned that in view of Vaughn's lengthy shift, having food was reasonably essential for Vaughn to perform his employment duties, just as having ice was reasonably essential for the oil drilling activities in *Janak*. Driving to the restaurant was not a personal activity because it was only necessary because of APF Co.'s instructions not to stop at the roadside restaurant on the second load. These factors, together with the fact that APF Co. directed Vaughn to drive to the restaurant, support the conclusion that driving to the restaurant was an activity in furtherance of Vaughn's employment.

How is the explanation for the conclusion that Vaughn's traveling was in furtherance of employment to be represented? The court did not enunciate a general characterization of what constitutes an activity in furtherance of employment. The court merely ruled that the facts of *Vaughn* were sufficient to support this conclusion, that is, that Vaughn's traveling was an instance of an activity in furtherance of employment. Since this inference connects the concrete facts of *Vaughn* to an abstract feature, it is a precedent constituent.

If nothing were known about the explanation of *Vaughn* other than the facts relevant to the conclusion that Vaughn's traveling was in furtherance of employment, the explanation would include only a single precedent constituent. However, the court reached two important intermediate conclusions: that having food was *reasonably essential* for Vaughn's job duties; and that his trip to the restaurant was *necessitated* by APF Co.'s actions. As with "activity in furtherance of employment," the court did not attempt to present a general definition of either of these predicates, but merely reasoned that each was satisfied by the facts of *Vaughn*. As a result, the justifications for each are also best represented as precedent constituents.

Figure 4.5 shows the material facts (under the above construction of *Vaughn*) for the conclusion that having food was "reasonably essential" for Vaughn's job duties. Having food was a prerequisite for eating lunch, an activity that would have decreased the intensity of Vaughn's hunger. Vaughn's hunger, in turn, would have impeded his job duties. This facts are a subset of the facts *Vaughn* shown in Figure 4.4.

To take advantage of precedent constituents for flexibility in matching, GREBE permits portions of the material facts of a precedent to be replaced by abstract features warranted by precedent constituents. For example, the material facts for the conclusion that APF Co.'s direction not to stop to eat necessitated his travel to restaurant2, shown in Figure 4.6, include that Vaughn having

Figure 4.5. The material facts of *Vaughn* for the conclusion that having food was "reasonably essential" for Vaughn's job duties, conveying sulfur.

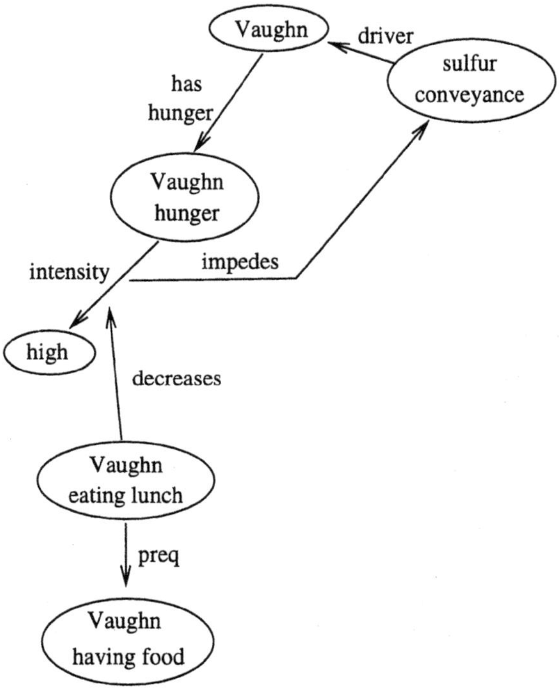

food was reasonably essential for Vaughn's employment duties. This abstract feature is warranted by the facts shown in 4.5. Other material facts for the conclusion that APF Co.'s direction not to stop to eat necessitated his travel to restaurant2 include that Vaughn's customary traveling back was of high typicality; that Vaughn's customary traveling back achieved the state of Vaughn having food but was the replaced activity in APF Co.'s direction not to stop to eat on return trip; and that traveling to restaurant2 was an alternative means of achieving the state of Vaughn having food. That Vaughn having food was reasonably essential for Vaughn's employment duties is an abstract fact not present in the facts *Vaughn* as represented in Figure 4.4. Note that the sequences of arcs connecting *customary traveling back* and *traveling to restaurant2* to *Vaughn having food* in Figure 4.4 have each been replaced by a single *achieves* arc.

Figure 4.7 shows GREBE's representation of the material facts of *Vaughn* for the conclusion that Vaughn's traveling was "in furtherance of employment." The specific facts relevant to the conclusion that Vaughn having food was reasonably essential for his job duties have been replaced by a single relation. Similarly, a single necessitation relation replaces the facts relevant to the conclusion that APF Co.'s direction not to stop to eat on Vaughn's return trip made Vaughn's lunch trip necessary if Vaughn was to have food.

A portion of the explanation for worker's compensation liability in *Vaughn* is shown in Figure 4.8. The top-level goal of worker's compensation liability is explained by a statutory rule (Art. 8309 §1, rule 1) having two antecedents: that Vaughn was employed, and that his injury was sustained in the course of his employment. Vaughn's employment is given in the facts of the case (*i.e.*, it was undisputed), and a second statutory rule (Art. 8309 §1, rule 2) has as its consequence that Vaughn's injury was sustained in the course of his employment. The second statutory rule has as one antecedent that the activity in which Vaughn was engaged when he was injured (traveling to a restaurant) was an activity in furtherance of employment. This conclusion was supported by Vaughn-ifo-pc, the precedent constituent warranting the conclusion that Vaughn's traveling was in furtherance of employment. There are 16 material facts for this conclusion, of which two—that having food was reasonably essential for employment and that APF Co.'s direction not to stop for food necessitated Vaughn's trip—are explained by additional precedent constituents.

GREBE does not explicitly retain the interconnections among individual inference steps in particular explanations as was done in Casey (Koton, 1988). Instead, as in Protos (Bareiss, 1988), all the inference steps of each precedent explanation are simply added to GREBE's general domain theory where they can be freely recombined to form new explanations.

Figure 4.6. A portion of the material facts of *Vaughn* for the conclusion that Vaughn's employer necessitated his traveling.

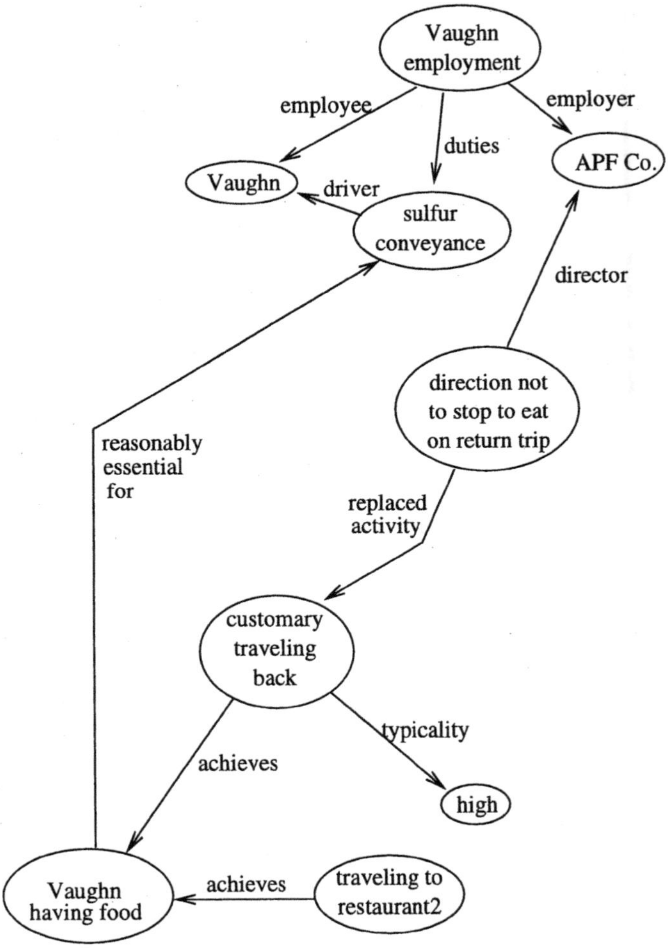

Figure 4.7. A portion of the material facts of *Vaughn* for the conclusion that Vaughn's traveling was "in furtherance of" his employment. These facts include the abstract features reasonably essential for and necessitation.

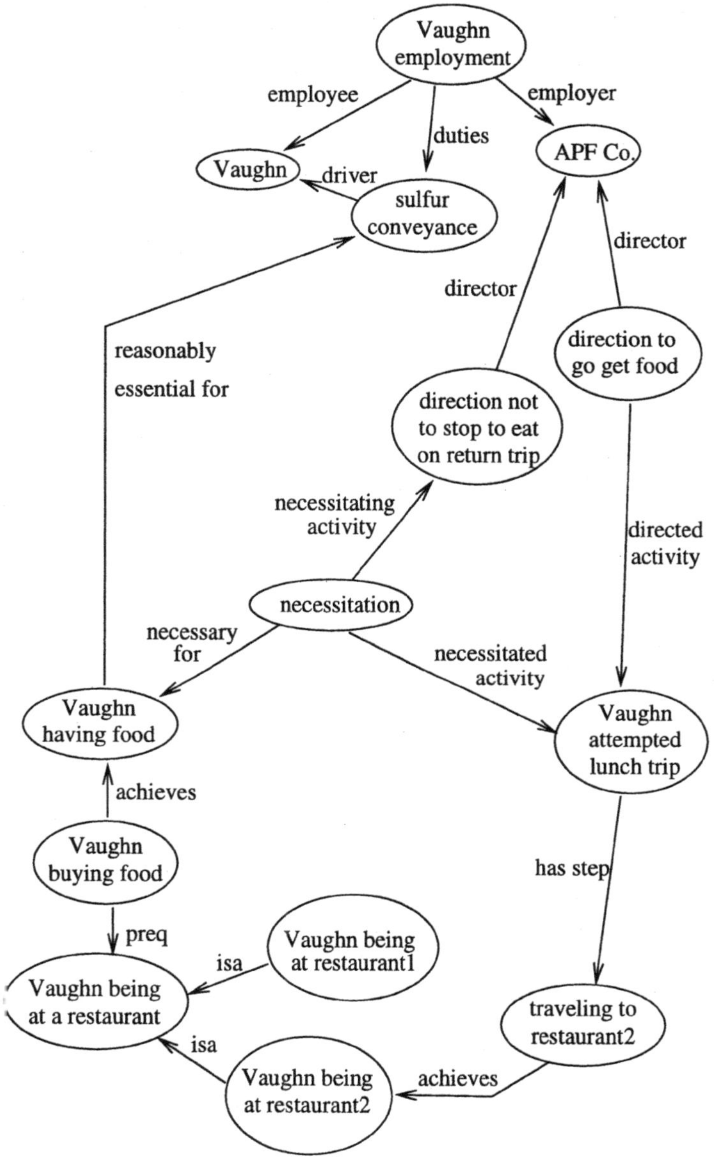

Figure 4.8. A portion of the explanation of *Vaughn* represented as a goal-reduction graph.

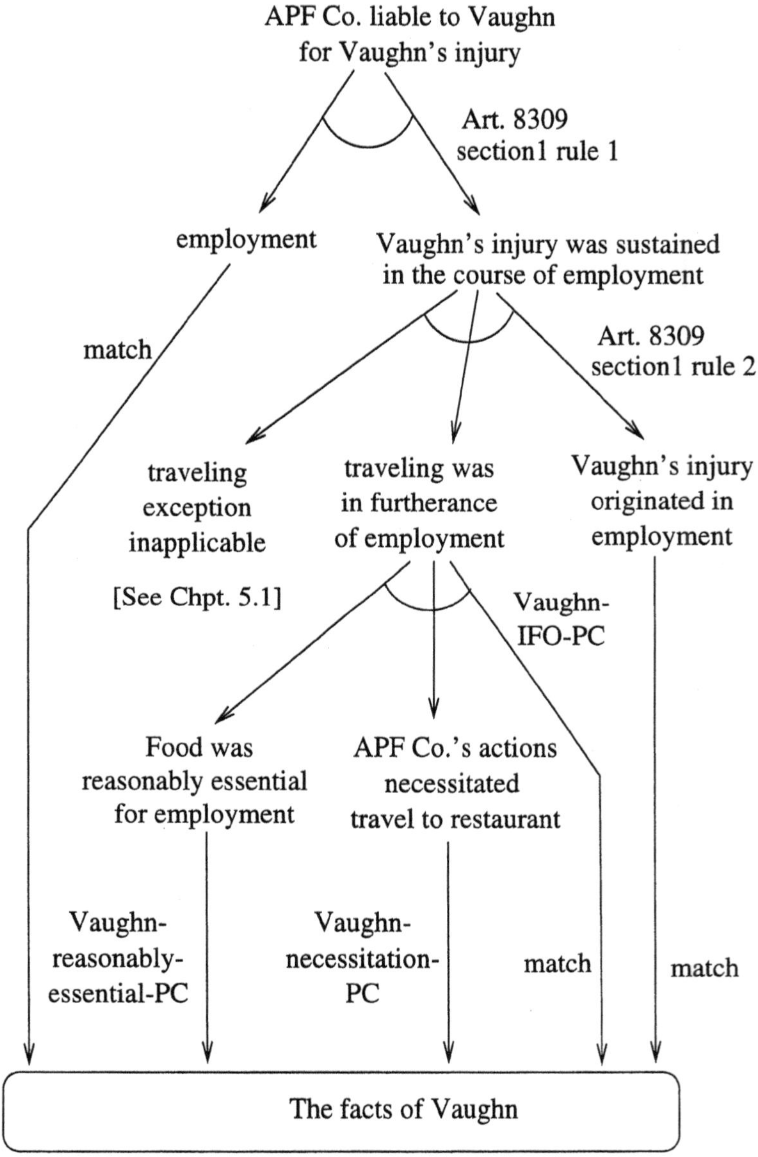

4.4 Case-Based Reasoning in GREBE

GREBE contains three case-based reasoning components, shown in Figure 4.1. The first, the precedent retriever, locates the instance and noninstance precedent constituents whose facts most closely match those of the new case. Next, the structure mapper determines the best mapping from the material facts to the new case. The match improver then attempts to infer any facts in the new case that would improve the match.

Because one of the algorithms for precedent retrieval is intimately connected to structure matching, the three components of GREBE's case-based reasoner are not presented in the order in which they are called by GREBE. Instead, the structure mapper is presented first, the match improver second, and the precedent retriever last.

Comparing Cases by Structure Matching

A central characteristic of structured representations is that it is the configuration of relations, rather than the individual relations themselves, that contains most of the information. For example, the fact that Vaughn was the driver in a certain traveling activity is of little significance standing alone. This fact is significant only in combination with a number of additional facts: that the destination of the traveling was a place where it was necessary to be in order to buy food, that lack of food would have prevented Vaughn from performing his job duties, etc. Because the configuration of relations is the most significant characteristic of a structured case representation, it follows that two structured representations of case facts are similar to the extent that they share similar configurations of relations.

Structural congruence as a similarity metric has been studied extensively by the analogical reasoning community (Winston, 1980, Gentner, 1989a, Falkenhainer et al., 1989, Holyoak and Thagard, 1989a). Two analogs are structurally congruent for the purposes of analogical matching if "objects in ... two analogs can be placed into correspondence so that relations also correspond" (Holyoak and Thagard, 1989a). This view of analogy focuses on "relational commonalities independently of the objects in which those relations are embedded" (Gentner, 1989b).

The correspondence between analogs is generally modeled as a mapping from the objects in one analog to those in another. The case constituting the domain of the mapping is customarily referred to as the *source* of the mapping, and the case constituting range of the mapping is referred to as the *target*. In case-based legal reasoning, a legal precedent is the source case and the new case is the target. The requirement of strict structural congruence of cases is equivalent to requiring an isomorphism between the cases. In practice, the requirement of isomorphism is usually relaxed to include approximations to isomorphisms in which there may fail to be relations in the target that correspond to some relations in the source. This relaxation is necessary because few pairs of distinct cases are isomorphic. In addition, as illustrated below, the constraint that each relation in the source analogue map onto an identical relation in the target can also be relaxed by permitting semantically similar relations to match (Holyoak and Thagard, 1989a).

If case-based legal reasoning is viewed as a form of analogical reasoning, the task of assessing the degree of similarity between a precedent constituent's facts and a new case is equivalent to the problem of finding the closest approximation to an isomorphism between representations of the two. This leaves open the question of what criterion should be used in deciding what constitutes the "closest approximation" to an isomorphism, that is, the best mapping. If there is not an isomorphism between the source and the target, the choice among mappings is equivalent to a choice among which relations in the source case are unmatched in the target case. This is a special case of the general problem, described in Chapter 2, of estimating the strength of matches formed by attribute dropping.

Ideally, one would like to choose the mapping for which the matched relations are of greatest importance. It has been argued, however, that it is usually impossible to assign an *a priori* weighting scheme to the facts of legal precedents (Ashley and Rissland, 1988). Unlike the representations studied in (Falkenhainer et al., 1989), systematicity and other syntactic characteristics of case representations are not reliable indicia of relevance of relations in GREBE's representation. As a result, GREBE uses the simple heuristic of choosing the mapping that minimizes the number of unmatched source relations. If there are several mappings that are optimal in this sense, GREBE chooses one arbitrarily.

Structure matching is potentially very computationally expensive. The general unlabeled subgraph isomorphism problem is NP-complete (Garey and Johnson, 1979). Finding the closest near-isomorphism is even more expensive, because in general there is no way to determine the best partial mapping without examining every consistent partial mapping. However, adding the restriction that only edges with identical labels can match makes matching much less expensive. If every edge of each graph has a unique label, then only a single consistent mapping is possible. By contrast, there are $n!$ consistent mappings between complete graphs having n vertices and unlabeled or identically labeled edges. Thus, the complexity is highly dependent on the details of particular case representations, and in particular on the number of identically labeled edges in each graph.

A representational heuristic that tends to minimize the number of identically labeled edges is to prefer specialized over generic relations between objects. For example, the **agent** slot in **permitting**, **directing**, and **driving** can be specialized to **permitter**, **director**, **driver**, to preclude consideration of every possible mapping between an agent of an activity in the source case and an agent of an activity in the target case.

Structure-Matching as Heuristic Search

GREBE's structure-matching algorithm determines the degree of structural congruence between the facts of a precedent constituent and the facts of a new case using the A* algorithm (Russell and Norvig, 1995). Each node in the search space represents a partial or complete mapping from the source facts to the target facts, and the cost function *f(N)* for each node N for a given mapping between cases is the proportion of source facts unmatched in the target under the best mapping that is consistent with the N's current mapping. The input to the algorithm is the following:

- a new case NC
- a proposition, $(Pred\ A_1 \ldots A_n)$, to be explained in NC, and
- a precedent constituent PC for predicate *Pred*, consisting of
  - a set of material facts represented as tuples, T, and
  - the proposition $(Pred\ B_1 \ldots B_n)$ that the precedent constituent explained

The frontier F of the search graph is initialized with a node containing a mapping representing the correspondence between the objects in the proposition explained by the precedent constituent and objects in the proposition that is to be explained, *i.e.*:

$B_1 \Rightarrow A_1$

...

$B_n \Rightarrow A_n$

This initial correspondence is a *pragmatic* constraint (Holyoak and Thagard, 1989a) on the permissible mappings between the source and target cases.

In each iteration of the main loop, the node N selected for expansion is the one for which the estimated cost function, $f(\mathrm{N}) = g^*(\mathrm{N}) + h(\mathrm{N})$ is least, where $g^*(\mathrm{N})$ is the proportion of tuples in T unmatched under the mapping in N, and $h(\mathrm{N})$ is an estimate of the number of unmatched tuples in the best completion of the mapping in N. The nodes for which $g^*(\mathrm{N})$ is least are first selected, then for each of these nodes, $h(\mathrm{N})$ is calculated to be the proportion of tuples of T not yet considered. By considering only the nodes for which $g^*(\mathrm{N})$ is least, $h(\mathrm{N})$

is treated as always being less than a single unmatched tuple. This insures the admissibility condition that $f(\text{N}) \leq f^*(\text{N})$ (Nilsson, 1980).

If no more tuples from T remain to be considered in N, the best mapping has been found. Otherwise, the next tuple $t \in T$ is selected, and all mappings from the objects in t to new case objects are determined under which t matches a tuple in NC. If no mappings can be found, then $g^*(\text{N})$ is incremented and t is added to the list of tuples unmatched under the mapping in N. Otherwise, N is removed from the frontier, and a new node is added for every distinct mapping under which t matches a tuple in NC. The complete algorithm is set forth in Appendix F.

The algorithm permits tuples with semantically similar relations to match, in a manner similar to ACME (Holyoak and Thagard, 1989a). Such matches are considered to be only partial matches, so $g^*(\text{N})$ is incremented by a fraction of the increment for a mismatch determined by the semantic distance between the relations. For example, the semantic similarity between had-hunger and had-thirst is estimated (based on their separation in a relation hierarchy) as 0.8. If under N's mapping

(had-hunger John John's-hunger)

matched the tuple

(had-thirst Mary Mary's-thirst)

$g^*(\text{N})$ would be incremented only 0.8 of the increment for a mismatch. The effect of this treatment of partial matches is to create a partial ordering of mappings: exact match > strong partial match > weak partial match > mismatch.

The algorithm constructs at least a part of every consistent mapping from the material facts of the precedent constituent to NC. However, only a small portion of unpromising mappings are constructed, so there is a considerable efficiency gain over completely constructing every possible mapping.[5]

Mapping *Vaughn* onto a New Case. The application of the structure-matching algorithm to GREBE's case representations can be illustrated by considering a match between a precedent of "activity in furtherance of employment," *Vaughn*, and the facts of *Jarek's Case,* 326 Mass. 182, 93 N.E.2d 533 (1950). The facts of *Jarek's Case* can be briefly summarized as follows:

> Jarek was employed as a railroad porter and normally worked from 8:00 A.M. to 5:00 P.M. Because of an unusual work-load, Jarek's employer asked him to work late. Jarek requested and was given permission to walk several blocks home to tell his wife that he would be working late. He slipped and was seriously injured while walking home.

[5]For example, when the structure mapper is in greedy mode (see Appendix F), heuristic search reduces the number of updates to F necessary to find the best mapping from *Vaughn-ifo-pc* to *Jarek's Case* from 58 updates for exhaustive search to 37. In nongreedy mode, best-first search reduces the number of updates necessary to find the best mapping from 1882 for exhaustive search to 247.

Figure 4.9 is a partial representation of the facts of *Jarek's Case*. At the top of the graph is a node representing the employment relation with Jarek as employee, a Railroad as employer, and duties of portering. The Railroad directed Jarek to engage in overtime portering, and this action gave rise to a family need on the part of Jarek. The intensity of this need would have been decreased by Jarek informing his wife of the schedule change. However, a prerequisite for informing his wife was that Jarek be at home. Being at home would have been achieved by Jarek's special trip home, and the Railroad gave permission for Jarek to make the trip. GREBE's actual representation of the facts of *Jarek's case* contains 89 propositions (corresponding to 89 relations among 26 objects).

Figure 4.7 shows the material facts of the precedent constituent in *Vaughn* that Vaughn's traveling was in furtherance of his employment, Vaughn-ifo-pc. The fact Vaughn-ifo-pc explains is:

```
(in-furtherance-of
    Vaughn-traveling-to-restaurant2
    Vaughn-employment)
```

and the proposition to be explained is

```
(in-furtherance-of
    Jarek-special-travel-home
    Jarek-employment)
```

The structure matching algorithm should only consider mappings in which there is a correspondence between objects in the fact explained by Vaughn-ifo-pc and objects in the proposition to be explained. Thus, the mapping of the initial node of the search frontier F is:

Vaughn-traveling-to-restaurant2 ⇒ Jarek-special-travel-home
Vaughn-employment ⇒ Jarek-employment

The structure-matching algorithm then incrementally expands this partial mapping. At completion, the algorithm returns the best mapping between the material facts of Vaughn-ifo-pc and the facts of *Jarek's Case:*

Vaughn-employment ⇒ Jarek-employment
traveling-from-factory-to-restaurant2 ⇒ Jarek-special-travel-home
Vaughn ⇒ Jarek
APF-Co ⇒ Railroad
Vaughn-sulfur-conveyance-activity ⇒ customary-portering-activity
APF-Co-direction1 ⇒ Railroad-direction
APF-Co-direction2 ⇒ Railroad-giving-permission
APF-Co-scheduling-goals ⇒ Railroad-scheduling-goal
Vaughn-modified-conveyance-back ⇒ overtime-portering-activity
Vaughn-eating-lunch ⇒ Jarek-informing-his-wife
Vaughn-food-need ⇒ Jarek-family-need

Figure 4.9. A portion of the facts of *Jarek's Case.*

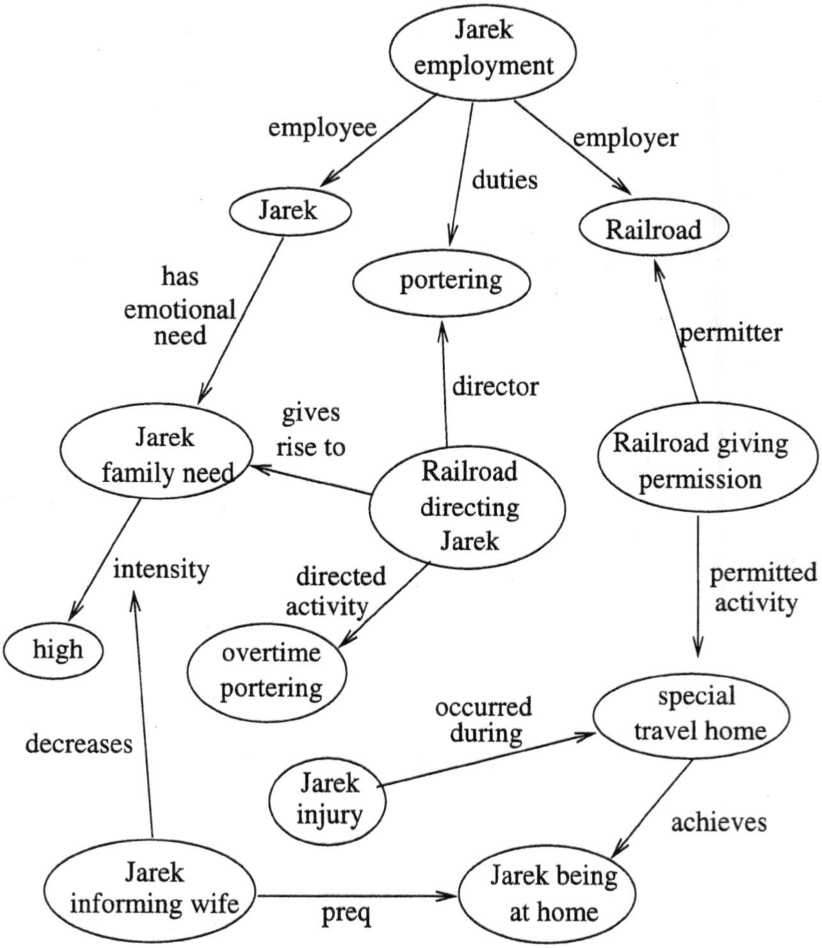

Vaughn-having-food ⇒ Jarek-being-at-home

Also returned are the material facts unmatched under this mapping:

```
(director
        APF-Co-direction2
        APF-Co)
(driver
       traveling-from-factory-to-restaurant2
       Vaughn)
(impedes
       (intensity Vaughn-food-need high)
       Vaughn-sulfur-conveyance-activity)
(reasonably-essential-for
       Vaughn-having-food
       Vaughn-sulfur-conveyance-activity)
(necessitation
       traveling-from-factory-to-restaurant2
       APF-Co-direction1 Vaughn-having-food)
(directed-activity
       APF-Co-direction2
       traveling-from-factory-to-restaurant2)
```

The match improver is then called to attempt to improve the match.

Match Improvement

GREBE's match improver is a mechanism for case elaboration. It first determines whether a match could be improved if additional facts were established about the target case. It then calls the explanation generator to attempt to infer each fact that would improve the match.

The first stage in match improvement is to determine what new case facts would improve the match if they could be inferred. This simply requires using the mapping returned by the structure-matcher to substitute for each object in an unmatched precedent fact the corresponding new case object under the mapping. Suppose, for example, that the structure-matcher returns mapping M and unmatched facts $(Pred_1\ A_{11} \ldots A_{1m}) \ldots (Pred_n\ A_{n1} \ldots A_{nk})$. Inferring any $(Pred_i\ M(A_{i1}) \ldots M(A_{ij}))$ in the new case would reduce the mismatch. Accordingly, the match improver calls the explanation generator with $(Pred_1\ M(A_{11}) \ldots M(A_{1m})) \ldots (Pred_n\ M(A_{n1}) \ldots M(A_{nk}))$ as goals.

The only complication of this process is that M may not be defined for one or more A_{ij}. In that case, the match improver creates a variable whose type is determined by the relation to replace the source object, *e.g.*, if

```
(achieves Vaughn-driving-home Vaughn-being-home)
```

is unmatched and Vaughn-being-home is not in the domain of M, it is replaced by the variable being-at-place.713.

Returning to the example of *Jarek's Case*, when the best mapping from the material facts of Vaughn-ifo-pc to the facts of *Jarek's Case* is used to substitute objects from *Jarek's Case* for objects from *Vaughn* in the unmatched tuples under the mapping, the following tuples result:

```
(director
        Railroad-giving-permission
        Railroad)
(directed-activity
        Railroad-giving-permission
        Jarek-special-travel-home)
(driver
        Jarek-special-travel-home
        Jarek)
(reasonably-essential-for
        Jarek-being-at-home
        customary-portering-activity)
(necessitation
        Jarek-special-travel-home
        Railroad-direction
        Jarek-being-at-home)
(impedes
        (intensity Jarek-family-need high)
        customary-portering-activity)
```

The match improver therefore calls the explanation generator with each of these goals.

The first three propositions have semantic explanations under the facts of *Jarek's Case*:

- director is semantically similar to permitter and the Railroad was the permitter in Railroad-giving-permission.

- directed-activity is semantically similar to permitted-activity and Jarek-special-travel-home was the permitted activity in Railroad-giving-permission.

- Being a driver is similar to walking, and Jarek walked in Jarek-special-travel-home.

For the next two propositions, GREBE has no rules for inferring necessitation or that something is reasonably-essential-for employment. These were intermediate conclusions by the court in *Vaughn* in the course of analogizing *Vaughn* to an earlier precedent, *Janak*. As discussed in Section 4.3, the reasoning behind these predicates is modeled in GREBE as precedent constituents that identify the facts that were relevant to the court's decision that each of these predicates was satisfied. GREBE therefore turns to case-based reasoning to attempt to infer these predicates in *Jarek's Case.*

Figure 4.10 illustrates the best mapping between the material facts of *Vaughn* for necessitation and the facts of *Jarek's Case.* Under this mapping, all the source relations are matched against relations in the target. Figure 4.11 illustrates the best mapping between the material facts of *Vaughn* for reasonably-essential-for and the facts of *Jarek's Case.* Under this mapping, one relation, an impedes relation between the high intensity of Vaughn's food need and Vaughn's ability to perform his job activities, is unmatched in *Jarek's Case.* GREBE has neither rules nor precedents to enable it to infer that Jarek's high family need impedes his work ability. As a result, this represents an unexplained relevant difference between *Vaughn* and *Jarek's Case.*

A match between two cases fails if the proportion of tuples that remain unmatched after match improvement exceeds a user-specifiable threshold. If the proportion of unexplained, unmatched tuples is less than this threshold, however, the match improver returns a case-based explanation consisting of the following:

- Warrant: a precedent constituent, in this case Vaughn-ifo-pc.
- Grounds:
  - The best mapping, M, from the material facts of the precedent constituent to the new case.
  - Inferences supporting the match, that is, explanations of any tuples unmatched under M.
- Qualification: any tuples unmatched under M that could not be explained by the match improver. These represent relevant differences between the precedent and the new case.

In *Jarek's Case*, the result of the mapping process is an explanation for the conclusion that Jarek's traveling was in furtherance of his employment in terms of the similarity of *Jarek's Case* to the relevant facts of the *Vaughn* case. This explanation shows the correspondences between objects in the two cases, and sets forth the inferences, both semantic and case-based, that support the analogy between the two cases. Figure 4.12 illustrates the explanation structure, which represents both the inferences that support the analogy and an important difference between the cases: that Jarek's need to tell his wife of the schedule change wouldn't impede his work to the degree that hunger would.

Figure 4.10. The best mapping from the material facts of *Vaughn* for "necessitation" to the facts of *Jarek's Case*. Horizontal dashed arrows represent object pairings.

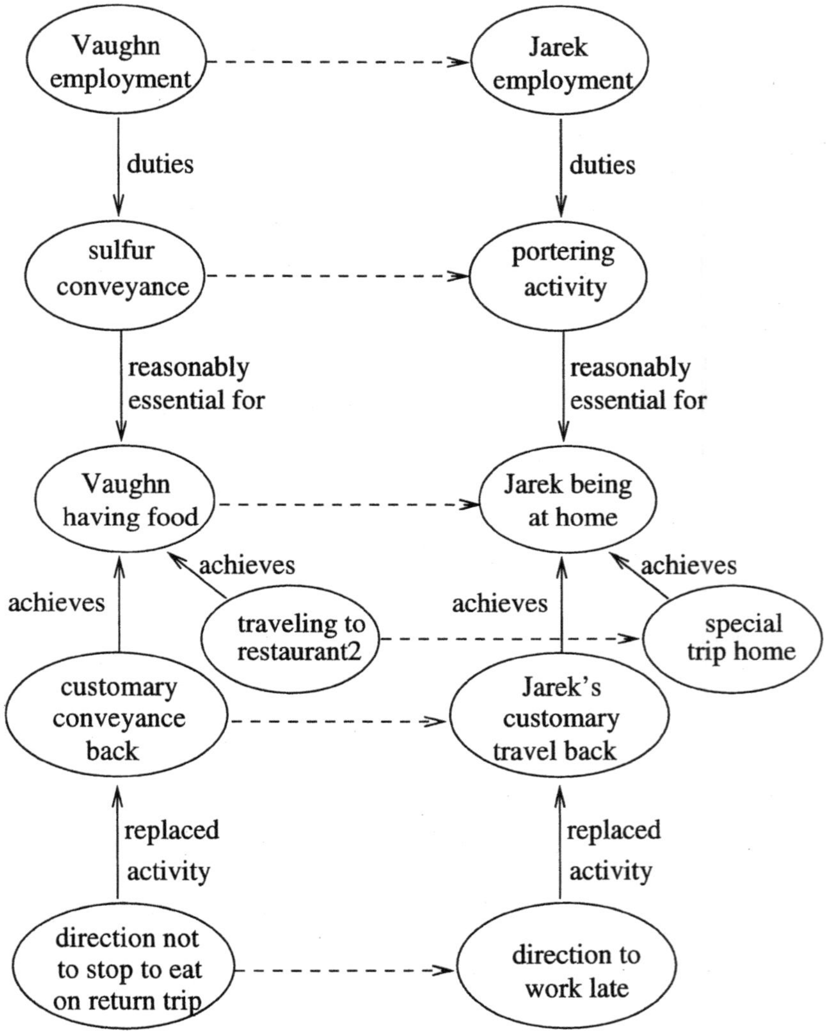

Figure 4.11. The best mapping from the material facts of *Vaughn* for "reasonably essential for employment" onto the facts of *Jarek's Case*. Under this mapping the impedes relation in *Vaughn* is unmatched.

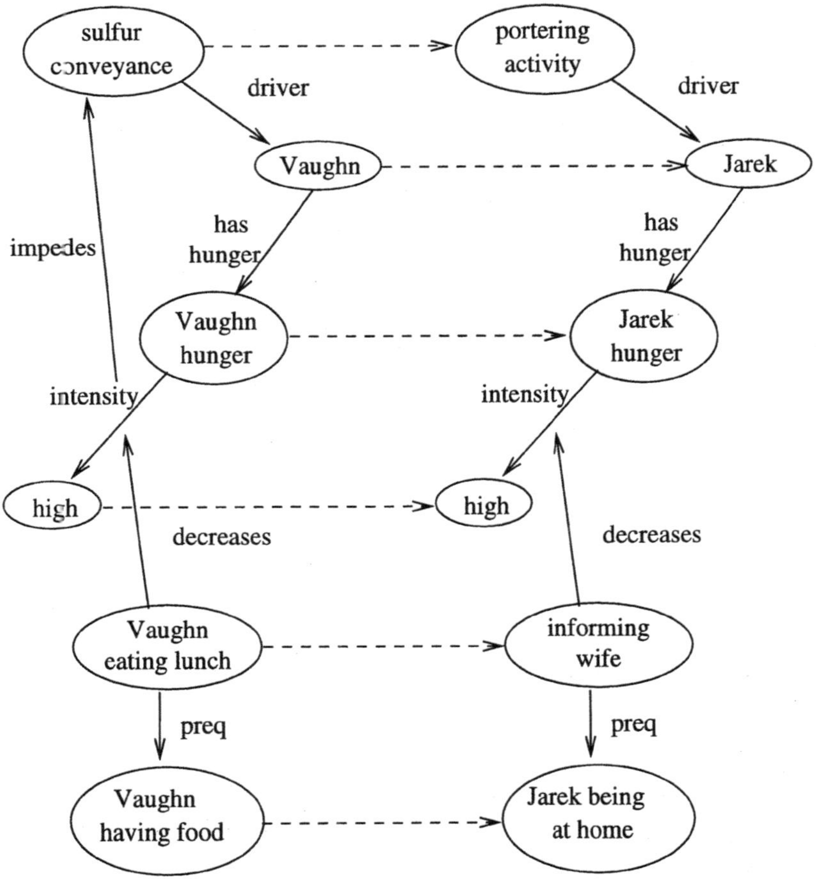

Figure 4.12. The explanation that Jarek's traveling was "in furtherance of" his employment.

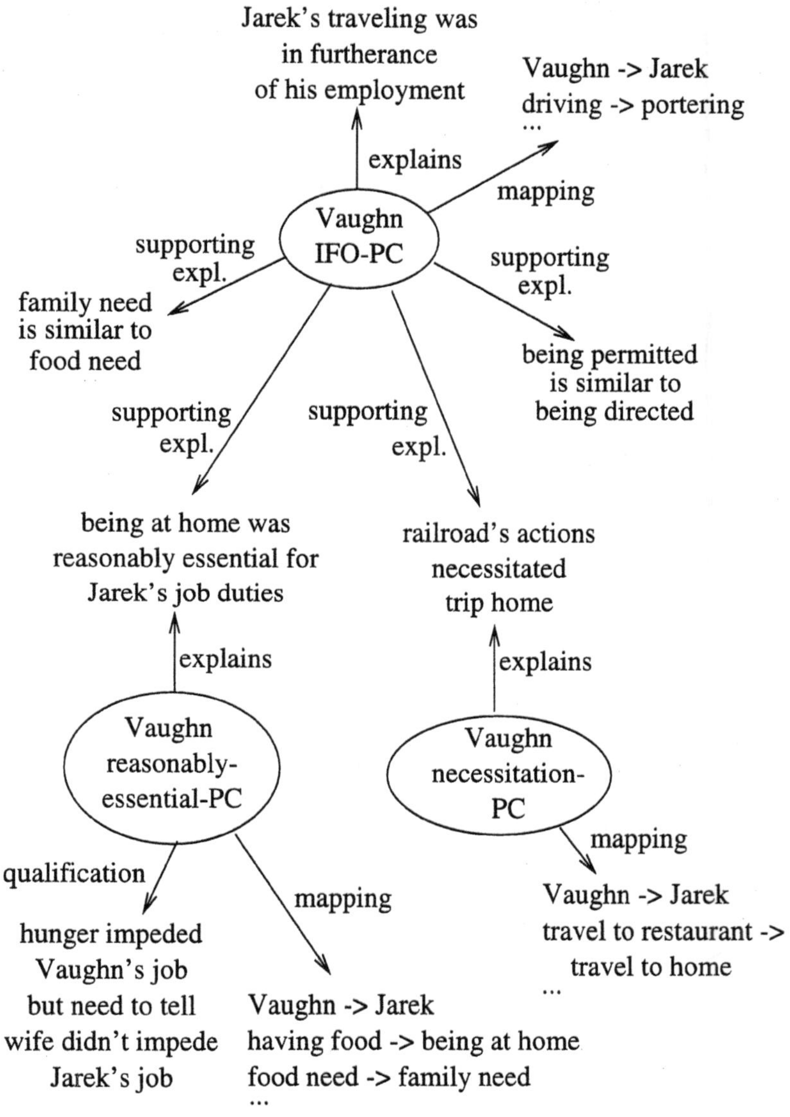

Exemplar Retrieval

> *Superior intelligence ... seems to consist in nothing so much as in a large development of the faculty of association by similarity.*
>
> —William James (James, 1902)

The task of exemplar retrieval is to locate and fetch the exemplars most relevant to a particular issue in a given case.[6] Specifically, given a new case NC and a proposition $(Pred\ A_1 \ldots A_n)$ to be explained by case-based reasoning, the retrieval task is to find exemplars that:

- Are instances or noninstances of $Pred$, that is, are explanations of propositions having $Pred$ or $\neg Pred$ as their predicate, and
- Have facts that most closely match the facts of NC.

It is important to retrieve both instances and noninstances of $Pred$ for several reasons. First, it can't be known *a priori* whether the most similar—and therefore most relevant—exemplar is an instance or a noninstance. Therefore, determining the most relevant exemplar requires considering both instance and noninstance exemplars. Second, a complete analysis of a legal issue should include arguments both for and against a given proposition, if tenable arguments can be made. It is particularly important to determine and present alternative arguments if both arguments are of comparable strength.

It is straightforward to form collections of the instance and noninstance exemplars for a predicate. The difficult part of exemplar retrieval is determining the exemplar from each collection whose material facts are most similar to NC. As discussed above, structured representations of case facts are similar to the extent that they have structurally similar configurations of relations. GREBE's criterion for the degree of structural similarity is the proportion of material facts that match new case facts under the best mapping from the material facts to the new case. The central problem of exemplar retrieval is therefore finding the exemplar constituent with the highest proportion of matches under the best mapping from its material facts to NC.

Numerous researchers have explored techniques for accurate case retrieval based on remindings triggered by individual case features. *See, e.g.,* (Porter et al., 1990, Kolodner, 1984, Hammond, 1989, Simpson, 1985). However, these techniques are depend strongly on propositional representations of case facts. In structured representations, individual relations are not, in general, capable of discriminating among dissimilar cases. This is because cases can differ structurally even if they contain identical relations. It follows that some al-

[6]As noted in Chapter 1, "case-based reasoning" subsumes both reasoning with exemplars and reuse of operators sequences or configurations. Retrieval of operator sequences or configurations entails a slightly different set of issues than exemplar retrieval, *e.g.*, goal regression to identify the relevant case features (Veloso, 1992). This chapter addresses the specific task of retrieving exemplars that are expressed in a relational representation.

ternative to feature-based indexing is necessary to determine the structurally most similar exemplar (Branting, 1990).

Two different approaches to structured case retrieval have been implemented in GREBE:

- Retrieval by best-first incremental matching, and
- Match refinement by structural difference links.

Retrieval by Best-First Incremental Matching. Retrieval by best-first incremental matching (BFIM) is a direct extension of GREBE's structure-matcher. The idea is to simultaneously construct mappings from the material facts of every exemplar constituent for the predicate (or its negation) to the new case. By performing a best-first search among mappings, only the best match need be carried to completion. BFIM is therefore potentially more efficient than sequentially comparing a new case to every exemplar constituent.

Only minor modifications of GREBE's structure-matcher are necessary for BFIM. No part of the structure mapper requires that all the nodes of the frontier, F, represent mappings from the same exemplar constituent. Each node of F contains separate records for the remaining facts to be matched, unmatched facts, and the amount by which the proportion remaining and proportion unmatched should be incremented during each node expansion. Thus, if F is initialized with a separate node for each exemplar for a predicate, the structure mapper can simultaneously find both the exemplar constituent and the mapping with the lowest proportion of unmatched material facts.

However, GREBE's match improver introduces a wrinkle into BFIM. The exemplar whose material facts most closely match NC before match improvement may not be the closest exemplar after match improvement. As a result, BFIM ordinarily doesn't stop when it returns the single exemplar having the structurally closest material facts, but continues until it has returned a user-definable number n of exemplars. After each exemplar is returned by the structure mapper, all nodes involving that exemplar are removed from F, and the structure mapper is then called again to find the best exemplar constituent in the remaining frontier. When the n best exemplar constituents have been selected, the match improver is applied to each. The exemplar with the lowest proportion of unmatched material facts after match improvement is then returned by BFIM.[7]

BFIM folds structure-matching into the retrieval process, returning not only the most similar exemplar but also the best mapping from the exemplar to NC. A drawback of BFIM is that its computational expense, while potentially

[7]This approach is analogous to MAC/FAC (many are called, few are chosen) (Gentner and Forbus, 1991), in which a group of candidate exemplars is selected on the basis of their degree of superficial similarity to the new case, and structure matching is used to discriminate among the candidates.

less than the expense of exhaustive matching, is at best linear in the number of exemplars for the predicate. Accordingly, it is appropriate only if the number of exemplars per predicate is limited in size. In many domains of law the number of viable exemplars on any single issue may never exceed a few dozen. In areas of the law where the number of exemplars can grow without limit, however, BFIM is probably not tractable.

A related approach using a different architecture is ARCS (analogical retrieval by constraint satisfaction) (Thagard et al., 1990). In ARCS, a constraint network is constructed from a set of candidate cases selected on the basis of pragmatic constraints. A connectionist algorithm is then applied until the network settles into a state that indicates the relative correspondence of the stored cases to the new case. In both ARCS and BFIM, computational resources are directed to the most promising partial matches at the expense of less promising matches.

Match Refinement by Structural Difference Links. An alternative approach to case retrieval used by GREBE involves match refinement using precomputed information about structural differences among cases. In match refinement by structural difference links (MRSDL), an initial candidate is selected on the basis of surface semantic similarity. Precomputed information on the structural relations among exemplars is then used to refine the match. Specifically, if the structural differences between an exemplar Ex_{cur} and a new case NC have been determined, difference links containing precomputed information about the structural differences between Ex_{cur} and alternative exemplars Ex_1 ... Ex_n can be used to estimate inexpensively the similarity between NC and each Ex_i. The idea behind this approach is that Ex_i is a better match to NC than Ex_{cur} to the extent that Ex_{cur} differs from Ex_i and NC in the same way. However, to the extent that Ex_i has additional differences from NC, the match between Ex_i and NC is worse. The most promising Ex_i is the case for which the differences with Ex_{cur} shared by Ex_i and NC are greatest and the additional differences between Ex_i and NC are least.

For the following discussion of MRSDL, it is helpful to introduce the following definitions and assumptions:

1. A *case* is a connected, directed graph consisting of a set $\{(r\ o_1\ o_2)\}$ of triples. $O(C_i)$ consists of the objects (vertices) in case C_i.

2. A mapping M from C_1 to C_2 is a set of ordered pairs $\{(s,t) | s \in O(C_1) \wedge t \in O(C_2)\}$ such that for all (s_1, t_1) and $(s_2, t_2) \in M$ (1) if $s_1 \neq s_2$, then $t_1 \neq t_2$, that is, M is 1 1 (injective)}, and (2) if $s_1 = s_2$, then $t_1 = t_2$. Thus, the inverse of a mapping is itself a 1–1 mapping.

3. The *difference* between two cases C_1 and C_2 under mapping $M : C_1 \Rightarrow C_2$, denoted $\delta(M)$, consists of the set of triples $\{(r\ o_1\ o_2) \mid (r\ M(o_1)\ M(o_2)) \notin C_2\}$. The *similarity* between two cases C_1 and C_2 under mapping $M : C_1 \Rightarrow C_2$, denoted $\sigma(M)$, consists of $\{(r\ o_1\ o_2) \mid (r\ M(o_1)\ M(o_2)) \in C_2\} = C_1 - \delta(M)$.

4. A mapping $M_2 : C_1 \Rightarrow C_2$ is an *extension* of mapping $M_1 : C_1 \Rightarrow C_2$ if $M_2 \supseteq M_1$.

5. A mapping $M : C_1 \Rightarrow C_2$ is a *best mapping*, denoted $M : C_1 \stackrel{B}{\Longrightarrow} C_2$, if $(\forall M_i : C_1 \Rightarrow C_2)|(\delta(M_i)| \geq |\delta(M)|)$.

6. A mapping $M_2 : C_1 \Rightarrow C_2$ is a *best extension* of mapping $M_1 : C_1 \Rightarrow C_2$, denoted $M_2 : C_1 \stackrel{B(M_1)}{\Longrightarrow} C_2$, if $(\forall M_i : C_1 \Rightarrow C_2)$ for which $M_i \supseteq M_1$, $|(\delta(M_i)| \geq |\delta(M_2)|)$.

7. C_1 is a *better match* to NC than C_2 if $\frac{|\delta(C_1 \stackrel{B}{\Rightarrow} NC)|}{|C_1|} < \frac{|\delta(C_2 \stackrel{B}{\Rightarrow} NC)|}{|C_2|}$, that is, if a lower proportion of C_1 triples than C_2 triples are unmatched under some best mapping to NC.

The algorithm for using a structural difference link to estimate the similarity between two cases is as follows:

Given:

- NC, a new case.
- Ex_{cur}, the currently best matching exemplar.
- Ex_i, the exemplar whose structural similarity to NC is to be determined.
- $\delta(M_1 : Ex_{cur} \stackrel{B}{\Rightarrow} NC)$, the structural difference between the current best match and the new case under best mapping M_1.
- $\delta(M_2 : Ex_i \stackrel{B}{\Rightarrow} Ex_{cur})$, the structural difference between the indexing case and a past case Ex_i under best mapping M_2 (stored as a difference link).

Do:

- Determine $M_3 : \delta(M_2) \stackrel{B(M_2 \circ M_1)}{\Longrightarrow} NC$, a best extension of $M_2 \circ M_1$.
- Return $|(\delta(M_1) - \delta(M_2^{-1})) \cup \delta(M_3)|$ as the predicted number of triples in Ex unmatched under a best mapping from Ex to NC, $\delta(Ex_i \stackrel{B}{\Rightarrow} NC)$.

Figure 4.13. The match refinement algorithm attempts to find the exemplar Ex_i that differs least from NC. The upper shaded region of Ex_i represents differences with NC that Ex_{cur} and Ex_i share. The lower shaded region of Ex_i represents differences between NC and Ex_i not shared with Ex_{cur}.

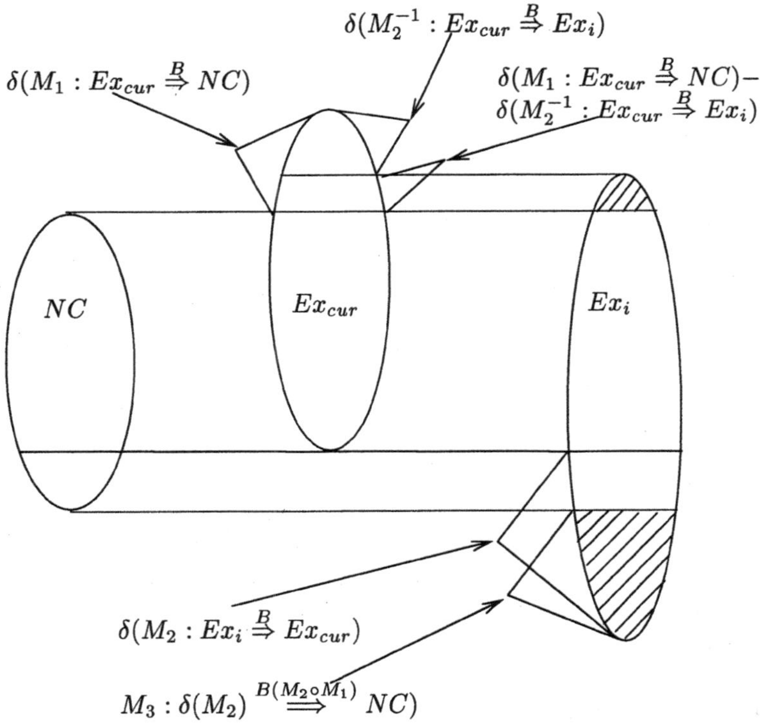

Figure 4.14. A new case.

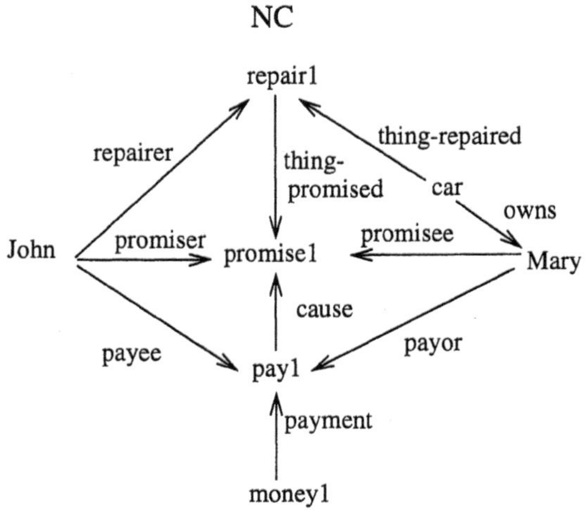

As shown in the upper shaded region of Figure 4.13, $|\delta(M_1 : Ex_{cur} \overset{B}{\Rightarrow} NC) - \delta(M_2^{-1} : Ex_{cur} \overset{B}{\Rightarrow} Ex_i)|$ represents the number of tuples in Ex_{cur} for which there are no corresponding tuples in NC under M_1 but for which there are corresponding facts in Ex_i under M_2^{-1}. This set represents the differences with NC that Ex_{cur} and Ex_i share.

$\delta(M_3 : \delta(M_2) \overset{B(M_2 \circ M_1)}{\Longrightarrow} NC)$ consists of the tuples of $\delta(M_2)$ (*i.e.*, Ex_i tuples unmatched in Ex_{cur} under the best mapping $M_2 : Ex_i \overset{B}{\Rightarrow} Ex_{cur}$) that are unmatched in NC under the best extension of $M_2 \circ M_1$, $M_3 : \delta(M_2) \overset{B(M_2 \circ M_1)}{\Longrightarrow} NC$. This set, which is an estimate of the differences between NC and Ex_i not shared with Ex_{cur}, is represented by the lower shaded region in Figure 4.13.

Consider a simple example involving the following brief narratives, represented in Figure 4.14 and Figure 4.15:

- NC. Mary paid John because John promised to repair Mary's car.
- Ex_1. Bill promised to pay Sally because Sally repaired Bill's watch.
- Ex_2. Fred paid Martha because Martha promised to repair the glasses of Junior, Fred's son.

Suppose that Ex_1 is the current best match to NC. Let us consider how knowledge of the best mappings from Ex_1 to NC and Ex_2 can be used to

Figure 4.15. Two exemplars.

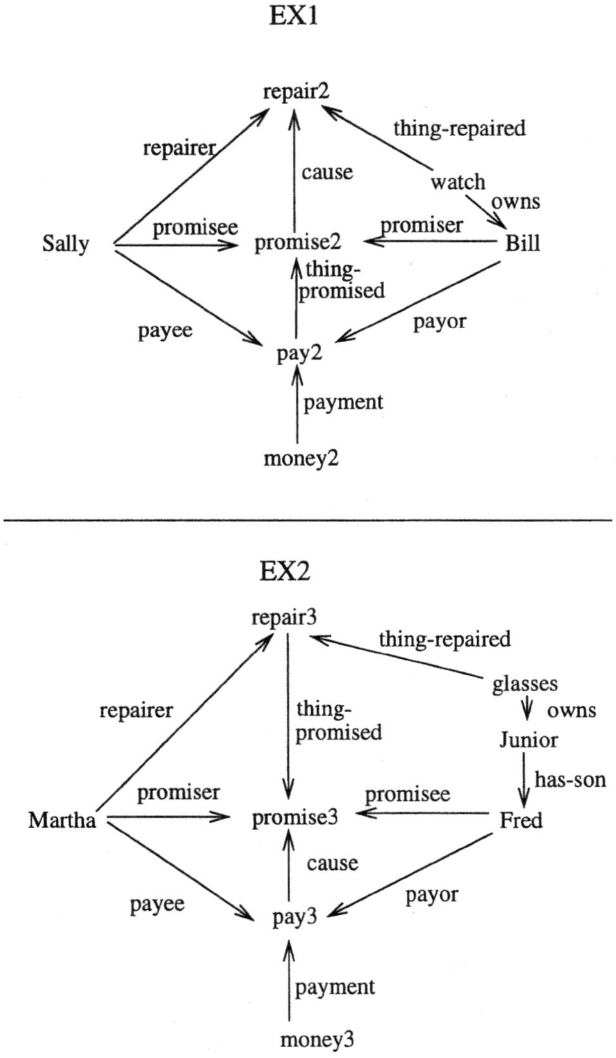

estimate the degree of match between Ex_2 and NC. There is a unique best mapping from Ex_1 to NC: $M_1 : Ex_1 \overset{B}{\Rightarrow} NC$ = {(Sally John)(Bill Mary)(pay2 pay1)(repair2 repair1)(money2 money1) (watch car)}. The difference under this mapping, $\delta(M_1)$, consists of the following triples: {(promiser promise2 Bill)(promisee promise2 Sally)(thing-promised promise2 pay2)(cause repair2 promise2)}.

Suppose that $M_2 : Ex_2 \overset{B}{\Rightarrow} Ex_1$ has been precomputed as a difference link.[8] If $\delta(M_1 : Ex_1 \overset{B}{\Rightarrow} NC) > \delta(M_2^{-1} : Ex_1 \overset{B}{\Rightarrow} Ex_2)$ then Ex_1 must match Ex_2 better than it matches NC. Thus, Ex_2 must share some triples with Ex_1 that NC lacks. $|\delta(M_1 : Ex_1 \overset{B}{\Rightarrow} NC) - \delta(M_2^{-1} : Ex_1 \overset{B}{\Rightarrow} Ex_2)|$ is the number of such triples.

In addition to triples that have matches in Ex_1 but not NC, Ex_2 may contain triples having no matches in either Ex_1 or NC. These triples consist of the set $\{(\text{r } o_1\ o_2) \in \delta(M_2) \mid (rM_4(o_1)M_4(o_2)) \notin NC\}$ where $M_4 : Ex_2 \overset{B}{\Rightarrow} NC$ is a best mapping from Ex_2 to NC (*i.e.*, the Ex_2 triples unmatched under the best mapping from Ex_2 to Ex_1 that are also unmatched in NC under the best mapping from Ex_2 to NC). Determining this set requires knowing $M_4 : Ex_2 \overset{B}{\Rightarrow} NC$, and determining M_4 is the potentially exponentially expensive problem that indexing was intended to obviate. However, we can use $\delta(M_3 : \delta(M_2) \overset{B(M_2 \circ M_1)}{\Longrightarrow} NC)$ as an estimate of this set. This estimate will be correct if $M_1 \circ M_2 \subseteq M_4$ for some $M_4 : \delta(M_2) \overset{B}{\Rightarrow} NC$, a best mapping from $\delta(M_2)$ to NC. If $M_1 \circ M_2 \not\subseteq M_4$ for any best mapping $M_4 : \delta(M_2) \overset{B}{\Rightarrow} NC$, then $\delta(M_3 : \delta(M_2) \overset{B(M_2 \circ M_1)}{\Longrightarrow} NC)$ may overestimate the size of the set $\{(\text{r } o_1\ o_2) \in \delta(M_2) \mid (rM_4(o_1)M_4(o_2)) \notin NC\}$. Accordingly, the difference link method is a heuristic method, not guaranteed to be accurate.

In the example above, $\delta(M_1 : Ex_1 \overset{B}{\rightarrow} NC) - \delta(M_2^{-1} : Ex_1 \overset{B}{\rightarrow} Ex_2) = \emptyset$. Thus, Ex_2 and Ex_1 share no triples that NC lacks. The number of Ex_2 triples having no matches in either Ex_1 or NC is estimated as follows: $M_1 \circ M_2$ is {(Martha Sally) (Fred Bill) (pay3 pay2) (repair3 repair2) (glasses watch) (money3 money2)} $\circ$ {(Sally John) (Bill Mary) (pay2 pay1) (repair2 repair1) (watch car)} = {(Martha John) (Fred Mary) (pay3 pay1) (repair3 repair1) (glasses car) (money3 money1)}, so $\delta(M_1 \circ M_2)$ is {(owns Junior glasses) (has-son Fred Junior)}. The extension of $M_1 \circ M_2$ which is a best mapping from $\delta(M_2)$ to NC is $M_1 \circ M_2$ itself, so the number of unmatched triples in $\delta(M_4 : Ex_2 \overset{B}{\rightarrow} Ex_1)$ is therefore $|\delta(M_1) - \delta(M_2^{-1})| + |\delta(M_1 \circ M_2)| = 0 + 2 = 2$.

The full algorithm for match refinement is as follows:

---

[8]It is unnecessary to explicitly represent $Ex_1 \overset{B}{\Rightarrow} Ex_2$ because $M_2^{-1} : Ex_1 \Rightarrow Ex_2$ is a best mapping from Ex_1 to Ex_2. **Proof**: Assume that $M_2 : Ex_2 \Rightarrow Ex_1$ is a best mapping, but that $M_2^{-1} : Ex_1 \Rightarrow Ex_2$ is not a best mapping. If M_2^{-1} is not a best mapping, then $\exists M_j : Ex_1 \Rightarrow Ex_2$ such that $|\delta(M_j)| < |\delta(M_2^{-1})|$, which implies that $|\sigma(M_j)| > |\sigma(M_2^{-1})|$. Since all mappings are 1–1, $|\sigma(M_j)| = |\sigma(M_j^{-1})|$ and $|\sigma(M_1)| = |\sigma(M_2^{-1})|$. So $|\sigma(M_j^{-1})| > |\sigma(M_2)|$, which implies that $|\delta(M_j^{-1})| < |\delta(M_2)|$, contradicting the assumption that M_2 is a best mapping.

Given:

- NC, a new case (*i.e.*, target exemplar)
- Ex_{cur}, the source exemplar that is currently the best match to NC
- $\delta(Ex_{cur} \overset{B}{\Rightarrow} NC)$, the propositions of Ex_{cur} that have no image in NC under $Ex_{cur} \overset{B}{\Rightarrow} NC$, the best mapping from Ex_{cur} to NC
- Precomputed difference links between Ex_{cur} and cases Ex_1 ... Ex_n containing the following information for each Ex_i:

  $Ex_{cur} \overset{B}{\Rightarrow} Ex_i$, the best mapping from Ex_{cur} to Ex_i, and $\delta(Ex_{cur} \overset{B}{\Rightarrow} Ex_i)$, the propositions of Ex_{cur} that have do not have an image in Ex_i under $Ex_{cur} \overset{B}{\Rightarrow} Ex_i$

Do:

1. Select the Ex_i for which $|\delta(Ex_i \overset{B}{\Rightarrow} NC)|/|Ex_i|$, the proportion of propositions unmatched under the best mapping from Ex_i to NC, is least as estimated by $|(\delta(M_1) - \delta(M_2^{-1})) \cup \delta(M_3)|$ (as described above).
2. Calculate the actual value of $\delta(Ex_i \overset{B}{\Rightarrow} NC)$.
3. If $|\delta(Ex_{cur} \overset{B}{\Rightarrow} NC)|/|Ex_{cur}| < |\delta(Ex_i \overset{B}{\Rightarrow} NC)|/|Ex_i|$, then NC matches Ex_{cur} better than any of the Ex_i's, so return Ex_{cur}. Otherwise, call the procedure again with Ex_i as the current best match (*i.e.*, replace Ex_{cur} with Ex_i).

The only search involved in determining $|(\delta(M_1) - \delta(M_2^{-1})) \cup \delta(M_3)|$ is the search to determine the best extension of $M_2 \circ M_1$, $M_3 : \delta(M_2) \overset{B(M_2 \circ M_1)}{\Longrightarrow} NC)$. If $M_1 \circ M_2$ is a significant subset of M_3 or if $\delta(M_2)$ is significantly smaller than Ex_i, this search will be significantly less expensive than a direct comparison between Ex_i and NC. However, this estimation is not guaranteed to be correct if either mapping $Ex_{cur} \overset{B}{\Rightarrow} NC$ or mapping $Ex_{cur} \overset{B}{\Rightarrow} Ex_i$ is an *incomplete mapping*, *i.e.*, a mapping in which the domain of the mapping is a proper subset of the tuples of the source. One source of inaccuracy is that incomplete mappings can lead to an overestimation of the differences with NC that Ex_{cur} and Ex_i share. Under the mappings shown in Figure 4.16,[9] for example, $\delta(M_1 : Ex_{cur} \overset{B}{\Rightarrow} NC)$ is {(r C_2 E_2) (r D_2 F_2) (r F_2 E_2)} and $\delta(M_2^{-1} : Ex_{cur} \Rightarrow Ex_i)$ is {(r B_2 A_2) (r A_2 C_2) (r B_2 D_2)}. As a result, $\delta(M_1 : Ex_{cur} \Rightarrow NC) - \delta(M_2^{-1} : Ex_i \Rightarrow Ex_{cur})$ is {(r C_2 E_2) (r D_2 F_2) (r F_2 E_2)} even though NC and Ex_i are isomorphic.

[9] In Figures 4.16 and 4.17 all arcs are implicitly labeled r.

Figure 4.16. A situation in which $\delta(M_1 : Ex_{cur} \Rightarrow NC) - \delta(M_2^{-1} : Ex_{cur} \Rightarrow Ex_i)$ is overestimated because the mappings are incomplete. All arcs are implicitly labeled **r**.

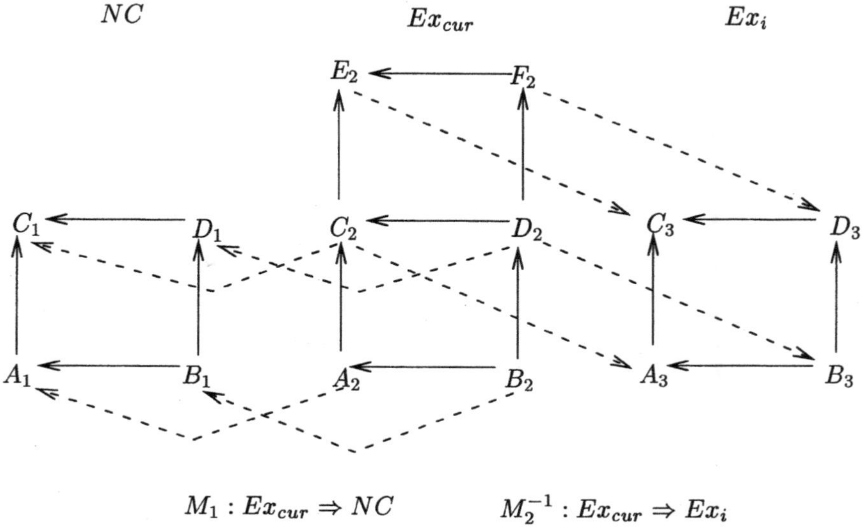

A second source of inaccuracy is that incomplete mappings can lead to an overestimation of the differences between NC and Ex_i not shared with Ex_{cur}. As illustrated in Figure 4.17, the composition of two best mappings is not necessarily itself the best mapping if either of the mappings being composed is incomplete. In this case, $\delta(M_3 : \delta(M_2) \stackrel{B(M_2 \circ M_1)}{\Longrightarrow} NC)$ is nonempty even though NC and Ex_i are isomorphic.

In general, the accuracy of the estimate of $\delta(Ex_i \Rightarrow NC)$ from $\delta(Ex_{cur} \Rightarrow NC)$, $\delta(Ex_{cur} \Rightarrow Ex_i)$, and $\delta(Ex_i \Rightarrow Ex_{cur})$ depends on the degree of pairwise structural similarity among NC, Ex_{cur}, and Ex_i. Thus, for this approach to work well, there must be a path of difference links stretching from the initial match to the actual closest case, consisting of pairwise similar cases. This condition is generally met when all cases are connected by difference links, but the space requirement of storing $O(n^2)$ links makes this approach unfeasible. Some structure must be imposed on the category so that the number of links can be reduced to the same order as the number of cases.

One approach to insuring that there is a sequence of pairwise similar cases from the initial match to the actual closest case is to identify a small collection of highly central cases such that every member of the case library has at least a moderate degree of similarity to at least one of the central cases. Each of the

Figure 4.17. A situation in which the composition of two best mappings is not itself a best mapping because $M_2 : Ex_i \Rightarrow Ex_{cur}$ is an incomplete mapping.

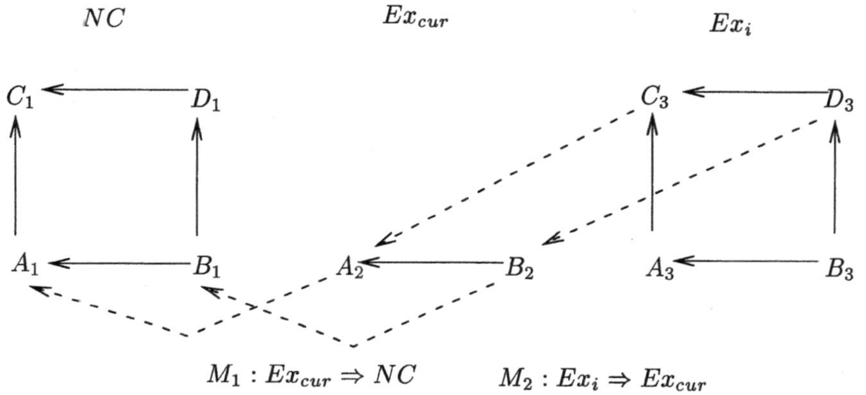

central cases is connected by difference links to every other central case and to every noncentral case to which it is at least moderately similar. As illustrated in Figure 4.18, the network of central cases provides a pathway of pairwise similar cases connecting every pair of cases in the case library. The number of links required for this arrangement is at most $m(m-1)/2 + m * (n-m)$, where n is the number of cases and m is the number of central cases. If the category represented by the case library is sufficiently cohesive, the number of central cases, and therefore the number of links, may be modest.[10]

In summary, two different approaches to structured case retrieval have been developed in GREBE. BFIM has the advantage of simplicity in that it involves only a straightforward extension of GREBE's basic structure-matching procedure and doesn't require setting up any indices. The match refinement approach has the potential for scaling up better than BFIM, but it gives rise to the problem of devising a configuration of difference links that is sufficient to insure that any initial match can be refined to the closest match, but which doesn't impose prohibitive storage requirements. Techniques for automatically creating appropriate difference link configurations are an area for future research. Performance data on the indexing methods are set forth in Chapter 6 on evaluation.

[10] An alternative approach to using the structural difference link approach would be to focus on the fact that $|(\delta(M_1) - \delta(M_2^{-1})) \cup \delta(M_3 : \delta(M_2) \overset{B(M_2 \circ M_1)}{\Longrightarrow} NC)|$ is an upper bound on $|\delta(Ex_i \Rightarrow NC)|$. A technique that uses upper and lower bounds on structural similarity for anytime retrieval is described in (Schaaf, 1995). See (Messmer and Bunke, 1998) for another approach to case matching by subgraph isomorphism detection.

Figure 4.18. A category organized by centrality. Highly central cases are labeled HC and less central cases are labeled LC. Difference links are indicated by solid lines. Dashed arrows represent the initial superficial match between new case NC and LC_{init} and subsequent refinement steps to the structurally most similar case, LC_{best}.

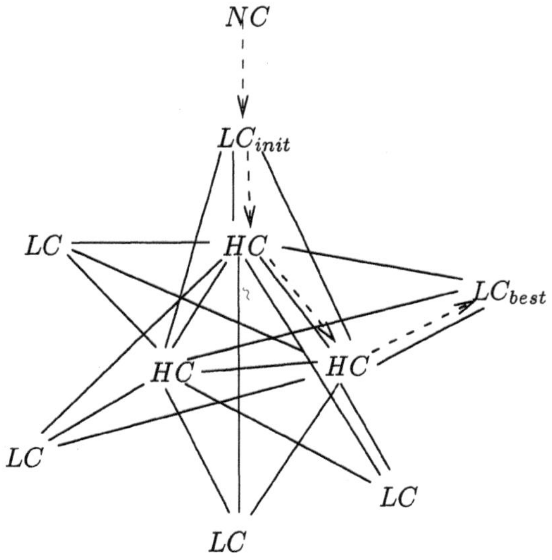

4.5 Presenting Explanation Structures as Memoranda

GREBE's explanation generator uses warrants that are derived from sources familiar to legal experts: statutes, the reasoning of exemplars, and the meanings of common terms. The objective of using such warrants is to produce explanations that are both as strong as possible and also as plausible as possible to users. If an inference path produced by the explanation generator corresponds to a strong, plausible explanation, then a straightforward syntactic transformation should be sufficient to transform the inference path into a natural language output that legal experts can comprehend and find persuasive. GREBE's memorandum generator is a mechanism for achieving this transformation.

The memorandum generator does not address the very difficult problem of converting between a case's natural language representation and the equivalent semantic network representation. Instead, GREBE addresses the far simpler problem of converting explanation structures into their natural language equivalent. GREBE's explanation structures have a simple recursive structure that lends itself well to template instantiation techniques.[11]

The memorandum generator operates in two steps. First, it sorts the explanations by a heuristic estimate of their strength. It then prints a natural-language equivalent of one or more of the explanations, starting with the strongest. The natural-language equivalent of each explanation is formed by instantiating natural-language templates corresponding to classes of predicates and types of warrants. The memorandum generator has both a verbose mode, in which it prints the complete explanation, and a comparison mode, in which it prints only those portions of an explanation that differ from the immediately preceding explanation.

Evaluating Explanations

GREBE's explanation generator produces multiple explanations whenever multiple warrants are applicable to a given goal. The first step of the memorandum generator is to order these explanations by an estimate of their strength. One explanation can be weaker than another either because it contains a case-based reasoning step involving attribute dropping or because it contains a semantic explanation. Neither attribute dropping nor semantic explanations are, in general, sound because both involve equating two entities solely on the basis of sharing a generalization. Estimating the strength of an explanation requires estimating the degree of violence done to the explanation by these unsound inferences.

[11]A more sophisticated ***document grammar*** approach to automated drafting of legal documents is set forth in (Branting and Lester, 1996b), (Branting and Lester, 1996a), (Branting et al., 1997), and (Branting et al., 1998). For a discussion of issues involved in drafting routine judicial documents, *see* (Branting, 1998).

GREBE calculates the strength of a semantic explanation to be the semantic similarity between the predicate in the explained fact and the predicate in the grounds. The semantic similarity between two predicates is, in turn, inversely proportional to the traversal distance between the predicates in a semantic hierarchy.[12]

No plausible scheme for assigning numerical measures of importance to the relevant facts of precedent constituents has been proposed (Ashley and Rissland, 1988). As a result, GREBE uses the heuristic of assigning equal weights to all the facts of a exemplar. The strength of a case-based explanation is thus calculated to be the proportion of facts that were matched under the best mapping following match improvement. A match explained by a semantic explanation counts as a partial match. For example, if a exemplar has 10 facts, of which 8 are matched under the best mapping onto a new case and one is matched by a semantic explanation of strength 0.2, the strength of the case-based explanation is calculated to be $(8 + 0.2)/10 = 0.82$.

However, the fact that exemplars can be nested, as described in Section 4.3, complicates the computation of the degree of match. For example, the material facts of the exemplar constituent in *Vaughn* for Vaughn's traveling being in furtherance of employment, shown in Figure 4.7, include two facts that are explained by case-based explanations: that food was reasonably essential for work and that the traveling was necessitated by Vaughn's employer. The proportion of matches in nested exemplars is determined by dividing the number of mismatches in any of the nested exemplars by the number of unique observable features in all of the exemplars. In effect, a hierarchy of exemplars is flattened into a single collection of observable facts for the purposes of determining the degree of match.

For example, suppose that the warrant for conclusion C in new case NC is exemplar Ex_1, with facts $F_1 \wedge AF_1 \wedge AF_2$, that the warrant for AF_1 is Ex_2, which has facts $F_2 \wedge F_3$, and that the warrant for AF_2 is Ex_3, having facts $F_4 \wedge F_5$. Suppose that NC has facts $F_1 \wedge F_2 \wedge F_5$. The strength of the explanation of C in NC is the ratio of the number of matches at any level to the number of observable features at any level: $\mid F_1, F_2, F_5 \mid / \mid F_1, F_2, F_3, F_4, F_5 \mid = 3/5 = 0.6$.

Calculation of the strength of other explanation types is straightforward: trivial explanations are calculated to have a strength of 1.0. The strength of a rule-based explanation is calculated to be the minimum of the strengths of the explanations of its antecedents. The strength of conjunctions and disjunctions is the minimum of the strengths of the conjuncts and the maximum of the strengths of the disjuncts, respectively.

[12]The formula used for determining semantic similarity is $S = 1.8 * d/2^d$, where d is the number of steps separating the predicates in the semantic hierarchy. The d in the numerator causes the semantic distance between siblings in a semantic hierarchy to be the same as the distance between a term and its parent, *e.g.*, the distance between *director* and *permitter* is the same as the distance between *director* and *speaker*, the parent of *director* and *permitter*. Under this formula, ten semantic explanations involving terms one or two steps apart in a hierarchy are equivalent to one mismatch. For example, the strength of the explanation: ((walker-in John traveling-to-store) similar-to (driver-in John traveling-to-store) is 0.9 because walker-in and *driver-in* are both children of traveler-in in a semantic hierarchy. Thus, they are separated by two steps in the hierarchy, and their similarity is $1.8 * 2/2^2 = 0.9$.

Instantiating Natural Language Templates

The natural language equivalent of an explanation is produced using conventional template instantiation techniques. The memorandum generator converts tuples into text strings using templates corresponding to classes of predicates, *e.g.*, amount-of and agent-of belong to a class having the template

<arg1 "was the" predicate arg2>

Text strings created from tuples are then used to instantiate templates for GREBE's explanation types. For example, the template for case-based explanations is

< "That" proposition "follows from the" (very strong, strong, moderate, weak) "analogy between the given case and the facts of" exemplar "that were relevant to the conclusion that" proposition-explained-by-the-exemplar "This analogy is supported by the following:" supporting-explanations "Relevant differences ... are that" unmatched-tuples >

Whether the analogy is "very strong," "strong," "moderate," or "weak," is determined by the strength of the case-based explanation, *i.e.*, the proportion of unmatched tuples. Note that part of the grounds of a case-based explanation, its mapping, is not included in this template. The entire mapping is at too low a level of detail to belong in a memorandum. On the other hand, it would be desirable for some high-level characterization of the correspondence to be presented. Generating such a summary poses a potentially difficult natural language production problem.

The template for conflicting case-based explanations includes language that depends on the relative strength of the two conflicting case-based explanations. If they are very close to the same strength, the memorandum generator produces

< "On one hand" CBE_1 "On the other hand" CBE_2 >

However, if one case-based explanation is much stronger than the other or if one case represents an exception to another[13] the output is

< "The stronger argument is that" CBE_1 "However, a weaker argument can be made that" CBE_2 >

[13]For example, driving to and from work is ordinarily not *in furtherance of employment*. However, traveling for a "special errand" is an exception that is *in furtherance of employment*. *Jecker v. Western Alliance Ins. Co.*, 369 S.W.2d 776 (Tex. 1963). Traveling under a separate contractual obligation to perform the special errand is, in turn, an exception to this exception. *Texas General Indem. Co. v. Bottom*, 365 S.W.2d 350 (Tex. 1963). The key property of exemplars that represent exceptions to one another is that if there is an equally close match to both a exemplar and an exception to that exemplar, the exception should control. This property is modeled in GREBE by slightly incrementing the estimate of match strength to a exemplar that is an exception to a conflicting exemplar. A proposal for using exception relations as a retrieval mechanism is described in (Branting, 1990).

5 EXAMPLES OF GREBE'S LEGAL ANALYSIS

This chapter presents examples of GREBE's legal analysis. The first section continues the analysis of *Jarek's Case*, which was begun in Chapter 4. The second section sets forth GREBE's analysis of four closely related cases, illustrating how small changes in facts can yield significant differences in analysis. Appendix B contains a brief summary of the precedent cases used by GREBE in the analyses of these cases.

5.1 Hard Cases Yield Strong Conflicting Arguments

In *Jarek's Case*, the Massachusetts Supreme Court ruled that Jarek was not entitled to workers' compensation benefits because his trip home was solely for the employee's benefit. This result was criticized by the leading authority on workers' compensation as "archaic" on the grounds that the employer's imposition of overtime work necessitated Jarek's trip home to relieve his wife's anxiety (Larsen, 1989). This conflict between a court and a leading commentator suggests that *Jarek's case* is a hard, and therefore interesting, case.

Let us consider how GREBE would analyze *Jarek's Case* under Texas law. The analysis is initiated by posing to GREBE the question whether Jarek's employer is liable under workers' compensation for Jarek's injury under the facts of *Jarek's Case.* Workers' compensation liability is not given in the facts of *Jarek's Case*, so GREBE's explanation generator attempts to find either rules or precedents that would enable it to establish workers' compensation liability. It finds only a single statutory rule, Vernon's Tex. Rev. Civ. Stat. Ann. art. 8309 §1, having workers' compensation liability as its consequent. It then attempts to establish the antecedent of this rule: that Jarek's injury was "sustained in the course" of that employment.

A second statutory rule, also contained in Art. 8309 §1, can warrant the conclusion that an injury is sustained in the course of employment. The antecedents of this rule are as follows:[1]

- The worker must be employed.
- The injury must occur while the worker is engaged in an activity "in furtherance of" his employment.
- The injury must "originate" in the employment.

The second antecedent restricts compensable injures to those that occur when the worker is engaged in an activity related to employment. For example, a worker injured by a chemical leak while picnicking near the plant where he worked could not recover, even though the injury was caused by a hazard of employment, because picnicking is unrelated to his work activities. The third antecedent restricts compensable injuries to those that are causally connected to the hazards of employment. For example, a worker punched in the nose by his girlfriend's ex-husband while at work would not have a compensable injury, because the injury would not have arisen from a hazard of employment, even though it occurred at work.

Art. 8309 §1b sets forth two additional requirements for injuries occurring during traveling:

- *The Statutory Traveling Rule.* Injuries occurring during traveling are compensable only if the transportation was "furnished as a part of the contract of employment, or ... paid for, ... or ... under the control of the employer" or if the worker was "directed in his employment" to engage in the traveling.
- *The Dual-Purpose Rule.* This rule precludes compensability of traveling that accomplishes some personal goal distinct from its employment purpose "unless the trip to the place of occurrence of said injury would have been made even had there been no personal [goal] and unless said trip would not have been made had there been no [employment related goal]."

[1] In relevant part, the text of this rule is:

> '[I]njury sustained in the course of employment' ... shall include all other injuries of every kind and character having to do with and originating in the work, business, trade or profession of the employer received by an employee while engaged in or about the furtherance of the affairs or business of his employer whether upon the employer's premises or elsewhere ....

The first antecedent, that the worker must be employed, was given in the facts of *Jarek's Case.* However, the next antecedent, that Jarek's traveling home was an activity "in furtherance of employment," is not given in the facts of the case and matches no rules. The explanation generator therefore turns to case-based reasoning.

The precedent retriever uses two invocations of retrieval by best-first incremental mapping or match refinement by structural difference links (depending on a user-specifiable parameter) to retrieve the structurally most similar precedent constituent for an activity "in furtherance of employment" and the structurally most similar precedent constituent for an activity not "in furtherance of employment." The precedent constituent for an activity "in furtherance of employment" most similar to *Jarek's Case* is *Vaughn-ifo-pc*, discussed in Section 4.3, and the most similar noninstance precedent constituent, *Typical-commuting-home-not-ifo-pc*, is from a paradigm case, *Typical commuting home.* A portion of GREBE's representation of the material facts of *Typical commuting home* are shown in Figure 5.1.

There is a perfect match between the material facts of *Typical commuting home* and *Jarek's Case*, indicating that *Jarek's Case* contains all the facts of an ordinary commuting trip. However, as discussed in Section 4.4, there are several unmatched relations in *Vaughn* under the best mapping from *Vaughn* to *Jarek's Case.* Figure 4.12 illustrated how three semantic and two case-based explanations can be created to improve the match between *Vaughn* and *Jarek's Case.* Since case-based explanations can be constructed both for and against the conclusion that Jarek's traveling was in furtherance of his employment (*i.e.*, the case matches both typical commuting home and *Vaughn*), the case-based reasoner returns a conflicting explanation for this antecedent.

The explanation generator then turns to the remaining antecedents of the rule for "injury sustained in the course of employment." The first is that Jarek's injury must have originated in his employment. Texas workers' compensation traveling cases seldom discuss this issue, apparently because the origination requirement is obviously satisfied whenever an injury results from a hazard of traveling and the traveling is itself in furtherance of employment. This rule, implicit in the cases, is made explicit in GREBE's rule base. The rule's requirement that the injury be a hazard of traveling is given in the facts of *Jarek's Case*, and there is an explanation, albeit conflicting, that Jarek's traveling was in furtherance of his employment.

The next rule antecedent is that the traveling must fall within some exception to the statutory rule barring compensation for accidents occurring during traveling. One exception is for traveling that is "directed in ... employment." Vernon's Tex. Rev. Civ. Stat. Ann. art. 8309 §1b. GREBE creates two different explanations for this conclusion. The first is a rule-based explanation using a

Figure 5.1. A portion of the material facts of *Typical commuting home* for the conclusion that commuting home is not an activity in furtherance of employment.

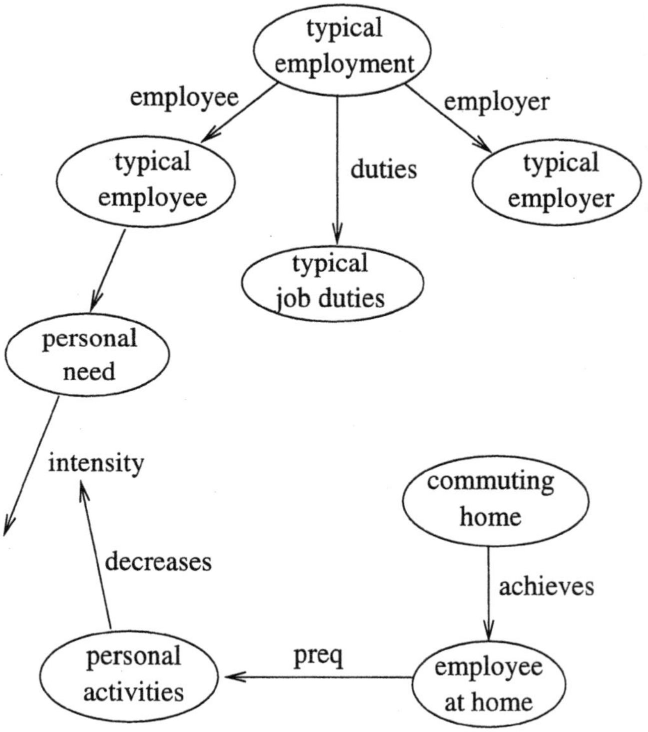

common-law rule from *Jecker v. Western Alliance Ins. Co.*, 369 S.W.2d 776 (1963), that an employee is implicitly "directed in ... employment" to travel whenever the traveling is in furtherance of employment.[2] The second is a semantic explanation based on the semantic similarity between being directed and being permitted.

The final rule antecedent, that the dual purpose rule be inapplicable, can be satisfied by either of two conditions:

- The traveling had no personal goal distinct from its employment purpose, or
- The traveling would have been made even had there been no personal goal and the trip would not have been made had there been no employment-related goal.

Here, there was no personal goal distinct from informing Jarek's wife of the schedule change, which was arguably an activity in furtherance of employment. Therefore, the dual purpose rule is inapplicable.

The explanation generator returns two explanations for workers' compensation liability differing only in how they explain that Jarek was "directed in his employment" to travel home. This pair of explanations is then passed to the memo generator.

When the memo generator evaluates the explanations of *Jarek's Case*, it finds that one explanation contains a weak semantic explanation of Jarek having been "directed in his employment" to travel home, *i.e.*, that being directed is similar to being permitted, and Jarek was permitted to travel home. However the other explanation has a strong explanation of this fact based on a common-law rule. It therefore converts the second, stronger explanation into its English equivalent.

The output of the memo generator begins by restating the proposition to be explained, followed by two rule-based reasoning steps:[3]

```
Query: Is Denver and Rio Grande railroad liable under worker
compensation to Jarek for Jarek's injury?

Under Vernon's Ann.Tex.Civ.St. article 8309 section 1b, Denver
and Rio Grande railroad is liable under worker compensation to
Jarek for Jarek's injury if:

    Jarek's injury was sustained by Jarek while engaged in the
    special trip home in the course of employment by Denver and
```

[2]Note that this rule renders the traveling exception superfluous, because it means that an exception to the statutory traveling rule is satisfied by any traveling that is "in furtherance of employment." It is not clear whether the *Jecker* court intended this effect, but no plausible narrower construction of this rule is obvious from the opinion.

[3]Each of the excerpts in this chapter, printed in typewriter font, is verbatim text from GREBE's memorandum generator.

Rio Grande railroad.

This conclusion follows from Vernon's Ann.Tex.Civ.St. article 8309 section 1b if:

a. Jarek was employed by Denver and Rio Grande railroad, as stated in the given facts.

b. Jarek's injury occurred during the special trip home, as stated in the given facts.

c. The special trip home was an activity in furtherance of Jarek's employment.

Jarek's Case is then analogized to the closest instance and noninstance precedent constituents that can warrant "activity in furtherance of employment:"

> Two conflicting arguments can be made concerning whether the special trip home was an activity in furtherance of Jarek's employment.
>
> The stronger argument is that:
>
> > The special trip home was not an activity in furtherance of Jarek's employment.
> >
> > This conclusion follows from the very strong analogy between the given case and the facts that are relevant to the conclusion that ordinary commuting from work is not an activity in furtherance of a typical employee's employment as held in American General Ins. v. Coleman, 157 Tx. 377, 303 S.W.2d 370.
> >
> > This analogy is supported by the following inference:
> >
> > > That Jarek walked during the special trip home, which is stated in the facts of the given case, is similar to the fact that a typical employee was the driver during ordinary commuting from work.

The semantic explanation of the equivalence of walking and driving is necessary because the paradigm case of commuting in the workers' compensation knowledge base involves an employee who drives to work. *American General Ins. v. Coleman*, 157 Tx. 377, 303 S.W.2d 370, is not itself a typical commuting case, but is a frequently cited authority for the proposition that ordinary commuting is not an activity in furtherance of employment.

The memo then continues with an argument that Jarek's traveling was in furtherance of his employment.

```
However, a weaker argument can be made that:

        The special trip home was an activity in
        furtherance of Jarek's employment.

        This conclusion follows from the strong analogy
        between the given case and the facts of Vaughn v.
        Highlands Underwriters Ins. Co., 445 S.W.2d 234
        (1969) that were relevant to the conclusion that
        the trip from the factory to a restaurant was an
        activity in furtherance of Vaughn's employment.
```

The memo sets forth the three semantic and two case-based explanations that support the match between *Jarek's Case* and *Vaughn*, together with the relevant differences between the cases.[4] Two propositions having semantic explanations—that the Railroad was the permitter and that Jarek was the permittee of Jarek's special trip home—are aggregated to form a single proposition that the Railroad permitted Jarek's special travel home.

```
        This analogy is supported by the following
        inferences:

          A.  That Denver and Rio Grande railroad
              permitted the special trip home, which is
              stated in the facts of the given case, is
              similar to the fact that Apf Co directed the
              trip from the factory to a restaurant.

          B.  Jarek's being at home was reasonably
              essential for Jarek's employment duties.
```

[4]Note that because of these differences the match between *Jarek's Case* and *Vaughn* requires attribute dropping as described in Chapter 2.

This conclusion follows from the weak analogy between the given case and the facts of Janak v. Texas Employer's Ins. Co., 381 S.W.2d 176 (1964) that were relevant to the conclusion that icewater being at Ecleto was reasonably essential for oil drilling by the Janak crew.

This analogy is supported by the following inference:

> That Jarek had the need to inform his wife, which is stated in the facts of the given case, is similar to the fact that the Janak crew had the need to keep cool.

Relevant differences between the given case and Janak v. Texas Employer's Ins. Co., 381 S.W.2d 176 (1964) with respect to the issue whether Jarek's being at home was reasonably essential for Jarek's employment duties are that:

- Jarek's employment duties was not impeded by the fact that the need to inform his wife was of high intensity.

Whereas in the Janak case:

- Oil drilling by the Janak crew was impeded by the fact that the need for cooling was of high intensity.

C. The special trip home was necessitated by Denver and Rio Grande's instruction to work late.

This conclusion follows from the very strong analogy between the given case and the facts of Vaughn v. Highlands Underwriters Ins.

```
Co., 445 S.W.2d 234 (1969) that were
relevant to the conclusion that the trip
from the factory to a restaurant was
necessitated by Apf. Co.'s instructions to
Vaughn.

This analogy is supported by the following
inference:

    Jarek's being at home was reasonably
    essential for Jarek's employment
    duties, as was shown above.

D.  That Jarek walked during the special trip
    home, which is stated in the facts of the
    given case, is similar to the fact that
    Vaughn was the driver during the trip from
    the factory to a restaurant.
```

Explanations of the remaining antecedents of Vernon's Tex. Rev. Civ. Stat. Ann. art. 8309 §1 are then presented. First is the explanation that Jarek's injury originated in his employment. This follows from the common-sense rule that an injury originates in employment if it results from a hazard of an activity that is in furtherance of employment. The first antecedent of this rule, that the injury was caused by a hazard of traveling, was undisputed. However, the second antecedent, that the traveling be in furtherance of employment, has conflicting explanations. The stronger of these explanations is that the antecedent is not satisfied.

```
d. Jarek's injury originated in Jarek's employment.

   i.  Jarek's injury was a hazard of the special trip
       home, as stated in the given facts.

   ii. The stronger argument is that the special trip
       home was not an activity in furtherance of
       Jarek's employment, as was shown above.
```

Finally, the inapplicability of the statutory traveling exception and dual-purpose rule is explained. The traveling exception is inapplicable when traveling is "directed in ... employment," and *Jecker* held that there is an implied direction to engage in traveling that is in furtherance of employment.

e. The rule barring compensation for accidents occurring during traveling is inapplicable to the special trip home.

This conclusion follows from Vernon's Ann.Tex.Civ.St. article 8309 section 1b if:

i. The special trip home falls within a statutory exception to the rule barring compensation for accidents occurring during traveling.

This conclusion follows from Vernon's Ann.Tex.Civ.St. article 8309 section 1b if:

Jarek was directed in his employment by Denver and Rio Grande railroad to engage in the special trip home.

This conclusion follows from the rule of Jecker v. Western Alliance Ins. Co., 369 S.W.2d 776 (1963), that there is an implied direction to perform activities in furtherance of employment if:

The stronger argument is that the special trip home was not an activity in furtherance of Jarek's employment, as was shown above.

ii. The dual purpose rule is inapplicable to the special trip home.

This conclusion follows from the dual purpose rule of article 8309 section 1b if:

The special trip home was not both in furtherance of the personal or private affairs of Jarek and in furtherance of Jarek's employment.

Under the facts of the given case, the

```
special trip home was not an activity
in furtherance of the personal or
private affairs of Jarek.
```

This analysis illustrates how two strong competing arguments can be made in *Jarek's Case*. On the one hand, *Jarek's Case* closely resembles ordinary commuting, which is not an activity in furtherance of employment. The Massachusetts Supreme Court found this argument persuasive and therefore denied benefits to Jarek. On the other hand, Jarek's traveling would not have been necessary except for the actions of his employer. This similarity argues that Jarek's traveling was, like Vaughn's, an activity in furtherance of employment.

From GREBE's analysis, it appears that the second argument is slightly weaker under Texas case law than the first because *Jarek's Case* fails to match *Vaughn* in two relevant respects. First, there was no evidence that Jarek's ability to perform his employment duties would have been impeded by his need to inform his wife of his schedule change. Second, Jarek was merely permitted, rather than directed, to go home. These differences are set forth in the GREBE's analysis and form the basis of GREBE's higher rating for the argument against workers' compensation liability.

GREBE's analysis is consistent with an analysis produced during a protocol study performed at the Colorado Court of Appeals on August 29–30, 1988 (Branting, 1988). The subjects of that study were experienced appellate staff attorneys who were presented with precedents and hypothetical cases and asked to analyze them aloud.

One subject was presented with *Vaughn*, a precedent of ordinary commuting, and the facts of *Jarek's Case*, and was asked to analyze *Jarek's Case* in terms of the precedents. Her analysis was that in order for a court to rule in favor of Jarek, the reasoning of *Vaughn* would have to be extended in two respects. First, there would have to be a determination, possibly based on public policy grounds, that an employee's family relations are as important as his/her need for food, water, or air. Second, the court would have to reason that whether a trip was requested or directed is not decisive, because sometimes a work necessity is known only to the employee. For example, the need to use the bathroom at a particular time is likely to be known only to the employee, but that doesn't mean that this need is any less important than the need for food. So the mere fact that the activity was requested rather than directed doesn't imply that it has no employment purpose.

GREBE lacks the world knowledge necessary to construct such imaginative extensions of existing legal doctrine. However, GREBE is able to show how conflicting arguments concerning a given legal issue can be constructed using existing legal authorities. Moreover, GREBE can recognize the stronger argument and identify the respects in which the weaker argument would need to be strengthened in order to prevail.

5.2 Small Changes in Facts Can Cause Large Changes in Analysis

Changing a few key facts of a case can often dramatically alter the case's legal consequences. This section illustrates how GREBE's impartial strategy for combining rules and cases leads GREBE to make large changes in its analyses based on small but important factual changes.

Car-pool Case 1

Consider the following hypothetical case:

> Joan and Donald were employed by the school district as teachers at a middle school and car-pooled together. Each workday, the driver of the car-pool was responsible for picking up some sandwiches on the way to work for both teachers to eat because there was no cafeteria at the school. On the day of the accident, Donald picked up Joan at her house and drove toward the school. Donald then deviated from the direct route to the school on his way to the sandwich shop. Before reaching the sandwich shop, Donald had an automobile accident in which Joan was injured. Does Joan have a claim for workers' compensation against the school district?

GREBE begins its analysis, as it did in *Jarek's Case*, by back-chaining through the statutory rules for workers' compensation liability. When it reaches the goal of showing that the traveling was within the scope of Joan's employment, however, it finds two distinct alternative analyses. The first uses a case-based explanation in which Joan's traveling is compared to the traveling of Draplia in the case of *Janak v. Texas Employer's Ins. Co.*, 381 S.W.2d 176 (1964). As mentioned in Section 4.3 and described in more detail in Appendix B, *Janak* involved an accident that occurred during a deviation from the direct route to Ecleto, a drill site where Draplia, the driver, and Janak, the passenger, worked on an oil drilling crew. The purpose of the deviation was to get ice to cool the crew's drinking water. The court found that the deviation was in furtherance of Draplia's employment because ice water was *reasonably essential* for oil drilling in a hot climate. The analogy to Draplia is weak, however, because, unlike Draplia, Joan was not the driver, nor was she responsible for picking up the sandwiches.

The alternative analysis applies a common-law rule enunciated in *Janak* that a passenger in a business car-pool is in the course of employment whenever the driver is in the course of employment. Subgoaling through this rule, the original problem of showing that Joan was within the scope of her employment is reduced to showing that Donald was within the scope of his employment at the time of the accident. Use of this rule is an example of goal reformulation. As described in Chapter 2, goal reformulation replaces a goal for which there is no closely matching exemplar with a new goal for which there are closer matches. Donald's traveling is much more closely analogous to Draplia's traveling, so a strong argument can be made that Donald, and therefore Joan, was acting in furtherance of employment. Donald's traveling also matches the facts of ordinary commuting, so a weaker argument can also be made that Donald's traveling was just ordinary commuting.

The stronger analysis identifies the business car-pool passenger rule from *Janak* and shows how its antecedents are satisfied:

```
...
The trip to the sandwich shop was an activity in
furtherance of Joan's employment.

This conclusion follows from the rule of Janak v.
Texas Employer's Ins. Co., 381 S.W.2d 176 (1964) that
a passenger in a business car-pool is in the course of
employment whenever the driver is in the course of
employment if:

  i.  Donald was employed by the school district, as
      stated in the given facts.

 ii.  Joan was the passenger in the trip to the
      sandwich shop, as stated in the given facts.

iii.  Donald was the driver during the trip to the
      sandwich shop, as stated in the given facts.

 iv.  Joan was a passenger in the trip to the sandwich
      shop pursuant to a business car-pool.

      This conclusion follows from the very strong
      analogy between the given case and the facts of
      Janak v. Texas Employer's Ins. Co.,
      381 S.W.2d 176 (1964) that were relevant to the
      conclusion that the Janak crew was a passenger in
      the deviation to Runge pursuant to a business
      car-pool.

  v.  The trip to the sandwich shop was an activity in
```

```
        furtherance of Donald's employment.
```

Having shown that Joan's status depends on whether Donald's traveling was in furtherance of his employment, the analysis turns to the latter question. Donald's traveling matches both Draplia's driving in *Janak* and ordinary commuting.

```
        Two conflicting arguments can be made concerning
        whether the trip to the sandwich shop was an
        activity in furtherance of Donald's employment.

        The stronger argument is that:

            The trip to the sandwich shop was an
            activity in furtherance of Donald's
            employment.

            This conclusion follows from the very strong
            analogy between the given case and the facts
            of Janak v. Texas Employer's Ins. Co.,
            381 S.W.2d 176 (1964) that were relevant to
            the conclusion that the deviation to Runge
            was an activity in furtherance of Draplia's
            employment.
```

An important intermediate conclusion in the reasoning of *Janak* was that ice water was *reasonably essential* for oil drilling. GREBE matches the facts that supported this conclusion to the facts of the Car-pool Case.

```
            This analogy is supported by the following
            inference:

                Sandwiches being at the middle school
                was reasonably essential for teaching
                children.

                This conclusion follows from the
                very strong analogy between the given
                case and the facts of Vaughn v.
                Highlands Underwriters Ins. Co.,
                445 S.W.2d 234 (1969) that were
                relevant to the conclusion that
                Vaughn's having food was reasonably
```

```
essential for Vaughn transporting
sulfur.
```

A relevant difference between *Janak* and the Car-pool Case 1 is identified: the crew's need to keep cool in *Janak* was a function of the temperature of the place where they worked, whereas the teachers' need for food was not influenced by the conditions of the workplace.

```
Relevant differences between the given case
and Janak v. Texas Employer's Ins. Co.,
381 S.W.2d 176 (1964) with respect to the
issue whether the trip to the sandwich shop
was an activity in furtherance of Donald's
employment are that:

  - It was not the case that the intensity
    of Teachers food need depended on the
    temperature of the middle school.

Whereas in the Janak case:

  - The intensity of Janak crew cooling
    need depended on the temperature of
    Ecleto.
```

Donald's traveling is then analogized to ordinary commuting.

```
However, a weaker argument can be made that:

     The trip to the sandwich shop was not an
     activity in furtherance of Donald's
     employment.

     This conclusion follows from the strong
     analogy between the given case and the facts
     that are relevant to the conclusion that
     ordinary commuting from work is not an
     activity in furtherance of a typical
     employee's employment as held in American
     General Ins. v. Coleman, 157 Tx. 377,
     303 S.W.2d 370.
```

However, the analogy to ordinary commuting is weak because Donald's traveling was not between home and work, but between home and the sandwich shop.

```
Relevant differences between the given case
and ordinary commuting home with respect to
the issue whether the trip to the sandwich
shop was an activity in furtherance of
Donald's employment are that:

  - It was not the case that the trip to
    the sandwich shop started at the middle
    school.

  - The sandwich shop was not the home of
    Donald.

Whereas in the typical commute back case:

  - Ordinary commuting from work starts at
    a typical workplace.

  - A typical home is the home of a typical
    employee.
```

```
vi. Joan was employed by the school district, as was
    shown above.
```

This example illustrates how goal reformulation leads to improved explanation. If GREBE were restricted to applying precedents to its top level goal, it couldn't produce the strongest explanation in the Car-pool Case 1 but would be restricted to a weaker argument analogizing Joan's traveling to the traveling of Draplia in the case of *Janak v. Texas Employer's Ins. Co.*, 381 S.W.2d 176 (1964).

Car-pool Case 2

Suppose that we present GREBE with a slightly altered version of the facts:

> The same facts as Car-pool Case 1 except that the deviation was to buy magazines for the teachers to read during their lunch break, rather than to buy food, and the teachers were compensated for their expenses in commuting to school.

As with Car-pool Case 1, GREBE is able to produce two distinct analyses depending on whether case-based reasoning or the business car-pool passenger rule is applied to the goal of establishing that the traveling was in furtherance of Joan's employment. As with Car-pool Case 1, the stronger analysis results from applying the rule. However, under this analysis, the strongest argument is that the traveling was *not* in furtherance of Donald's employment, because Donald's traveling closely resembled that in the case of *U.S. Fire Ins. Co. v. Eberstein*, 711 S.W.2d 355 (1986).

In *Eberstein*, a physician was killed when he was returning from a golf tournament to which he had deviated on his way to the hospital where he worked. This entire deviation was held not to be an activity in furtherance of employment because it was for personal purposes unrelated to Eberstein's job duties. GREBE also constructs an argument that Donald's traveling was like that of the driver in *Janak*, but this argument is weak because there is no evidence that magazines were reasonably essential for the teacher's job duties.

GREBE's analysis in comparison mode begins by restating the goal, stating whether the stronger argument is for or against the goal, and comparing the stronger argument to the analysis in the previous case:

```
Query: Is the school district liable under worker compensation
to Joan for Joan's injury under the facts of Car-pool Case number
2?

The stronger argument in Car-pool Case number 2 is that the
school district is not liable under worker compensation to Joan
for Joan's injury. Moreover, this argument is stronger here than
under the facts of Car-pool Case number 1.

The analysis in Car-pool Case number 2 is identical to the
analysis in Car-pool Case number 1 except for the following
issues:

1.  Whether the trip to the magazine shop was an activity in
furtherance of Donald's employment.
...
The analysis of these issues in Car-pool Case number 2 is as
follows:

1.  The trip to the magazine shop was an activity in
    furtherance of Donald's employment.

    Two conflicting arguments can be made concerning whether
    the trip to the magazine shop was an activity in
    furtherance of Donald's employment.
```

The argument comparing Car-pool Case 2 with *Eberstein* is presented first.

```
The stronger argument is that:

     The trip to the magazine shop was not an activity in
     furtherance of Donald's employment.

     This conclusion follows from the very strong analogy
     between the given case and the facts of U.S. Fire Ins.
     Co. v. Eberstein, 711 S.W.2d 355 (1986) that were
     relevant to the conclusion that the trip to the golf
     course was not an activity in furtherance of
     Eberstein's employment.
```

Eberstein drove to the golf course to satisfy a recreational need. GREBE improves the match with *Eberstein* by inferring how buying magazines helps to satisfy the teacher's recreational needs.

```
     This analogy is supported by the following inference:

          Donald purchasing magazines led to a decrease in
          the intensity of the need for recreation.

           A.  Donald transporting magazines required
               Donald possessing magazines which was
               achieved by Donald purchasing magazines, as
               stated in the given facts.

           B.  Donald transporting magazines led to a
               decrease in the intensity of the need for
               recreation.

                 I.  Teachers reading magazines required
                     magazines being at the middle school
                     which was achieved by Donald
                     transporting magazines, as stated in
                     the given facts.

                II.  Teachers reading magazines led to a
                     decrease in the intensity of the need
                     for recreation, as stated in the given
                     facts.
```

The analogy between Donald's traveling and Draplia's traveling in *Janak*, which was strong in Car-pool Case 1, is weaker here, even though the magazines satisfy a need on the part of the teachers. Unlike the oil driller's need for ice in *Janak* the teacher's need for magazines wouldn't interfere with their ability to teach, nor would it be produced by the conditions under which the teachers work. Moreover, bringing magazines to work is not an industry custom, unlike bringing ice to drill sites.

```
However, a weaker argument can be made that:

    The trip to the magazine shop was an activity in
    furtherance of Donald's employment.

    This conclusion follows from the strong analogy
    between the given case and the facts of Janak v. Texas
    Employer's Ins. Co., 381 S.W.2d 176 (1964) that were
    relevant to the conclusion that the deviation to Runge
    was an activity in furtherance of Draplia's
    employment.

    This analogy is supported by the following inference:

        Magazines being at the middle school was
        reasonably essential for teaching children.

        This conclusion follows from the weak analogy
        between the given case and the facts of Janak v.
        Texas Employer's Ins. Co., 381 S.W.2d 176 (1964)
        that were relevant to the conclusion that
        icewater being at Ecleto was reasonably essential
        for oil drilling by the Janak crew.
```

GREBE improves the match to *Janak* with a semantic explanation.

```
        This analogy is supported by the following
        inference:

            That Donald had the need for recreation,
            which is stated in the facts of the given
            case, is similar to the fact that Draplia
            had the need to keep cool.
```

However, a number of unexplained relevant differences remain.

Relevant differences between the given case and Janak v. Texas Employer's Ins. Co., 381 S.W.2d 176 (1964) with respect to the issue whether magazines being at the middle school was reasonably essential for teaching children are that:

- Teaching children was not impeded by the fact that the need for recreation was of high intensity.

Whereas in the Janak case:

- Oil drilling by the Janak crew was impeded by the fact that the need to keep cool was of high intensity.

Relevant differences between the given case and Janak v. Texas Employer's Ins. Co., 381 S.W.2d 176 (1964) with respect to the issue whether the trip to the magazine shop was an activity in furtherance of Donald's employment are that:

- Donald transporting magazines was not customary in the education industry.

- It was not the case that Teachers reading magazines consisted of consuming magazines.

- Some human was not engaged in consumption in Teachers reading magazines.

- It was not the case that Teachers reading magazines occurred during teaching children.

- It was not the case that the intensity of the need for recreation depended on the temperature of the middle school.

Whereas in the Janak case:

```
   - Transporting icewater was customary in the
     petroleum industry.

   - The crew's water consumption consisted of
     consuming ice water.

   - The Janak crew was engaged in consumption in the
     crew's water consumption.

   - The crew's water consumption occurred during oil
     drilling by the Janak crew.

   - The intensity of the need to keep cool depended
     on the temperature of Ecleto.
 ...
```

Car-pool Case 3

A second variation on Car-pool Case 1 is an accident that occurs after the conclusion of the deviation to get sandwiches:

> The same facts as Car-pool Case 1, but the accident occurred after Donald had purchased the sandwiches and was back on a direct route to the middle school.

GREBE's representation of the facts of Car-pool Case 3 is almost identical to that of Car-pool Case 1. Out of 127 propositions in the representation of Car-pool Case 3, only 4 are not also in Car-pool Case 1.

As in the previous two cases, both the business car-pool passenger rule and case-based reasoning are applicable to the goal of showing that Joan's traveling was in furtherance of her employment. Unlike the previous two cases, however, the business car-pool passenger rule does not lead to the stronger analysis. This is because the accident occurred after the deviation from the direct route to the school in Car-pool Case 3, whereas in *Janak* and in the previous cases, it occurred during the deviation. As a result, the match between Donald's traveling and Draplia's traveling in *Janak* is weaker than in the previous cases. The strongest analysis involves instead, a direct match of Joan's traveling to ordinary commuting.

```
Query: Is the school district liable under worker compensation
to Joan for Joan's injury under the facts of Car-pool Case number
3?

The stronger argument in Car-pool Case number 3 is that the
```

school district is not liable under worker compensation to Joan for Joan's injury. However, this argument is weaker here than under the facts of Car-pool Case number 2.

The argument against workers' compensation liability is weaker here than in Car-pool Case 2 because, as shown below, the match between Joan's traveling in Car-pool Case 3 and typical commuting requires a semantic explanation, whereas the match between Donald's traveling in Car-pool Case 2 and *Eberstein* requires no weak explanations.

The analysis in Car-pool Case number 3 is identical to the analysis in Car-pool Case number 2 except for the issue whether the trip to the Middle School was an activity in furtherance of Joan's employment.

Two conflicting arguments can be made concerning whether the trip to the Middle School was an activity in furtherance of Joan's employment.

The argument comparing Car-pool Case 3 with ordinary commuting is presented first.

The stronger argument is that:

> The trip to the Middle School was not an activity in furtherance of Joan's employment.
>
> This conclusion follows from the very strong analogy between the given case and the facts that are relevant to the conclusion that ordinary commuting to work is not an activity in furtherance of a typical employee's employment as held in American General Ins. v. Coleman, 157 Tx. 377, 303 S.W.2d 370.
>
> This analogy is supported by the following inference:
>
> > That Joan was the passenger in the trip to the Middle School, which is stated in the facts of the given case, is similar to the fact that a typical employee was the driver during ordinary commuting to work.

Then an argument comparing Donald's driving in Car-pool Case 3 to Draplia's driving in *Janak* is presented.

```
However, a weaker argument can be made that:

    The trip to the Middle School was an activity in
    furtherance of Joan's employment.

    This conclusion follows from the analogy between the given
    case and the facts of Janak v. Texas Employer's Ins. Co.,
    381 S.W.2d 176 (1964) that were relevant to the conclusion
    that the deviation to Runge was an activity in furtherance
    of Draplia's employment.
    ...
    Relevant differences between the given case and Janak v.
    Texas Employer's Ins. Co., 381 S.W.2d 176 (1964) with
    respect to the issue whether the trip to the Middle School
    was an activity in furtherance of Joan's employment are
    that:
      ...
      -  It was not the case that the trip to the Middle School
         was a deviation from transporting the teachers to
         school.

      -  The sandwich shop was not the destination of the trip
         to the Middle School.
      ...
    Whereas in the Janak case:
      ...
      -  The deviation to Runge was a deviation from traveling
         to Ecleto.

      -  Runge was the destination of the deviation to Runge.
      ...
```

These examples illustrate how impartiality leads to improved explanations. A system that was restricted to applying precedents to the goal of establishing that Joan's traveling was within the scope of her employment couldn't produce the strongest explanation in the Car-pool Case 1. The strongest explanation in the first hypothetical case required goal reformulation, *i.e.*, using a rule to replace the goal of showing that Joan's traveling was in furtherance of employment with the goal of showing that the driver's traveling was in furtherance of employment. Nor could this explanation have been produced by a system that was incapable of case elaboration. Matching the hypothetical case to the *Janak* case required inferring a fact—that sandwiches were reasonably essential for the activity of teaching—that was not given in the facts of the case. Similarly, a system that was restricted to applying rules to its top level goal couldn't have produced the strongest explanation in Car-pool Case 3. The strongest explanation in that case required applying a precedent to the top level goal. Only an impartial system has the flexibility to produce explanations of both types.

Car-pool Case 4

A final example illustrates a weakness of GREBE's approach to constructing explanations. Consider the following variation on Car-pool Case 2:

> The same facts as Car-pool Case 2, except that Donald decided that as long as he was in the shopping center buying magazines, he would pick up a sandwich for lunch. Does Donald have a claim for workers' compensation against the school district?

The analysis produced by GREBE is the following:

```
The goal cannot be explained under these facts.
```

GREBE is unable to build an explanation for liability under these facts because this case fails to satisfy the dual-purpose requirement of Vernon's Tex. Rev. Civ. Stat. Ann. art. 8309 §1b. Recall that for the dual-purpose requirement to be fulfilled, either there must be no personal goal distinct from an employment purpose, or it must be the case that "the trip to the place of occurrence of said injury would have been made even had there been no personal [goal] and ... would not have been made had there been no [employment-related goal]."

In Car-pool Case 4, there is both a personal goal (getting magazines) and a business purpose (getting sandwiches). Moreover, the trip would not have been made had there been no personal purpose. As a result, the dual-purpose requirement is not satisfied.

GREBE is able to construct arguments against a conclusion if they are based on a match between the new case and a noninstance precedent. However, if the argument against a conclusion is that some antecedent of every rule for that conclusion is unsatisfied, GREBE can do nothing but simply fail to make an explanation. This asymmetry between rules and precedents in GREBE contrasts with the behavior of human reasoners, who are equally adept at justifying the negation of propositions using either rules or precedents. Chapter 8 proposes a modification of GREBE's control strategy to address this asymmetry.

6 EVALUATION

Two distinct aspects of the performance of a system for legal analysis can be evaluated. The first is the quality of the analysis produced by the system. The quality of an analysis is evaluated by determining the extent to which the analysis identifies the relevant issues, determines the legal authorities applicable to those issues, and constructs sound and persuasive arguments based on those authorities. The second aspect of a legal-analysis system that can be evaluated is the efficiency of the system, that is, the computational resources necessary to produce an analysis.

The first section of this chapter describes an experimental evaluation of the quality of GREBE's legal analysis. This evaluation showed that GREBE's performance was generally superior to the performance of a group of law students on the same problems. However, both the students and GREBE appeared to lack sufficient breadth of knowledge about worker's compensation for expert performance.

The second section turns to the issue of efficiency. The simplest approach to precedent retrieval is simply to compare the new case to every precedent of the category of interest and to choose the best match. However, GREBE's relational representation makes each comparison between a new case and a precedent potentially very expensive. Thus, as the size of the knowledge base increases, the expense of exhaustive matching may quickly become prohibitive. More efficient alternative techniques for precedent retrieval are therefore essential for a full-scale implementation of systems using relational representations. The second section compares the performance of GREBE's two retrieval algorithms: retrieval by best-first incremental matching (BFIM) and match refinement by structural difference links (MRSDL).

6.1 Evaluating GREBE's Legal Analysis

This section describes an experimental evaluation of GREBE in which GREBE's analysis of 18 worker's compensation hypotheticals was compared to the analysis of the same hypotheticals by law students. The purposes of the evaluation were (1) to show that analysis of worker's compensation cases is a challenging task, even for humans with legal training, and (2) to assess the overall effectiveness of GREBE in addressing this task.

Design of the Experiment

Five students at the University of Texas Law School responding to an advertisement for several "short legal-research projects" were each presented with a group of related hypothetical worker's compensation cases. None of the students had any prior experience in Texas worker's compensation law. For each hypothetical, the students were to determine the applicable legal authorities, construct the strongest arguments for and against worker's compensation liability based on those authorities, and set forth the arguments in a short memorandum. Their instructions were as follows:

> Your task is to determine, for each of the following hypothetical cases, whether the employee, if living, or the employee's survivors, if the employee is not living, has a claim for worker's compensation benefits under Texas statutory and case law. For each case, please write a brief but complete memorandum setting forth the best sound arguments for and against worker's compensation liability in terms of the relevant Texas authorities. It is unnecessary to repeat the facts of each hypothetical case in the memoranda.

The subjects were asked to record the length of time they spent on each problem. In addition, the subjects were asked to record the reference materials that they consulted, and each "rule, statute, precedent or other authority" considered during the course of analyzing each hypothetical. The 18 hypothetical cases, divided into 5 problem sets, appear in Appendix D (a sixth problem set, 1b, was not used in this experiment but was used in the evaluation of retrieval algorithms, discussed in the next section). Three of the subjects were second-year Juris Doctor students, and two had foreign law degrees and were enrolled

Table 6.1. Student solution times in hours for each worker's compensation hypothetical. Each student received one problem set. An asterisk indicates that the data was not reported.

Problem Set	Problem				Total	Average
	1	*2*	*3*	*4*		
Car-pool 1–3	3.5	.75	2.25	-	6.5	2.17
Journey 1–3 & Jarek	2.0	0.5	1.0	1.0	5.0	1.67
Goodwrench 1–3	5.0	2.5	1.5	-	9.0	3.0
Goodwrench 4–6	*	*	*	-	15.0	5.0
Stanley 1–4	10.0	2.0	2.0	1.0	15.0	3.75

in the Masters of Comparative Law program. Each student was paid for his or her participation.

The times required for the student's analyses are summarized in Table 6.1. The average solution time for all problems was 2.77 hours. The solution time for the first problem in a set was always longer than solution times for subsequent problems: the average time for the first problem in each set was 5.12 hours, whereas the average for the remaining problems was 1.45 hours. The long solution time for initial problems probably reflects the student's lack of experience in worker's compensation law. A researcher unfamiliar with a given area of law may require several hours simply to locate and become familiar with the relevant authorities. The improvement on subsequent problems probably results from the similarity of cases within a single problem set. Once a single hypothetical from a given problem set has been analyzed, little additional research may be necessary to analyze other cases that differ in only a few facts.

The memoranda produced by the students, together with GREBE's analysis of the same 18 hypotheticals, were then given to a domain expert, an attorney who is a recognized authority on Texas worker's compensation law. The domain expert was asked to grade all of the analyses, applying the following criteria:

1. **Issues.** Does the memorandum correctly identify the relevant legal issues?

2. **Authorities.** Have the legal authorities (rules and cases) applicable to the issues been identified?

3. **Arguments.** Are the arguments contained in the memorandum complete, sound, and persuasive? That is:

Table 6.2. Grades for analyses of 18 worker's compensation hypotheticals by students (St.) and GREBE (Gr.). Letter grades have been converted into their numeric equivalent on a 4-point scale.

Problem Set	Issues		Authorities		Arguments		Overall	
	St.	Gr.	St.	Gr.	St.	Gr.	St.	Gr.
Car-pool 1–3	2.0	3.0	2.0	2.0	2.0	2.75	2.0	2.75
Journey 1–3 & Jarek	2.25	2.25	1.75	2.0	1.75	2.0	1.75	2.0
Goodwrench 1–3	2.0	1.33	2.0	1.33	2.0	1.33	2.0	1.33
Goodwrench 4–6	1.5	1.75	1.5	1.75	1.5	1.75	1.5	1.75
Stanley 1–4	1.75	2.0	1.75	2.0	1.75	2.75	1.75	2.0
Average	1.94	2.11	1.78	1.88	1.78	2.22	1.78	2.0

- Does the memorandum show how conclusions about the issues follow logically from the facts of the case and the relevant authorities?
- Were precedents used appropriately to assist in the interpretation of unclear statutory language?
- Were sound analogies drawn between the given case and the applicable precedents?
- Does the memorandum present arguments on both sides of the issues?

The domain expert was asked to use the three criteria to assign the analysis an overall grade. The results of domain expert's grading for the students and GREBE are summarized in Table 6.2.

Discussion

Analyzing the worker's compensation hypotheticals was clearly a challenging task for the law students. It took them, on average, over 5 hours to analyze the first hypothetical of each problem set, and the overall grade on the analyses they produced was only 1.78, equivalent to a C−. GREBE's analyses almost always received a slightly higher grade, receiving an average overall grade of 2.0. GREBE received 9 C's, 4 B's, and 4 F's, whereas the students received 12 C's, 5 F's and 1 B.

In only one problem, Goodwrench Case 1, did GREBE receive a lower grade than a student. In that case GREBE received an F for not identifying the issue that the employee might have been an independent contractor rather than an employee, whereas the student identified this issue. GREBE failed to identify this issue because its knowledge base simply has no information about the distinction between employees and independent contractors.[1] In two other cases, both a student and GREBE were down-graded for failing to identify potentially relevant authorities that were outside of GREBE's knowledge base. In one case, the missing authority was a portion of the worker's compensation statute that had not been represented in GREBE, and in the other case it was a federal statute that potentially could apply. These examples suggest that simply broadening the worker's compensation knowledge base to include a small number of additional legal authorities would significantly improve GREBE's performance.

It was anticipated that since most of GREBE's knowledge base consists of representations of the factual details of precedents, GREBE would be strong in comparison with the students in precedent retrieval. Similarly, it was anticipated that GREBE would suffer in comparison with the students in argument creation because GREBE has little knowledge of discourse structure and presents arguments in a very rigid, formulaic fashion. These expectations were not borne out by the data. The greatest difference between GREBE and the students was in grades for argument quality, where GREBE's average grade was 2.22 and the student's average grade was 1.78, a difference of .34. By contrast, there was only a difference of .1 between GREBE's grade for identifying the correct authorities (1.88) and the average grade for the students (1.78). This suggests that both the students and GREBE were hindered by incomplete knowledge of the domain, but that GREBE was somewhat better at assembling its knowledge into arguments.

A criticism that might be directed at this evaluation is that the students and GREBE appeared to have different precedent retrieval tasks in that GREBE had a relatively small set of precedents against which to compare new cases, whereas the students had an almost unlimited number of precedents to consider. The response to this argument is that legal reference materials, such as digests and treatises, drastically reduce the number of precedents that legal researchers need to consider. This is evidenced by the student's records of the precedents that they in fact considered. None read even half as many precedents as are in GREBE's precedent library. Moreover, the alternative procedure of giving the students a list of authorities with which to analyze the hypotheticals would

[1] The wording of Goodwrench Case 1 attempted to preclude the possibility of the claimant being an independent contractor by stating that he was "employed." However, a description of a claimant as an "employee" or as a "contractor" are not, in practice, necessarily dispositive of the claimant's actual status, so it is probably legitimate to raise this issue.

have presented a task very different from the research tasks that an attorney actually faces.

In summary, GREBE consistently performed somewhat better at identifying issues, determining the applicable authorities, and constructing arguments than law students assigned to the same tasks. However, GREBE's performance is still below the level of an expert in this domain. The paucity of comments by the domain expert makes it difficult to clearly identify GREBE's particular weaknesses, but an important factor appears to be that GREBE's knowledge base is still too narrow to cover all the issues that an expert in worker's compensation needs to be familiar with. That GREBE received a grade of B on 4 of the problems indicates that GREBE is capable of producing sound and informative analyses on problems for which the knowledge base is adequate.[2]

6.2 Evaluating GREBE's Retrieval Algorithms

This section describes an empirical evaluation of GREBE's two precedent retrieval algorithms: retrieval by best-first incremental matching (BFIM); and match refinement using structural difference links (MRSDL). The purpose of the evaluation was to determine whether these retrieval algorithms perform more efficiently than exhaustive matching with comparable levels of accuracy. Devising accurate retrieval algorithms that are more efficient than exhaustive matching is important because exhaustive matching may be prohibitively expensive in large knowledge bases.

In *exhaustive case matching*, a new case is matched against every relevant exemplar in the case library using structure matching. In *surface similarity retrieval* the new case is compared to each exemplar in the case library using the proportion of predicates in a precedent constituent that are also present in the new case, without regard to the connections among the predicates, as the similarity metric. Surface similarity retrieval is used as the first stage of two-stage retrieval algorithms such as MAC/FAC algorithm (Gentner and Forbus, 1991) (*see also* (Rau, 1988)). The surface similarity algorithm represents a lower limit on retrieval time, since it is linear in both the case size and the size of the case library.

Design of the Experiment

BFIM, MRSDL, exhaustive matching, and surface similarity retrieval were compared on four sets of precedents. The first two consisted of 100 fables and 26 plays (25 Shakespearean plays and West Side Story), generously shared by Paul Thagard, consisting on average of approximately 21 propositions per fable and

[2] *See* (Berman and Hafner, 1993) for a critical comparison of GREBE's output with discourse typical of an attorney or judge.

55 propositions per play. The remaining two sets of precedents consisted of 11 precedents of employment activities (averaging 29 propositions per case) and 10 precedents of near-miss noninstances of employment activities (averaging 30 propositions per case) from GREBE's worker's compensation precedent library.

In each retrieval trial, the fables and plays were randomly divided into 5 or 3 (respectively) approximately equal partitions. Each analog of each partition was then used as a new case with the cases of the remaining partitions as the case library. Thus, each retrieval of each fable was tested using 80 other fables as the case library, and retrieval of each play was tested using 17 or 18 other plays as the case library. A set of 21 worker's compensation hypotheticals, including the 18 hypotheticals used in the comparative evaluation of GREBE's analysis, were used to test retrieval of the instance and noninstance precedents of employment activities. These hypotheticals averaged 89 propositions per case.

Before MRSDL could be run on each collection of cases, some set of difference links had to be installed among them, since the behavior of MRSDL depends heavily upon the configuration of difference links among cases. For example, if there is no sequence of difference links connecting an initial surface match with the closest case, then clearly no series of match refinements can retrieve the closest case.

In this experiment, no effort was made to achieve an optimal configuration. Instead, a configuration of cases connected by difference links was incrementally built up in a manner consistent with the following scenario of human learning:

> Suppose that a law student is asked to analyze a hypothetical *H1*, and the student recalls a superficially similar precedent *P1*. Suppose that the student is then told that the controlling precedent is instead *P2* because of the greater structural similarities between *H1* and *P2*. To profit from this lesson, the student must understand the structural differences both between *H1* and *P1* and between *H1* and *P2* in order to appreciate that the former are greater than the latter. The student must therefore also understand the structural differences between *P1* and *P2* that led to the differences in their degree of structural similarity to *H1*. If on a later occasion the student encounters hypothetical *H2* that is superficially similar but structurally dissimilar to *P1*, the student can use knowledge of the structural differences between *P1* and *P2* to recover from the spurious match to *P1* and find the structurally most similar precedent *P2*.

Consistent with this scenario, each configuration was initialized with a single randomly selected case. The remaining cases were added in random order. For each new case c, a difference link was installed between c and the case with the greatest surface similarity, $SS(c)$. Exhaustive search was then used to determine the case structurally most similar case, $Ex(c)$. If $Ex(c)$ and $SS(c)$ were distinct, then difference links were installed between $Ex(c)$ and $SS(c)$,

Table 6.3. The proportion of MRSDL retrievals that were identical to the best match as determined by exhaustive match, the proportion of retrievals that returned an case whose degree of match was within 5% of the closest case, and the average number of structural comparisons required in each of the data sets. "EA+" and "EA−" represent instances and near-miss noninstances of employment activities, respectively.

Data Set	**MRSDL**		
	% exact	% close	comparisons
fables (80)	51.0	81.3	9.0
plays (17-18)	73.1	94.2	5.3
EA+ (11)	76.2	78.6	3.1
EA− (10)	78.6	92.9	2.5

and between c and $Ex(c)$. A distinct configuration of difference links was constructed for each set of partitions used as source cases.

In each of the retrieval approaches (except surface semantic retrieval) structure matching was performed by GREBE's structure matching algorithm running in greedy mode (described in Appendix F). To isolate the task of finding the structurally most similar case from the contribution of various mapping constraints and to expedite the trials, the algorithm was run with information concerning semantic similarity among relations and case elaboration rules removed. The degree of structural similarity was measured by the proportion of propositions in the source case that had an image in the target under the mapping that maximized structural congruence.

The experiment compared the retrieval accuracy of MRSDL and retrieval by surface similarity to the accuracy of exhaustive matching and BFIM (which is guaranteed to find the same match as exhaustive search). Table 6.3 sets forth the performance of MRSDL averaged across four trials. The first column sets forth the proportion of MRSDL retrievals for each data set that were identical to the best match as determined by exhaustive search (or equivalently, BFIM). There are often several cases having an almost identical degree of match with a case. The second column sets forth the proportion of MRSDL retrievals that returned a case whose degree of match was within 5% of that of the closest case found by exhaustive search. The third column contains the average number of structural comparisons required for each MRSDL retrieval.

Table 6.4. Min-exact$_c$ is the minimum number of candidates that must be retrieved by surface s milarity to insure that the case closest to case c is in the candidate set. Min-dl$_c$ is the smallest candidate set size guaranteed to contain an case whose degree of match is at least as great as the degree of match of the case returned by MRSDL.

Data Set	Surface Similarity		
	$AV_{c \epsilon Cases}$ *Min-exact$_c$*	$MAX_{c \epsilon Cases}$ *Min-exact$_c$*	$MAX_{c \epsilon Cases}$ *Min-dl$_c$*
fables	14.9	71.3	68.0
plays	4.3	12.5	8.5
EA+	3.3	9.0	9.0
EA−	3.1	6.0	6.0

The first two columns of Table 6.4 contain information concerning *Min-exact$_c$*, the minimum number of candidates that must be retrieved by surface similarity to insure that the case closest to case c is in the candidate set. If $Ex(c)$ is the case found by exhaustive search of a given case set with case c, and if $SS(c, n)$ is the set of n closest surface matches to c, then *Min-exact$_c$* = $\min\{n | Ex(c) \epsilon SS(c, n)\}$. The first column sets forth the average of *Min-exact$_c$* for all cases c in each data set. This represents the average number of candidates that would be necessary for surface-similarity retrieval if one somehow knew *Min-exact$_c$* for every case c. The second column sets forth the maximum of *Min-exact$_c$* for all cases c. This represents the smallest candidate set size that would guarantee for all cases that the candidate set would contain the best case. The last column represents the maximum of *Min-dl$_c$*, the smallest candidate set size guaranteed for all cases c to contain an case whose degree of match is at least as great as the degree of match of the case returned by MRSDL. If $Dl(c)$ is the case found by MRSDL, *Min-dl$_c$* = $\min\{n |$ SS(c, n) contains some case that matches c at least as well as $Dl(c)\}$.

Table 6.5 three sets forth the average retrieval time in seconds of user CPU time for exhaustive search, BFIM, and MRSDL.

6.3 Discussion

Table 6.3 shows that MRSDL performs reasonably well, although not as accurately as exhaustive matching or BFIM. In the fable and employment activity

Table 6.5. Mean retrieval times (in seconds of user CPU time) for exhaustive search, BFIM, and MRSDL.

Data Set	**Exh.**	**BFIM**	**MRSDL**
fables	10.7	2.9	5.0
plays	5.8	4.7	6.3
EA+	4.1	2.6	1.7
EA−	2.9	1.4	1.1

noninstance data sets MRSDL was over 90% accurate in retrieving cases that were within 5% of the optimal match. Table 6.4 illustrates the shortcomings of surface-similarity retrieval. Although the average value of $\mathit{Min\text{-}exact}_c$ was comparable to the average number of structural comparisons performed by MRSDL, each data set contained some case c for which $\mathit{Min\text{-}exact}_c$ was at least half the size of the data set. Thus, on these data sets at least, no surface-similarity retrieval scheme can simultaneous ensure correctness and search less than half of the cases in memory. The last column of Table 6.4 illustrates that the smallest initial candidate set size guaranteed to equal the accuracy of MRSDL is at least half the size of the case library.

Table 6.5 illustrates that BFIM was consistently faster than exhaustive matching, more than three times as fast in the fable data set. MRSDL was usually also substantially faster than exhaustive matching. The surprising exception was in the plays data set where MRSDL was actually slower than exhaustive matching. Surprisingly, BFIM was also faster than MRSDL in two of the data sets. Parallel competitive matching has been criticized on grounds of psychological implausibility (Gentner and Forbus, 1991), but these data suggest that this retrieval technique can be relatively efficient.[3]

[3]The experimental results in precedent retrieval described in this chapter were first reported in (Branting, 1992b).

7 RELATED WORK

This book has presented an approach to classification and explanation in weak-theory domains—typified by legal analysis—under which rules and precedents are viewed as mutually supporting warrants. Under this approach, precedents can compensate for inadequate reduction rules, while rules can improve matching through case elaboration and goal reformulation.

This view of the relation between rules and precedents provides a framework for discussing related work on classification in weak-theory domains. Previous systems for classification in weak-theory domains can be divided among those that use rules exclusively, those that use cases exclusively, and those that are able to use both. Systems that use both rules and cases can be further subdivided based on whether they use case elaboration or goal reformulation.

This chapter argues that systems that use rules exclusively are limited by their inability to reason about open-textured predicates appearing in rule antecedents. Similarly, systems that use cases exclusively are limited by their inability to reason about the equivalence of cases with factual differences. Case matching is improved by either case elaboration or goal reformulation, but the best performance requires both.

The discussion of systems that use case-based reasoning is limited to those in which precedents are used to extend the range of problems that can be solved in a weak-theory domain. There are two other important purposes for case-based reasoning: reducing search by permitting reuse of past solutions (Veloso, 1992, Hammond, 1989, Lehnert, 1987, Blumenthal and Porter, 1994), and facilitating knowledge acquisition by permitting knowledge specific to solving particular problems to be acquired (Klahr, 1996, Bareiss et al., 1989). However, since these purposes for case-based reasoning are secondary to the focus of this book, they will not be addressed here.

7.1 Rule-Based Systems

Rule-based reasoning is sufficient for problem solving only in domains in which rule antecedents are operational in the case description language. Weak-theory domains, however, lack sufficient abstraction rules to connect rule antecedents to the case-description language. As a result, rule-based reasoning in isolation is seldom sufficient in such domains. The insufficiency of rule-based reasoning in weak-theory domains is well illustrated by the domain of legal reasoning.

There is a broad consensus within the automated legal reasoning community that rule-based reasoning is insufficient to model the problem solving of attorneys because of the problem of open-textured legal predicates (Gardner, 1987, McCarty, 1990)[1]. A number of rule-based legal reasoning systems have been constructed, *e.g.,* AustLII (a web-based legal knowledge base and rule-based inferencing system) (Greenleaf et al., 1997), the Latent Damage System (Capper and Susskind, 1988), LDS (Legal Decision-making System) (Peterson and Waterman, 1985), SAL (System for Asbestos Litigation) (Paul, 1991), the British Nationality Act Program (Sergot et al., 1986), and various systems for tax law, *e.g.,* (Fisher, 1997) and (Sherman, 1991). The purpose of these programs is generally to produce a computer model of a particular set of related legal rules. The limitation of such systems is that whenever the antecedent of a rule contains an open-textured predicate, the system must simply ask the user whether the predicate is satisfied. This is because these systems lack the reduction rules necessary to determine whether open-textured predicates are satisfied by particular case descriptions. Thus, the task addressed by these systems is a drastic simplification of the legal reasoning task described in Chapter 1.

For example, researchers at the Imperial College formalized the British Nationality Act (BNA) as a PROLOG program (Sergot et al., 1986). The BNA program back-chains from the goal of establishing citizenship under the Act through Horn clauses representing specific statutory provisions, generating queries as needed.

This research effort showed that statutory rules can often be represented as Horn clauses with only slight modifications of the original statutory language

[1]However, *see* (Bench-Capon and Sergot, 1988) for a proposal for using conflicting rule-based arguments to model open-textured legal concepts.

(important exceptions being rules involving counterfactuals, default inferences, or negation). However, the BNA system is unable to reason about whether open-textured predicates appearing in statutory rules are satisfied by the particular facts of a given case. Instead, the system depends upon the user to make this determination.[2]

Another typical rule-based system for legal analysis is LDS, a system for determining the settlement value of personal injury suits (Peterson and Waterman, 1985). LDS chained forward from the facts of a new case to five distinct factors bearing on the settlement value, including the loss suffered by the plaintiff, the likelihood of establishing liability, and the relative degrees of responsibility of the plaintiff and defendant. These factors were then combined to produce an estimate of the expected judgment in a law suit. As with the BNA program, LDS forced onto the user the task of determining whether open-textured predicates were satisfied. For example, LDS asked the user whether the use of the product was "foreseeable," an issue that is arguably at the heart of reasoning in the domain of negligence (Rissland, 1990).[3]

In summary, rule-based reasoning in isolation is insufficient for problem solving in weak-theory domains such as law because such domains lack sufficient reduction rules to connect open-textured rule antecedents to the facts of new cases.

7.2 Case-Based Reasoning Systems

Precedents can bridge the gap in generality between open-textured predicates and case facts in weak-theory domains. This is because the facts of precedents, like those of new cases, are expressed in the case-description language. Case-based reasoning is effective, however, only if either there are sufficient precedents that every new case is identical to some precedent or there is sufficient match knowledge that every new case can be matched to a precedent of the category to which it belongs. There are few domains in which it is possible to anticipate all possible cases. As a result, case-based reasoning is highly dependent upon match knowledge.

Chapter 2 discussed how rule-based reasoning could assist the matching process, either by permitting new-case attributes to be inferred or by refining a goal to one for which there are precedents that more closely match the new

---

[2]For example, a typical question posed by the system is whether the person in question has ever "renounced" British citizenship. There may be a variety of different ways of renouncing citizenship, each of which is highly context dependent. A putative renunciation might be the result of mistake, duress, intoxication, or a joke. Each of these factors is itself open-textured, *e.g.*, how substantial must a threat be to constitute duress? What if the person's own carelessness led to the mistake? How intoxicated must a person be for his renunciation to be ineffective? In some cases, determining whether there has been renunciation may be the most complex part of the analysis of citizenship.

[3]For a more recent rule-based system for claim evaluation, see (Paul, 1991). For a discussion of the social implications of the widespread adoption of predictive legal expert systems typified by LDS, see (Berman and Hafner, 1989).

case. A system that is unable to use explicit rules to assist in matching must depend instead on weaker forms of general knowledge. Chapter 3 demonstrated that any matching scheme that focuses exclusively on the facts of a case and not at all on the explanation for the membership of the case in a category is inadequate as a model of legal precedent. However, case matching is an essential component of the reduction-graph model of legal precedent set forth in Chapter 3.

One approach to case matching, *weighted feature matching* (which was introduced in Section 3.4), calculates the overall similarity between cases as a function of numerical estimates of the *salience*, or importance, of the features they share (or, equivalently, calculates the distance between cases in feature space as a function of the salience of the the features on which they differ) (Wettschereck and Aha, 1995, Stanfill and Waltz, 1986, Bradshaw, 1987, Kibler and Aha, 1987). The classification of the precedent with the highest overall match strength is then applied to the new case. Match knowledge under this approach consists of the weights that are assigned to each case feature and the function used to combine feature weights.

A key drawback of this approach is that it is, in general, impossible to determine a set of feature weights that leads to correct matching behavior. In general, the salience of a given case feature can be a function of the particular problem-solving context or of the value of other case features (Murphy and Medin, 1985). For example, some combinations of feature values may make other features irrelevant or highly important. Although the context sensitivity of weights can be improved by making feature weights specific to particular categories (Bareiss et al., 1988) or precedents (Wettschereck and Aha, 1995, Aha and Goldstone, 1990), weighted feature matching is poorly suited for representing interactions among features or for comparing cases in which not all relevant facts have been made explicit.

An alternative approach, called the *dimensional* (Ashley, 1990) or *argument* (Clark, 1988b) approach, is not dependent on a context-independent similarity metric, but instead uses knowledge of which features (called *dimensions* in (Ashley, 1990) and *arguments* in (Clark, 1988b)) tend to establish a conclusion and which tend to establish its negation. The most important difference between the dimensional and argument versions of this approach is that dimensions can vary in magnitude, whereas arguments are boolean. Discussion of this approach will focus on the dimensional version, since it has been implemented in an automated legal reasoning system, HYPO.

Under the dimensional approach, a precedent is similar to a new case if the two cases share one or more dimensions. One precedent is more similar to a new case than a second precedent if the dimensions shared by the first precedent and the new case are a superset of those shared by the second precedent and the new case. The most similar precedents are those which are similar and for which there is no more similar case. Arguments for a classification of a new case can be based on a comparison between a new case and the most similar precedents.

The classification of a new case is the same as that of a most similar precedent for which:

- The magnitude of each dimension in support of the classification is at least as high in the new case as in the precedent.
- The magnitude of each dimension in support of the negation of the classification is no higher in the new case than in the precedent.

Even if these conditions can not be met, precedents may nevertheless be a source of arguments for or against a given classification. HYPO generates *3-ply arguments* consisting of the following:

1. An argument in favor of a given classification for a new case, consisting of a precedent to which the classification applied and the factors in support of the classification shared by the two cases.
2. A response to the argument, consisting either of distinguishing the precedent or identifying counterexamples. A counterexample is a precedent having a contrary classification. A precedent is distinguished by adverting to:
    - Factors that support the classification that are present in the precedent but absent in the new case, or
    - Factors that negate the classification that are present in the new case but absent in the precedent.
3. A rebuttal, consisting of a response to any counterexamples identified in second ply.

HYPO is an implementation of the dimensional approach in the domain of trade secrets misappropriation. A new case is entered into HYPO by instantiating "legal case frames," templates for the parties to the dispute, the products giving rise to the dispute, and the alleged trade secret information and disclosures. The system then determines which of 30 "factual predicates" are satisfied by the case. Based on the factual predicates, the system determines which of 13 dimensions are present in the new case. A dimension is present if its prerequisites are a subset of the factual predicates satisfied by the case. The system uses the dimensions to retrieve the most similar precedents and generate 3-ply arguments from those precedents. HYPO's dimensional analysis approach has been incorporated into CATO, a tutorial system for law students (Aleven and Ashley, 1997, Aleven and Ashley, 1996).

HYPO is unable to use rule-based reasoning for goal reformulation and has only a rudimentary case elaboration mechanism. HYPO's inability to perform goal reformulation means that rules for combining separate case-based reasoning steps into a single argument cannot be explicitly represented in HYPO. The limitations resulting from this inability to combine multiple case-based reasoning steps were observed in TAX-HYPO, an application of HYPO's basic architecture to the domain of the home office deduction:[4]

> What TAX-HYPO lacks is the capacity to combine the analyses of individual predicates to generate an argument that takes into account the statute as a whole. The program fails to argue or evaluate the claim for a deduction: it can merely argue the pros and cons of specific individual predicates. Particularly, TAX-HYPO is not cognizant of the Boolean connectives in the statute, and it treats it merely as a set of unrelated predicates (Rissland and Skalak, 1989a).

The inability of HYPO to perform goal reformulation motivated the development of CABARET, discussed below.

In addition to its incapacity for goal reformulation, HYPO has only rudimentary case elaboration ability. HYPO uses factual predicates to determine what dimensions are present in a new case. However, HYPO lacks any mechanism for reasoning about whether factual predicates are present. HYPO's factual predicates are not, in general, elements of the case description language and thus require the user to provide an interpretation of the case facts. For example, one factual predicate is "exists disclosures info1," meaning that "[t]here is data that plaintiff made disclosures to outsiders." One can easily imagine cases in which the critical issue was whether a disclosure was made or whether the disclosees were "outsiders" or not.[5] Moreover, HYPO's model of arguments has no role for inferences about whether factual predicates were satisfied. Thus, even if HYPO's domain theory could be called upon to assist in determining whether factual predicates are satisfied, the resulting inferences would not be reflected in the arguments produced by HYPO.

In summary, HYPO represents a detailed computational model of how knowledge of the factors that tend to support or negate legal classifications and the magnitude of these factors in a set of precedents and new cases can be used to generate a variety of arguments (*e.g.*, citing and distinguishing cases, "trump-

[4] I.R.C. §280A(c)(1)

[5] For example, how much and what type of information must be revealed to constitute a disclosure? Does unintentionally revealing information constitute a disclosure? Does it matter whether reasonable care was taken to prevent a disclosure? If so, what constitutes reasonable care? Does the category "outsiders" include technical staff, contractors, members of the board of directors, or employees of subsidiaries? All of these potential issues and many others might have to be addressed to determine whether the "exists disclosures info1" predicate is satisfied in any given case.

ing," citing counterexamples). HYPO does not address the tasks of combining case-based reasoning steps or reasoning about whether factual predicates that are prerequisites for dimensions are present.

7.3 Hybrid Systems

The previous sections discussed the limitations of systems that rely exclusively on rules or precedents for reasoning in weak-theory domains. This section addresses hybrid systems that can reason with both rules and cases. The emphasis of the discussion is on the control structure of these systems.

Unlike GREBE, which permits rules and precedents to be combined in whatever order leads to the strongest explanation, previous hybrid systems have generally constrained case-based and rule-based reasoning to apply in a predefined order. A convenient division among previous systems can be made between those in which case-based reasoning is required to precede rule-based reasoning in problem solving (the *CBR-first* approach) and those in which case-based reasoning can never precede rule-based reasoning (the *CBR-last* approach).

CBR-First Systems

Several hybrid systems require case-based reasoning to be applied to the top-level goal of the system and restrict rules to the assessment of similarity between cases. Such systems can perform case elaboration, but not goal reformulation.

Protos and Casey. Protos (Bareiss et al., 1990) and Casey (Koton, 1988), which were briefly described in Chapter 2, are diagnostic systems whose domain theories include both precedents and rules. Protos assigns a new case to the same diagnostic category as the precedent that it most closely matches. Protos uses causal, associational, and definitional rules to reason about the equivalence of cases with differing features. Protos acquires these rules as an apprentice from teacher-provided explanations. Similarly, Casey assigns a causal explanation and diagnosis to patients based on the explainable similarity of their symptoms to those of precedent cardiac cases. Casey uses causal rules derived from the Heart Failure program, a model-based expert system for cardiac disorder diagnosis, to reason about whether the symptoms of a new case are consistent with the causal model that accounted for the symptoms of a precedent.

Protos and Casey are alike in not permitting rules to be applied to their top-level goals of diagnosing hearing disorders and cardiac disorders, respectively. As a result, neither system can compare portions of cases but instead must compare cases as monolithic wholes. The importance of goal reformulation was implicitly recognized by Koton when she noted that several cases involving "multiple noninteracting diagnoses" could not be solved because the particular combination of diagnoses had not been seen before. Koton suggested that developing the ability to combine solutions from several precedents is logical piece of future work.[6]

TAXMAN II. There is a trade-off between the quantity of matching knowledge that a case-based reasoning system possesses and the minimum number of cases necessary for effective problem solving (Porter et al., 1990). At one extreme are systems that have no matching knowledge at all, which require an exhaustive case library to be effective. At the other extreme is the *prototype* approach, in which domain knowledge for matching is so extensive that a single precedent may be sufficient to match all instances of a category. The prototype approach to case-based reasoning is exemplified by TAXMAN II (McCarty and Sridharan, 1982).

In TAXMAN II, McCarty and Sridharan sought to develop a representation of open-textured legal concepts and a model of the "construction and modification of legal concepts during the analysis of a difficult case." TAXMAN II used a "prototype-plus-deformation" model of concept structure described in Section 3.4. Under this model, a concept has three components. First, there is an optional invariant component that provides necessary, but not sufficient, conditions for satisfying the concept. Second is a set of exemplars providing sufficient conditions. Third, there is a set of transformations expressing various relationships among the exemplars. The result is an "ordered space of exemplars" in which a partial ordering is imposed on the exemplars by the transformations. Such a space can sometimes be represented by a single prototype together with a series of transformations, which act as "deformations."

A legal argument for a particular classification is modeled as a set of transformations that includes all the exemplars and the given case. A counter-argument consists of a set of transformations that includes the exemplar but excludes the given case. The most persuasive argument is the one that "imposes the greatest degree of coherence on the set of exemplars."

Since the theory of legal argument set forth in TAXMAN II was never completely implemented,[7] a meaningful evaluation is difficult. However, it is worth observing that a particular structure matching followed by match improvement, as performed by GREBE, would probably constitute a transformation under the TAXMAN II scheme. If so, the TAXMAN II theory is general enough to subsume the matching and case-elaboration portions of GREBE (although apparently not goal reformulation).

However, essential components of the TAXMAN II approach have yet to be completely specified. The very generality of the notion of transformations gives rise to the problem of eliminating those that are meaningless. Ongoing research

[6]Koton somewhat surprisingly justified case-based reasoning in Casey entirely on the basis of its contribution to efficiency, rather than as extending the range of problems that can be solved with the existing set of rules. This apparently followed from her decision to treat the Heart Failure model as embodying a complete and correct set of first principles. However, Koton speculated that if this assumption were relaxed, Casey would be able to improve on the performance of the Heart Failure program (Koton, 1988).

[7]See (McCarty, 1995) for a description of a partial implementation.

is directed to the task of identifying criteria for constraining transformations (McCarty, 1995, McCarty, 1990). However, these constraints, and the notion of argument persuasiveness as well, ultimately depend on a criterion for "conceptual coherence." As a result, realization of the TAXMAN II model awaits the development of an explication of conceptual coherence in the context of legal reasoning. The peer commentary in (Thagard, 1989) indicates that there is not yet a consensus as to the nature of a satisfactory theory of conceptual coherence.

CBR-Last Systems

Several hybrid systems are unable to perform rule-based reasoning to assist in matching. These systems can perform goal reformulation, but not case elaboration.

Meldman's Dissertation. Meldman's dissertation (Meldman, 1975) proposed the first computer model of legal analysis that attempted to incorporate both rules and precedents. The domain of the system was intentional torts, *e.g.*, assault and battery. The system used a frame-like representation for factual situations to represent both legal doctrine, *i.e.*, legal rules and precedents, and the facts of new cases. However, the system was never actually implemented.

Gardner's System. An early CBR-last system in the domain of legal reasoning was Anne Gardner's system, which analyzed problems about the formation of contracts by offer and acceptance (Gardner, 1987). The objective of the program was to identify the issues upon which the outcome of a contract case depends and to distinguish those that are "hard" from those that are "easy." Hard issues, which arise from open-textured predicates, are those on which legal experts might disagree, whereas easy issues are those on which experts would agree. The system's domain knowledge included legal and common-sense rules, and precedents represented as abstract fact-patterns.

Gardner's system treated a question as easy if a new case exactly matched the antecedent of a legal or common-sense rule or the facts of a precedent and didn't match any rule or case having an opposite outcome. If a situation matched conflicting cases or rules, the case was hard. The analysis produced by program did not attempt to resolve, but instead merely branched on, each hard issue. The output of the program was a graph structure in which each node corresponded to a hard issue and terminal nodes represented alternative analyses of an entire new case.

By permitting rule-based reasoning to precede case-based reasoning, Gardner's system performed goal reformulation. However, the system lacked any provision for case elaboration: precedent cases applied only to new cases that matched them exactly. Moreover, Gardner's system had no apparatus for generating arguments on either side of a given question or for analyzing, even in a summary way, the factors on which the evaluation of a hard question might depend.

CABARET. HYPO's inability to perform goal reformulation is addressed by CABARET, a system that uses an agenda-based approach to integrating rule-based and case-based reasoning (Skalak and Rissland, 1992, Rissland and Skalak, 1989c, Rissland and Skalak, 1989b). The case-based reasoning component of CABARET is modeled after HYPO, while the rule-based reasoning component includes mechanisms for both forward and backward chaining. The behavior of the two components is coordinated through a blackboard architecture by a collection of approximately 30 heuristic control rules.

CABARET's control rules are divided into categories, such as "Near Miss," "Ways to Broaden a Rule," and "Ways to Discredit a Rule." Specific control rules within these categories may make use of the particular "point of view" (*i.e.*, as proponent or opponent of a particular proposition) held by the system. For example, one control heuristic is to attempt to broaden a rule if the current point of view is in favor of the consequences of the rule and the rule has an unsatisfied antecedent. Another heuristic is to attempt to discredit a rule if the point of view is against the consequences of the rule and its antecedents are satisfied.

Since the case-based component of CABARET is derived from HYPO, CABARET's capacity for case elaboration is extremely limited. However, CABARET's control heuristics are independent of the details of the case-based and rule-based reasoning components. Thus, CABARET could presumably accommodate a case-based reasoning component that performed case elaboration if its heuristics were augmented with rules applicable to goals arising during case matching.

Apart from the issues of case elaboration, however, GREBE's approach to integrating rules and precedents differs from that of CABARET in two respects. First, GREBE's design reflects the view that rules and precedents should be treated as equivalent for the task of constructing explanations, even if some implementation differences are necessary. The design of CABARET, by contrast, reflects the view that rules and precedents differ sufficiently in their explanatory function that an agenda-based controller is necessary to manage their interaction. Underlying GREBE's approach is the assumption that the relative strength of the explanations resulting from applying a rule or a case at a given argument stage can be determined only in retrospect. For example, in Car-pool cases 1 and 2, described above in Chapter 5, the strongest arguments result from using a common-law rule to reformulate the goal of showing that Joan's traveling was within the scope of her employment to the goal of showing that the driver, Donald, was within the scope of his employment. However, in Car-pool case 3 the strongest argument results from applying case-based reasoning to the goal of showing that Joan's traveling was within the scope of her employment. None of the heuristics mentioned in connection with CABARET would be useful in making an *a priori* choice between rule-based and case-based reasoning in the Car-pool cases.

Second, GREBE's design is based on the assumption that conflicting arguments can be constructed about open-textured rule antecedents, but not about the elements or persuasive force of rules themselves. By contrast, CABARET uses heuristics such as "Ways to Broaden a Rule" and "Ways to Discredit a Rule" that contradict this assumption. CABARET's heuristics therefore include an aspect of argumentation that GREBE does not attempt to address.

In summary, CABARET as implemented does not perform case elaboration and may fail to find the strongest explanation in situations typified by the Car-pool cases. On the other hand, CABARET is capable to generating arguments about the elements or persuasive force of rules themselves, a task that GREBE does not address.

Impartial Systems

GREBE is distinguished from previous systems in that it does not impose a rigid ordering on the use of rules and precedents (Branting and Porter, 1991, Branting, 1991). GREBE permits precedents to operationalize rule antecedents and rules to assist in case matching. Moreover, if both a rule and a precedent are applicable to a goal, the choice is based on the strength of the resulting explanation, rather than on an arbitrary ordering scheme. A control strategy that permits rules and precedents to be used in this complementary fashion, imposing no arbitrary ordering restrictions, is *impartial.*

EXPANDER is an impartial blackboard-based architecture described in (Walker, 1992). The EXPANDER architecture was an extension of the PROLEXS system, which used a blackboard architecture to integrate the four knowledge sources in the domain of Dutch landlord-tenant law: legislation; legal doctrine derived from treatises; expert knowledge; and cases (Oskamp et al., 1989). The case-based reasoning component of PROLEXS—the "abstraction finder"—works by "detecting analogies between the case at hand and the cases stored in the case-law knowledge [base]." However, it does not appear that the abstraction finder is able to invoke rule-based reasoning, so PROLEXS is a CBR-first system. The EXPANDER architecture did not have this restriction, but only those EXPANDER elements shared with PROLEXS were actually implemented.

In summary, previous systems have implemented only portions of the framework for integrating rules and precedents advocated in this book. Systems confined to rule-based reasoning have little ability to reason about open-textured predicates appearing in rule antecedents. Systems that use only case-based reasoning are limited in their ability to reason about the equivalence of cases with factual differences or to combine separate case-based reasoning steps into a single explanation. By contrast, systems capable of case elaboration, such as Protos, Casey, and TAXMAN II, are able to direct a large portion of their domain theories to the task of assessing the relevant similarities between cases. Similarly, systems capable of goal reformulation, such as CABARET and PROLEXS, are able to combine multiple case-based reasoning steps. GREBE's impartial control strategy permits both case elaboration and goal reformulation. This gives GREBE the flexibility to combine rules and precedents in whatever manner leads to the strongest explanations.

8 RESEARCH CONTRIBUTIONS

This book has presented an approach to integrating rules and precedents for classification and explanation in weak-theory domains. This approach was used in the construction of GREBE, a system for legal analysis in the domain of Texas worker's compensation law. The research contributions of the GREBE approach and various avenues of future research suggested by the experience of developing GREBE are summarized in this chapter.

8.1 Contributions

This research has both theoretical and practical contributions. The theoretical contribution is a general account of the manner in which rules and precedents can be integrated to improve classification and explanation. Such an account is important because there are many domains for which neither rules nor precedents, standing alone, are sufficient for reliable classification. Expertise in such domains therefore depends on integrating both.

The practical contribution is a demonstration of how this general framework can be applied to the legal analysis task. GREBE is a system for legal analysis in the domain of worker's compensation that can accurately determine the legal rules and precedents that are relevant to a given question about a case, combine these authorities into arguments pro and con, and express these arguments in an intelligible memorandum form. The effectiveness of GREBE at addressing the legal analysis task is a confirmation of the utility of the general framework for integrating rules and precedents.

A General Framework for Integrating Rules and Precedents

Chapter 2 presented a framework under which rules and precedents are viewed as being alike in that each is a warrant connecting facts to conclusions. The generality of rules sometimes leads to a gap between abstract predicates in rule antecedents and the case-description language in which new cases are described. Weak-theory domains are those in which this gap causes classification uncertainty.

The general framework treats rules and precedents as complementary knowledge sources in weak-theory domains. Precedents can bridge the gap in abstraction between rule antecedents and new cases because the facts of precedents are expressed in the case description language. Conversely, rules can improve case matching through case elaboration, the process of inferring case facts in order to increase the similarity between cases, or goal reformulation, the process of replacing a goal by subgoals for which there are precedents that more closely match the new case. This framework is applicable to any classification task in a weak-theory domain, independent of the particular search control strategy or case representation.

A Formal Model of Ratio Decidendi

The relationship between the framework for integrating rules and precedents and the task of legal analysis was explicated in Chapter 3, which set forth a formal model of *ratio decidendi*. Under this model, the authoritative elements of a precedent include (1) each warrant for the ultimate result appearing in the warrant-reduction graph of the precedent's justification and (2) each reduction operator connecting successive warrants in this reduction graph. The reduction-graph model accounts for most of the important characteristics of *ratio decidendi* identified in the jurisprudential literature. In particular, the reduction-graph model shows how the theory under which a case is decided controls its precedential effect.

Chapter 3 showed that a purely exemplar-based model of precedent is unable to represent the reasoning under which a decision follows from the material facts of the case. By contrast, the reduction-graph model explicitly represents this reasoning. This permits a new case to be matched against the smallest collections of case facts that justified a legal conclusion in a precedent rather than requiring a new case to match the entire facts of any one precedent.

An Application of the Framework for Legal Analysis

GREBE is a system that applies the general framework for integrating rules and precedents to the legal analysis task. GREBE differs from previous systems for classification and explanation in two important respects. First, while previous systems implemented portions of this framework, *e.g.*, case-based reasoning to compensate for weak domain theories (Ashley, 1990, Clark, 1988b, McCarty and Sridharan, 1982), case elaboration (Koton, 1988, Porter et al., 1990), or goal reformulation (Gardner, 1987, Rissland and Skalak, 1989c, Oskamp et al., 1989), GREBE differs from earlier systems in incorporating all these components.

Second, GREBE differs from previous implemented case-based reasoning systems in using a relational case-description language. An adequate case-description language for legal analysis should fulfill two criteria. First, it should be rich enough to express the almost limitless variability of possible cases. Second, it should be free from bias toward any particular classification, so that conflicting arguments can be made in hard cases. Previous implemented systems were typically limited to propositional representations that usually fail to satisfy these criteria. By contrast, GREBE uses a case-description language in which arbitrary orderings of causal, temporal, and intentional relations can be stated explicitly.[1]

While GREBE's relational case-description language can express subtle factual distinctions among cases, it requires a different approach to case comparison than the simple feature matching used by most previous case-based reasoning systems. GREBE extends the structure-matching paradigm developed by the analogical reasoning community by incorporating case elaboration. Facts unmatched under the best mapping from a precedent constituent to a new case become subgoals to which either rule-based or case-based reasoning can be applied.

As shown below, the contributions of GREBE to the task of automated legal analysis are the direct result of its implementation of the general framework for integrating rules and precedents in conjunction with a highly expressive case-description language.

Accurate Precedent Retrieval. A fundamental problem in legal analysis is accurate retrieval of relevant legal precedents (Dick, 1987). GREBE's perfor-

[1](Ashley and McLaren, 1995) describes a system, TRUTH-TELLER, that uses a similar relational representation for case-based ethical reasoning. See also (McCarty, 1995) for a partial implementation of Eisner v. Macomber.

mance in retrieving legal precedents stems from three factors: a case-description language capable of expressing subtle distinctions among cases; algorithms for efficient and accurate retrieval of cases represented in this case-description language; and the ability to generate and evaluate alternative explanations.

The first factor is that GREBE's relational representation permits subtle distinctions among cases to be represented. This is important because the ability of the case-description language to express relevant similarities and differences between a new case and legal precedents is a limiting factor in accurate discrimination among precedents.

An adequate case-description language is of little use, however, without the second factor, algorithms for retrieval of cases represented in a relational case-description language. The price of the added expressiveness of relational representations is that retrieval techniques developed for less expressive propositional representations are, in general, insufficient. GREBE contains two algorithms for retrieving relational cases. The first, retrieval by best-first incremental matching, is a straightforward extension of GREBE's basic structure-matching procedure. The second, match refinement by structural difference links (MRSDL), makes use of precomputed information about structural differences among cases. Preliminary empirical evidence indicates that both retrieval methods perform faster than exhaustive matching and that MRSDL is only slightly less accurate.

The final factor is the ability to generate and evaluate alternative explanations. As illustrated by GREBE's analysis of the Car-pool Cases set forth in Chapter 5, GREBE produces alternative explanations depending on whether case-based reasoning is applied directly to a goal or instead to a subgoal formed by goal reformulation. The precedents relevant in one such explanation may differ from those relevant in an alternative explanation. By generating and then evaluating alternative explanations, GREBE is able to recognize the particular combination of rules and precedents that leads to the strongest arguments pro and con.

Producing Cogent Arguments. The output of GREBE is an explanation structure that shows how a legal conclusion can be justified in terms of the relevant legal authorities and the specific facts of the new case. Specifically, the explanations produced by GREBE:

- Identify the issues relevant to the question posed by the user.

- Determine the legal rules and precedents applicable to each issue.

- Show how conclusions about the issues follow from the facts of the case and the relevant authorities.

- Identify the relevant differences between a given case and applicable precedents.
- Present arguments on both sides of the issues, if conflicting precedents exist.

These characteristics of GREBE's output result from its expressive case-description language, which permits arguments to be closely tied to the particular facts of a new case, and its flexibility in combining rules and precedents in whatever manner leads to the strongest arguments.

Evaluation. The effectiveness of GREBE's performance was evaluated by comparing its analysis of 18 related worker's compensation hypotheticals to the analysis produced by law students. This evaluation showed that GREBE's performance was generally superior to the performance of a group of law students on the same problems.

8.2 Limitations and Future Work

The implementation of GREBE demonstrates that the general framework for integrating rules and precedents, in conjunction with a highly expressive case-description language, can lead to a high level of performance at the legal analysis task. This section begins by discussing issues that must be addressed if GREBE is to be extended into an automated legal assistant of practical value to attorneys. This section concludes with a discussion of several broader issues raised by this research beyond the particular application of legal analysis.

Issues in Automated Legal Reasoning

Overcoming Representational Sensitivity. Much of GREBE's effectiveness results from the richness of its case-description language. However, the benefits of an expressive case-description language come at a cost. Earlier chapters discussed how case comparison and retrieval are much more complex when cases are represented relationally than if they are represented propositionally. Another cost of relational case representations is that their expressiveness leads to a multiplicity of different ways of representing the same set of facts. This creates the danger of inconsistent analysis of equivalent cases.

Consider, for example, the problem of representing the fact that John rode to work in Mary's car. One representation of this fact would be that Mary is the *agent* and John the *patient* of a transporting activity. One alternative is that Mary and John could both be *agents* of a traveling activity, but in addition Mary could be the *driver* and John the *passenger*. A variant of this approach is to specialize the *agent* relation into *driver* and *passenger* relations, so that John and Mary occupy just one role each in the traveling activity. Another alternative is to represent two traveling activities, one by John and another by Mary. The dependence of John's traveling on Mary's traveling could be expressed by representing that John's traveling was a concurrent subprocess of Mary's traveling or by stating that Mary's traveling together with John's presence in Mary's car jointly caused John's traveling. A third alternative is to specialize *traveling* into *traveling-as-passenger* and *traveling-as-driver*. John would be the *agent* of a *traveling-as-passenger*, and Mary would be the *agent* of a *traveling-as-driver*. These examples hardly exhaust all the possibilities for representing this single fact. This plethora of choices indicates that relational representations are underconstrained.

The proclivity of relational case-representations to multiple representations for equivalent facts gives rise to the possibility of representational inconsistencies across different precedents or between new cases and precedents, particular if there are multiple case enterers. Representational inconsistencies can, in turn, cause inconsistent analyses because structure matching is sensitive only to the relational structure of case representations and not at all to their underlying semantics.

Case elaboration is a mechanism that addresses representational inconsistency. GREBE can reason about the equivalence of different representations of equivalent facts if it has the rules to do so. However, case elaboration is unlikely to be sufficient in itself to overcome representational inconsistency. Devising a sufficient set of rules would require anticipating every alternative representation that might be used for any given factual element. Moreover, GREBE's current approach to case elaboration is to use structure matching to focus the case elaboration process on just those facts that are relevant to a match. If case representations were sufficiently different that case elaboration had to be performed before structure matching, the elaboration would be very unfocused and therefore very expensive, especially if there was a vast collection of elaboration rules.

If representational inconsistency results from the absence of conventions for representing common factual patterns, such as a person riding to a destination in a car driven by someone else, inconsistency could be reduced by developing a library of conventions for fact patterns occurring in a given domain. These conventions would provide a set of constraints on what is otherwise an underconstrained representation. The difficulty of this approach is that it may be difficult to anticipate all of the factual patterns that might arise in a legal domain involving detailed human actions and intentions. The difficulty of devising an adequate library of factual patterns might be substantially reduced in domains, such as corporate taxation, negotiable instruments, or secured transactions, that are relatively isolated from the complexities of human life.

Another approach is to incorporate consistency enforcement into the case entry mechanism. For example, if GREBE had a natural language interface containing a grammar for a subset of English in which every worker's compensation case could be expressed, the grammar itself could enforce consistency across multiple occurrences of the same factual patterns. A more general approach to incorporating consistency enforcement into the case entry mechanism, *case-based formulation*, is described below.

In summary, GREBE's sensitivity to relational inconsistencies must be addressed if GREBE is to become a practical system for legal analysis. While explicitly representing knowledge of equivalence between different representations is a possible approach to this problem, adding constraints to the representation language or incorporating consistency enforcement into the case entry mechanism seem more promising.

Methodology for Determining Material Facts. The cogency of GREBE's explanations is very sensitive to the selection of material facts of precedents. However, GREBE does not itself provide any guidance for this selection process. Determining material facts requires imposing a particular construction on a precedent and using that construction to create a reduction graph representing the explanation of the case under that construction. A key requirement for creating larger scale knowledge bases is the development of a knowledge acquisition tool for creating reduction graphs and recording the material facts appearing in the antecedents of any exemplars in those reduction graphs.

Justifications Based on Legal Principles. An important form of justification in legal reasoning not addressed in GREBE is an appeal to general policies and principles of justice. Principles differ from rules in that conflicting principles can apply to the same case (Dworkin, 1977). GREBE can represent only those principles that are amenable to representation by paradigm cases. This approach is similar to modeling graded structure in categories by resemblance of actual cases to an "ideal" (Barsalou, 1985). The applicability of conflicting principles is modeled as partial matches to paradigm cases of the principles. Whether this approach to reasoning with principles is sufficient is a question open to future research.

Improved Models of Legal Discourse. GREBE produces detailed memoranda that identify the relevant legal issues and the rules and precedents applicable to each issue, show how how conclusions about the issues follow from the facts of the case and the relevant authorities, and identify the relevant differences between a given case and applicable precedents. However, as pointed out in (Berman and Hafner, 1993), these memoranda differ significantly from discourse typical of an attorney or judge. One source of difference is that GREBE's memorandum generator lacks any model of argument salience. The structure of GREBE's memoranda reflects the subgoaling structure of GREBE's inference process: issues are presented in the order in which they were reached during subgoaling. However, human discourse tends to order issues by factors such as novelty or the degree to which the issues are in contention. Rather than systematically presenting a long series of uncontroversial argument steps an attorney tends to focus immediately on the issues that are most in dispute.

GREBE also lacks a model of Gricean maxims of discourse (Grice, 1975). For example, GREBE sometimes belabors that obvious because it lacks any model of shared human information (although in comparison mode GREBE omits the portions of an explanation that are identical to the immediately previous explanation).

Human attorneys tend to frame their arguments in terms of stereotypical formulations of social goals (Berman and Hafner, 1993). GREBE, in contrast, can only argue in terms of similarities and differences between case facts.

While models of the discourse structure of routine legal documents have been developed, *e.g.,* (Branting and Lester, 1996b), (Branting and Lester, 1996a), (Branting et al., 1997), and (Branting et al., 1998), a theory of the discourse structure of legal argumentation has yet to be developed.

Extending the GREBE Approach

Retrieval of Structured Cases. There is a fundamental tradeoff between the expressiveness of a case-description language and the computational expense of retrieving precedents represented in that language. Efficient indexing and retrieval algorithms have been devised for cases with propositional representations. However, such representations are insufficient for complex domains. Retrieval of cases expressed in a relational case-description language is potentially much more expensive. In the worst case, when cases are simply arbitrary graphs, this problem requires considering every consistent partial mapping between every precedent and the new case, a clearly intractable problem. The challenge is to exploit knowledge that relational cases are not arbitrary graphs, but instead reflect the regularities of the real world, to avoid the full-blown graph-matching problem.

GREBE presents two alternative approaches to retrieval of structured cases. However, neither approach directly addresses the problem of using domain knowledge to obviate graph matching, and each approach has limitations. Retrieval by best-first incremental matching is much more efficient than exhaustive matching for small case libraries, but is not feasible for very large case libraries because retrieval time is proportional to the library size. Match refinement scales up better, but it is very sensitive to the choice of structural difference links. An important research issue is determining what configurations of difference links lead to the most accurate and efficient match refinement and automating the creation of such configurations. The broader problem of devising general techniques for exploiting domain knowledge to avoid graph matching has scarcely been addressed.

Completing the Integration of Rules and Precedents. A basic assumption underlying this book is that rules and precedents should be treated in a commensurate fashion. However, GREBE's treatment of rules and cases differs in one fundamental way: rule antecedents are matched by unification, whereas precedent facts are matched by structure matching.

The original motivation for this distinction was the view that partial matches between cases are inevitable and should therefore be permitted, whereas the failure to match a rule antecedent should lead to failure. However, in weak-theory domains it may be impossible to construct a complete explanation for either a proposition or its negation. Under these circumstances, the best that can be done is to determine the most complete partial explanations and identify the missing portions of each explanation. Knowledge of the missing parts of the strongest partial explanation for a conclusion can be useful to guide acquisition of additional information or as an argument that the conclusion is false.

GREBE finds the closest partial match to a precedent and identifies the respects in which the match is incomplete. As illustrated by GREBE's analysis of Car-pool Case 4 in Chapter 5, however, GREBE simply fails if a rule antecedent cannot be established. Thus, there is an asymmetry in GREBE's treatment of rules and cases. This asymmetry would be corrected if unification were replaced by structure matching as the mechanism for rule matching.

Using structure matching for both rules and cases would require modification of GREBE's search control strategy. Currently, GREBE tries all rules applicable to a goal but only the single precedent of the goal that matches the new case most closely. This difference in treatment reflects the fact that precedents are usually much more numerous than rules (since a single rule may have many instances). If the distinction between rules and precedents were eliminated, however, a uniform strategy would have to replace this two-track treatment.

One suitable strategy would be best-first search through the warrant hierarchy, where the evaluation function is the strength of the partially constructed inference chain. This would require some scheme for evaluating the strength of rule-based explanations involving unmatched rule antecedents to permit comparison of alternative partial explanations. It is unclear whether GREBE's heuristic of calculating the strength of case-based explanations as the proportion of precedent facts that are matched in the new case would be appropriate for rules, or whether some alternative would have to be devised.

Case-Based Formulation. The traditional model of case-based reasoning involves a rigid separation of case entry, retrieval of the most relevant precedents, and comparison between the new case and each of the precedents. Each of these steps is fraught with potential difficulty. Entering a complex case represented in a relational case-description language is time consuming and prone to inconsistency. The computational cost of retrieval and comparison can be, in the worst case, exponential in the size of a new case.

However, both the risk of representational inconsistencies and the expense of comparing cases is exacerbated by postponing the retrieval and comparison steps until a new case is entered in its entirety. An alternative approach, termed *case-based formulation*, starts retrieval as soon as a meaningful portion of a new case had been entered. The central tenet of this approach is that existing information should act as a model and a guide for expressing new information.

Case-based formulation has four potential benefits. First, it can reduce the time necessary to express new information because modifying an existing representation is often much simpler than creating a new representation *ab initio*. Second, it can reduce the danger of representational inconsistency because conventions for representing particular patterns of facts can be reused rather than having to be recreated in every new case. Third, it permits knowledge acquisition to improve, rather than degrade, as the size of a knowledge base increases. Finally, by expressing new cases in terms of old, the relevant similarities and differences between new and old cases can be determined *a fortiori* by the very process of formulating each new case. An initial implementation of case-based formulation is described in (Branting, 1992a).

8.3 Guide to Further Research

The research described in this book is in the intersection of two research communities: the case-based reasoning community; and the artificial intelligence and law community. This section briefly overviews the resources for additional research in each of these communities.

Case-Based Reasoning

At the time of this writing, there is not a journal of case-based reasoning research. The most important sources for current research in case-based reasoning are therefore workshops and conferences.

In the U.S., the earliest research related to case-based reasoning includes Janice Aiken's Centaur program (Aikins, 1979, Aikins, 1983), early work by

Edwina Rissland on reasoning with examples (Rissland and Soloway, 1981), and McCarty and Sridharan's work on TAXMAN (McCarty and Sridharan, 1982). The publication of "Dynamic Memory" by Roger Schank (Schank, 1982) stimulated research on computational models of episodic memory, including work by Kolodner (Kolodner, 1984), Simpson (Simpson, 1985), and Sycara (Sycara, 1985). DARPA sponsored workshops on case-based reasoning in 1988 (Kolodner, 1988), 1989 (Kolodner, 1989), and 1991 (Bareiss, 1991).

In Europe, the origins of case-based reasoning research seem to be more closely associated with machine learning than in the U.S. Workshops in case-based reasoning were held in Europe in 1993 (Wess et al., 1993), 1994 (Manago, 1994), 1996 (Smith and Faltings, 1996), and 1998 (Smyth and Cunningham, 1998).

The U.S. and European case-based reasoning communities joined in sponsoring international conferences on case-based reasoning in 1995 (Veloso and Aamodt, 1995), 1997 (Leake and Plaza, 1997), and 1999 (Althoff et al., 1999). The International Conferences on Artificial Intelligence contain the broadest coverage of current research in case-based reasoning.

The proceedings of the National Conferences on Artificial Intelligence (AAAI) and of the International Joint Conferences on Artificial Intelligence (IJCAI) typically contain several papers on case-based reasoning, and articles also occasionally appear in AI journals such as *Artificial Intelligence* and the *International Journal of Human-Computer Studies.* Proceedings of the International Conferences on Machine Learning often contain papers on "instance-based learning," a general term for nearest-neighbor and prototype-based learning systems. General surveys of case-based reasoning are set forth in (Aamodt and Plaza, 1994) and (Kolodner, 1993), and (Ashley, 1993) contains an overview of case-based reasoning as applied to legal problem solving.

Artificial Intelligence and Law

The earliest research in AI and law antedates the first work in case-based reasoning by a number of years. Logical models of legal reasoning date back at least to (Allen, 1957). The first rule-based legal systems were implemented in the early 1970's (Maggs and deBessonet, 1972, Popp and Schlink, 1975), and an early nearest-neighbor approach was implemented in 1974 (MacKaay and Robillard, 1974). Meldman's dissertation, which set forth a computational model of legal analysis that included a relational case representation and case similarity assessment by structural matching, was completed in 1975 (Meldman, 1975). Carole Hafner's conceptual retrieval system, LIRS, was completed in 1978 (Hafner, 1981).

The first international workshop on applications of artificial intelligence to law was held in Swansea, Wales, in 1979 (Niblett, 1979). The International Association for Artificial Intelligence and Law (IAAIL) has sponsored a series of biennial International Conferences on Artificial Intelligence and Law (ICAILs) starting in 1987 (ICAIL-87, 1987, ICAIL-89, 1989, ICAIL-91, 1991, ICAIL-93, 1993, ICAIL-95, 1995, ICAIL-97, 1997, ICAIL-99, 1999). *Artificial Intelligence and Law* journal is published by Kluwer Academic Publishers. The ICAIL conferences and the journal of *Artificial Intelligence and Law* are the primary international forums for current research in AI and law. In addition, the Foundation for Legal Knowledge Systems has sponsored a series of annual JURIX conferences in the Netherlands every year since 1989.

GLOSSARY

Argument A sequence of reasoning steps that justifies the classification of a case. "Argument" is preferred to "explanation" when referring to a justification for one of several inconsistent conclusions.

Atomic sentence An expression consisting of an n-ary predicate applied to an n-tuple of terms.

Attribute A single case fact. Synonymous with "feature."

Case A collection of propositions representing an actual or hypothetical entity or situation.

Category A collection of all entities that satisfy some predicate.

Conclusion A proposition whose truth may be at issue.

Contrast set The set of entities that are not members of a category.

Exemplar A case with a known classification. An exemplar can be used as a warrant in which the antecedent consists of the facts of the exemplar and the consequent is the classification.

Explanation A sequence of reasoning steps that justifies the classification of a case.

Fact A proposition known or assumed to be true.

Feature A single case fact. Synonymous with "attribute."

GREBE Generator of Recursive Exemplar-Based Explanations

Incomplete mapping A mapping in which the domain of the mapping is a proper subset of the tuples of the source.

Instance exemplar An exemplar known to be an instance of a category.

Legal analysis The task of determining and explaining the legal classification of a set of facts.

Legal predicate A predicate appearing in a proposition that was at issue in a legal dispute or that determines the rights, obligations, or liabilities of one or more persons.

Mapping A mapping from C_1 to C_2, denoted $M : C_1 \Rightarrow C_2$, is a set of ordered pairs $\{(s,t) | s \in O(C_1) \wedge t \in O(C_2)\}$, where $O(C_i)$ consists of the objects in case C_i.

Material facts The facts of an exemplar that are relevant to a classification of that exemplar.

New case A given collection of facts whose classification is at issue.

Noninstance exemplar An exemplar known to be an noninstance of a category.

Precedent A legal case that has given rise to a judicial decision, *i.e.,* a legal dispute that has been resolved. A precedent is a kind of exemplar, since it is an instance of the category of cases that satisfy some legal predicate. However, if resolution of the legal dispute required multiple reasoning steps, a precedent may contain multiple exemplars, called *precedent constituents.*

Predicate A term that expresses a characteristic of an object or a relationship among objects.

Precedent constituent An exemplar whose facts are a subset of the facts of an entire case. A precedent constituent of a legal precedent is an exemplar in the *ratio decidendi* of the precedent.

Proposition An atomic sentence or a sentence formed by applying a truth functional operator to a proposition.

Relation A predicate of arity at least 2.

Term An object, variable, or functional expression.

Theory Knowledge for problem solving, typically expressed as a set of propositions.

Tuple A lisp representation of an atomic sentence.

References

Aamodt, A. and Plaza, E. (1994). Case-based reasoning: Foundational issues, methodological variations, and system approaches. *AI Communications*, 7(1):39-59.

Aha, D. (1990). *A Study of Instance-Based Algorithms for Supervised Learning Tasks*. PhD thesis, University of California at Irvine.

Aha, D. W. and Goldstone, R. L. (1990). Learning attribute relevance in context in instance-based learning algorithms. In *Twelfth Annual Conference of the Cognitive Science Society*, pages 141–149.

Aho, A., Hopcroft, J., and Ullman, J. (1974). *The Design and Analysis of Computer Algorithms*. Addison-Wesley Publishing Co.

Aikins, J. (1979). Prototypes and production rules: An approach to knowledge representation for hypothesis formation. In *Proceedings of the Sixth International Joint Conference on Artificial Intelligence*, pages 1–3.

Aikins, J. (1983). Prototypical knowledge for expert systems. *Artificial Intelligence*, 20(2):163–210.

Aleven, V. and Ashley, K. (1996). Doing things with factors. In *Proceedings of the Third European Workshop on Case-Based Reasoning (EWCR-96)*, pages 76–90, Lausanne, Switzerland.

Aleven, V. and Ashley, K. (1997). Evaluating a learning environment for case-based argumentation skills. In *Proceedings of the Sixth International Conference on Artificial Intelligence and Law*, pages 170–179, University of Melbourne, Melbourne, Australia. ACM Press.

Allen, L. (1957). Symbolic logic: A razor-edged tool for drafting and interpreting legal documents. *Yale Law Journal*, 66:833–879.

Allen, L. and Saxon, C. (1991). More IA needed in AI: Interpetation assistance for coping with the problem of multiple structural interpetations. In *Pro-*

ceedings of the Third International Conference on Artificial Intelligence and Law, pages 53–61, Oxford, England.

Althoff, K., Bergmann, R., and Branting, K., editors (1999). *Case-Based Reasoning Research and Applications, Lecture Notes in Artificial Intelligence 1650*. Springer Verlag.

Amarel, S. (1968). On representations of problems of reasoning about actions. In Michie, D., editor, *Machine Intelligence*, volume 3, pages 131–171. Edinburgh University Press.

Ashley, K. (1990). *Modelling Legal Argument: Reasoning with Cases and Hypotheticals*. MIT Press, Cambridge, Massachusetts.

Ashley, K. (1993). Case-based reasoning and its implications for legal expert systems. *Artificial Intelligence and Law*, 1(2–3).

Ashley, K. and McLaren, B. (1995). Reasoning with reasons in case-based comparisons. In *Lecture Notes in Artificial Intelligence 1010*, pages 133–144, Sesimbra, Portugal. Springer.

Ashley, K. and Rissland, E. (1988). Waiting on weighting: A symbolic least commitment approach. In *Proceedings of AAAI-88*, Minneapolis. American Association for Artificial Intelligence.

Baade, H. (1963). *Jurimetrics*. Basic Books, New York.

Bareiss, E. R. (1988). *Protos: A Unified Approach to Concept Representation, Classification, and Learning*. PhD thesis, The University of Texas at Austin.

Bareiss, E. R., Porter, B. W., and Murray, K. S. (1989). Supporting start-to-finish development of knowledge bases. *Machine Learning*, 4(3):259–284.

Bareiss, E. R., Porter, B. W., and Wier, C. C. (1988). Protos: An exemplar-based learning apprentice. *International Journal of Man-Machine Studies*.

Bareiss, E. R., Porter, B. W., and Wier, C. C. (1990). Protos: An exemplar-based learning apprentice. In Kodratoff, Y. and Michalski, R., editors, *Machine Learning*, volume 3, pages 112–139. Morgan Kaufmann Publishers, Inc., San Mateo, California.

Bareiss, R., editor (1991). *Proceedings of the Third DARPA Case-Based Reasoning Workshop*. Morgan Kaufmann, Washington, D.C.

Barr, A. and Feigenbaum, E. A. (1982). *The Handbook of Artificial Intelligence*, volume 1. William Kaufmann.

Barsalou, L. W. (1985). Ideals, central tendency, and frequency of instantiation as determinants of graded structure in categories. *Journal of Experimental Psychology: Learning, Memory, and Cognition*, 11(4):629–649.

Bellairs, K. (1989). *Contextual Relevance in Analogical Reasoning: A Model of Legal Argument*. PhD thesis, University of Minnesota.

Bench-Capon, T. and Sergot, M. (1988). Towards a rule-based representation of open texture in law. In Walter, C., editor, *Computing Power and Legal Language*. Greenwood/Quorum Press, New York, NY.

Berman, D. and Hafner, C. (1989). The potential of artificial intelligence to help solve the crisis in our legal system. *Communications of the ACM*, 32:928–938.

Berman, D. and Hafner, C. (1993). Representing teleological structure in case-based legal reasoning: The missing link. In *Proceedings of the Fourth International Conference on Artificial Intelligence and Law*, pages 50–59, Amsterdam, The Netherlands. ACM Press.

Berman, D. and Hafner, C. (1995). Understanding precedents in a temporal context of evolving legal doctrine. In *Proceedings of the Fifth International Conference on Artificial Intelligence and Law*, pages 42–51.

Blumenthal, B. and Porter, B. (1994). Analysis and empirical studies of derivational analogy. *Artificial Intelligence*, 67:287–327.

Bodenheimer, E. (1974). *Jurisprudence*. Harvard University Press, Cambridge, MA.

Bradshaw, G. (1987). Learning to recognize speech sounds: The nexus project. In *Proceedings of the Fourth International Workshop on Machine Learning*, pages 1–11.

Branting, K. (1988). Protocol analysis of five worker's compensation problems. Unpublished protocol analysis of problem solving by attorneys at the Colorado Court of Appeals.

Branting, K. (1990). Techniques for retrieval of structured cases. *Working Notes of the AAAI Spring Symposium on Case-Based Reasoning*, Palo Alto, California.

Branting, K. (1991). Exploiting the complementarity of rules and precedents with reciprocity and fairness. In *Proceedings of the Third DARPA Case-Based Reasoning Workshop*. Morgan Kaufmann.

Branting, K. (1992a). A case-based approach to problem formulation. In *Proceedings of the Fourteenth Annual Conference of the Cognitive Science Society*, Bloomington, Indiana.

Branting, K. (1992b). A model of the role of expertise in analog retrieval. In *Proceedings of the Fourteenth Annual Conference of the Cognitive Science Society*, Bloomington, Indiana.

Branting, K. (1994a). A computational model of *ratio decidendi*. *Artificial Intelligence and Law*, 2(1):1–31.

Branting, K. (1994b). Four challenges for a computational model of legal precedent. *THINK (Journal of the Institute for Language Technology and Artificial Intelligence at Katholike Universiteit Tilburg)*, 3:62–69. Special Issue on legal knowledge-based systems.

Branting, K., Lester, J., and Callaway, C. (1997). Automated drafting of self-explaining documents. In *Proceedings of the Sixth International Conference on Artificial Intelligence and Law (ICAIL-97)*, pages 72–81, University of Melbourne, Melbourne, Australia. ACM Press.

Branting, K. and Porter, B. W. (1991). Rules and precedents as complementary warrants. In *Proceedings of Ninth National Conference on Artificial Intelligence*, Anaheim. AAAI Press/MIT Press, Menlo Park, California.

Branting, L. and Lester, J. (1996a). A framework for self-explaining legal documents. In *Proceedings of the Ninth International Conference on Legal Knowledge-Based Systems (JURIX-96)*, pages 77–90, Tilburg University, the Netherlands.

Branting, L. and Lester, J. (1996b). Justification structures for document reuse. In *Proceedings of the Third European Workshop on Case-Based Reasoning (EWCR-96)*, pages 76–90, Lausanne, Switzerland.

Branting, L., Lester, J., and Callaway, C. (1998). Automating judicial document drafting: A unification-based approach. *Artificial Intelligence and Law*, 6(2–4):111–149.

Branting, L. K. (1998). Techniques for automated drafting of judicial documents. *International Journal of Law and Information Technology*, 6(2):214–229.

Burton, S. J. (1985). *An Introduction to Law and Legal Reasoning.* Little, Brown and Company.

Capper, P. N. and Susskind, R. E. (1988). *Latent Damage Law — The Expert System.* Butterworths.

Cardozo, B. (1921). *The Nature of the Judicial Process.* Yale University Press, New Haven.

Christie, G. C. (1969). Objectivity in law. *Yale Law Journal*, 78:1311–1350.

Clark, P. (1988a). A comparison of exemplar-based and rule-based learning systems. In *Proceedings of the International Workshop on Machine Learning, Meta-Reasoning and Logic*, Portugal.

Clark, P. (1988b). Representing arguments as background knowledge for constraining generalization. In *Proceedings of the European Working Session on Learning.*

Collier, C. W. (1988). Precedent and legal authority: A critical history. *Wisconsin Law Review*, pages 771–825.

Cross, R. (1991). *Precedent in English Law.* Oxford University Press, Oxford, fourth edition.

Cueto-Rua, J. C. (1981). *Judicial Methods of Interpretation of the Law.* The Publications Institute, Paul M. Hebert Law Center, Louisiana State University.

Dick, J. P. (1987). Conceptual retrieval and case law. In *Proceedings of the First International Conference on Artificial Intelligence and Law*, pages 106–113, Boston, Massachusetts.

Dietterich, T. G. (1990). Machine learning. *Annual Review of Computer Science*, 4.

Dietterich, T. G. and Michalski, R. S. (1983). A comparative review of selected methods for learning from examples. In Carbonell, J. G., Michalski, R. S., and Mitchell, T. M., editors, *Machine Learning*, volume 1, pages 41–81, 46. Tioga, Palo Alto, CA.

Dworkin, R. (1977). *Taking Rights Seriously*. Harvard University Press.

Falkenhainer, B., Forbus, K., and Gentner, D. (1989). The structure-mapping engine: Algorithm and examples. *Artificial Intelligence*, 41(1).

Farley, A. and Freeman, K. (1995). Burden of proof in legal argumentation. In *Proceedings of the Fifth International Conference on Artificial Intelligence and Law*, pages 156–164.

Feinman, J. M. (1989). The jurisprudence of classification. *Stanford Law Review*, 41:661–717.

Fisher, R. (1997). Determination of residence status for taxation law: Development of a rule-based expert system. In *Proceedings of the Sixth International Conference on Artificial Intelligence and Law*, pages 161–169, University of Melbourne, Melbourne, Australia. ACM Press.

Freeman, K. and Farley, A. (1996). A model of argumentation and its application to legal reasoning. *Artificial Intelligence and Law*, 4(3–4):163–197.

Gardner, A. (1987). *An Artificial Intelligence Approach to Legal Reasoning*. Bradford Books/MIT Press, Cambridge, MA.

Gardner, H. (1985). *The Mind's New Science*. Basic Books Inc., New York.

Garey, M. R. and Johnson, D. S. (1979). *Computers and Intractability*. Freman, New York.

Gentner, D. (1989a). Finding the needle: Accessing and reasoning from prior cases. In *Proceedings of the Second DARPA Case-Based Reasoning Workshop*. Morgan Kaufmann.

Gentner, D. (1989b). The mechanisms of analogical learning. In Vosniadu, S. and Ortony, A., editors, *Similarity and Analogical Reasoning*. Cambridge University Press, London.

Gentner, D. and Forbus, K. (1991). MAC/FAC: A model of similarity-based retrieval. In *Thirteenth Annual Conference of the Cognitive Science Society*, pages 504–509.

Golding, A. and Rosenbloom, P. (1991). Improving rule-based systems through case-based reasoning. In *Proceedings of Ninth National Conference on Artificial Intelligence*, pages 22–27, Anaheim. AAAI Press/MIT Press, Menlo Park, California.

Golding, A. and Rosenbloom, P. (1996). Improving accuracy by combining rule-based and case-based reasoning. *Artificial Intelligence*, 87(1–2):215–254.

Golding, M. P. (1980). *Legal Reasoning*. Commission on Undergraduate Education in Law and the Humanities of the American Bar Association.

Goodhart, A. (1930). Determining the *ratio decidendi* of a case. *Yale Law Review*, 40:161.

Goodhart, A. (1959). The *ratio decidendi* of a case. *Modern Law Review*, 22:117.

Greenleaf, G., Mowbray, A., King, G., Cant, S., and Chung, P. (1997). More than *wysh*ful thinking: AustLII's legal inferencing via the World Wide Web. In *Proceedings of the Sixth International Conference on Artificial Intelligence and Law*, pages 47–55, University of Melbourne, Melbourne, Australia. ACM Press.

Grice, H. (1975). Logic and conversation. In Cole, P. and Morgan, J., editors, *Syntax and Semantics 2: Speech Acts*, pages 41–58. Academic Press, New York, N.Y.

Hafner, C. (1981). *An Information Retrieval System Based on a Computer Model of Legal Knowledge.* UMI Research Press.

Hammond, K. J. (1989). *Case-Based Planning: Viewing Planing as a Memory Task.* Academic Press, Inc., San Diego, California.

Hart, H. L. A. (1958). Positivism and the separation of law and morals. *Harvard Law Review*, 71:593–629.

Hart, H. L. A. (1961). *The Concept of Law.* Clarendon Press.

Holmes, O. W. (1906). *Lochner v. New York*, 198 U.S. 45, 76 (Holmes, J., dissenting).

Holyoak, K. and Thagard, P. (1989a). Analogical mapping by constraint satisfaction. *Cognitive Science*, 13(3).

Holyoak, K. and Thagard, P. (1989b). A computational model of analogical problem solving. In Vosniadou, S. and Ortony, A., editors, *Similarity and Analogical Reasoning.* Cambridge University Press, Cambridge.

ICAIL-87 (1987). *First International Conference on Artificial Intelligence and Law*, Boston, Massachusetts. ACM Press.

ICAIL-89 (1989). *Second International Conference on Artificial Intelligence and Law*, Vancouver, B.C. ACM Press.

ICAIL-91 (1991). *Third International Conference on Artificial Intelligence and Law*, Oxford, England. ACM Press.

ICAIL-93 (1993). *Fourth International Conference on Artificial Intelligence and Law*, Amsterdam, The Netherlands. ACM Press.

ICAIL-95 (1995). *Fifth International Conference on Artificial Intelligence and Law*, College Park, MD. ACM Press.

ICAIL-97 (1997). *Sixth International Conference on Artificial Intelligence and Law*, Melbourne, Australia. ACM Press.

ICAIL-99 (1999). *Seventh International Conference on Artificial Intelligence and Law*, Oslo, Norway. ACM Press.

James, W. (1902). *The Varieties of Religious Experience.* Collier MacMillan Publishers, London.

Kibler, D. and Aha, D. W. (1987). Learning representative exemplars of concepts: an initial case study. In *Proceedings of the 4th International Workshop on Machine Learning*, pages 1–11.

Klahr, P. (1996). Global case-based development and deployment. In *Proceedings of the Third European Workshop on Case-Based Reasoning (EWCR-96)*, pages 519–530, Lausanne, Switzerland.

Kolodner, J. (1984). *Retrieval and Organizational Strategies in Conceptual Memory: a Computer Model.* Lawrence Erlbaum Associates, Hillsdale, NJ.

Kolodner, J., editor (1988). *Proceedings of the DARPA Case-Based Reasoning Workshop.* Morgan Kaufmann, Clearwater Beach, Florida.

Kolodner, J., editor (1989). *Proceedings of the Second DARPA Case-Based Reasoning Workshop.* Morgan Kaufmann, Pensacola Beach, Florida.

Kolodner, J. (1993). *Case-based reasoning.* Morgan Kaufmann Publishers, San Mateo, California.

Koton, P. (1988). *Using Experience in Learning and Problem Solving.* PhD thesis, Massachusetts Institute of Technology, Cambridge, Massachusetts. Department of Electrical Engineering and Computer Science.

Lakoff, G. (1987). *Women, Fire, and Dangerous Things.* University of Chicago Press. Chicago and London.

Larsen, A. (1989). *The Law of Workmen's Compensation*, volume 1. Matthew Bender, New York.

Leake, D., Kinley, A., and Wilson, D. (1997). A case study in case-based CBR. In *Proceedings of the Second International Conference on Case-Based Reasoning*, pages 371–382, Providence, Rhode Island. Springer.

Leake, D. and Plaza, E., editors (1997). *Case-Based Reasoning Research and Development: First International Conference on Case-Based Reasoning (ICCBR-97), Lecture Notes in Artificial Intelligence 1266.* Springer Verlag, Providence, Rhode Island, USA.

Lehnert, W. G. (1987). Case-based problem solving with a large knowledge base of learned cases. In *Proceedings of the National Conference on Artificial Intelligence*, pages 301–306.

Levi, E. H. (1949). *An Introduction to Legal Reasoning.* University of Chicago Press, Chicago.

Llewellyn, K. (1960). *The Bramble Bush: On Our Law and Its Study.* Oceana Publications, Dobbs Ferry, NY.

Loevinger, L. (1963). Jurimetrics: The next step forward. *Minnesota Law Review*, 46:255–275.

MacCormick, N. (1987). Why cases have rationes and what these are. In Goldstein, L., editor, *Precedent in Law*, pages 155–182. Clarendon Press, Oxford.

MacKaay, E. and Robillard, P. (1974). Predicting judicial decisions: The nearest neighbor rule and visual representation of case patterns. *Datenverarbeitung im Recht*, pages 301–332.

Maggs, P. and deBessonet, C. (1972). Automated logical analysis of systems of legal rules. *Jurimetrics*, 12:158–169.

Mallory, R. S. (1989). Sources of classification accuracy in Protos. Technical Report AI-TR89-118, Artificial Intelligence Laboratory, Department of Computer Sciences, University of Texas at Austin.

Manago, M., editor (1994). *Advances in Case-Based Reasoning: Second European Workshop on Case-Based Reasoning (EWCR-94), Lecture Notes in Artificial Intelligence 984*. Springer Verlag.

Marshall, C. (1989). Representing the structure of a legal argument. In *Proceedings of the Second International Conference on Artificial Intelligence and Law*, pages 121–127, Vancouver, B.C.

McCarty, L. T. (1989). A language for legal discourse 1. Basic features. In *Proceedings of the Second International Conference on Artificial Intelligence and Law*, Vancouver, B.C.

McCarty, L. T. (1990). Artificial intelligence and law: How to get there from here. In *Ratio Juris*, volume 3, pages 189–200. Also in *Workshop Notes from the Eighth National Conference on Artificial Intelligence: Adversarial Reasoning and Artificial Intelligence and Legal Reasoning*, Boston, American Association for Artificial Intelligence.

McCarty, L. T. (1991). Invited Address, Third International Conference on Artificial Intelligence and Law, June 28, Oxford, England.

McCarty, L. T. (1995). An implementation of Eisner v. Macomber. In *Fifth International Conference on Artificial Intelligence and Law*, pages 276–286, College Park, MD. ACM Press.

McCarty, L. T. and Sridharan, N. S. (1982). A computational theory of legal argument. Technical Report LRP-TR-13, Laboratory for Computer Science Research, Rutgers University.

Meldman, J. A. (1975). *A Preliminary Study in Computer-Aided Legal Analysis*. PhD thesis, Massachusetts Institute of Technology.

Messmer, B. and Bunke, H. (1998). A new algorithm for error tolerant subgraph isomorphism detection. *PAMI*, 20(5):493–504.

Moore, M. S. (1981). The semantics of judging. *Southern California Law Review*, 54:151–294.

Morgan, E. M. (1948). *Introduction to the Study of Law*. Chicago, second edition.

Murphy, G. L. and Medin, D. L. (1985). The role of theories in conceptual coherence. *Psychological Review*, 92:289–316,299.

Murray, J. L. (1982). The role of analogy in legal reasoning. *UCLA Law Review*, 29:833–871,852.

Newell, A. (1982). The knowledge level. *Artificial Intelligence*, 18:87–127.

Niblett, B., editor (1979). *Proceedings of a Workshop on Computer Science and Law: An Advanced Course, University College of Swansea, Wales, UK.*

Nilsson, N. J. (1980). *Principles of Artificial Intelligence.* Tioga Publishing Company.

Oliphant, H. (1928). A return to stare decisis. *American Bar Association Journal*, 14.

Oskamp, A., Walker, R. F., Schrickx, J. A., and van den Berg, P. H. (1989). Prolexs, divide and rule: a legal application. In *Proceedings of the Second International Conference on Artificial Intelligence and Law*, Vancouver, B.C.

Paul, J. (1991). Expert systems, legal decision making, and self-revealing software. In Narayanan, A. and Bennun, M., editors, *Law, Computer Science, and Artificial Intelligence*, pages 216–232. Ablex Publishing Corporation, Norwood, NJ.

Peterson, M. and Waterman, D. (1985). Rule-based models of legal expertise. In Walters, C., editor, *Computing Power and Legal Reasoning*, pages 627–659. West Publishing Company, Minneapolis, Minnesota.

Pople, H. E. (1973). On the mechanization of abductive logic. In *International Joint Conference on Artificial Intelligence*, pages 147–152.

Popp, W. and Schlink, B. (1975). Judith, a computer program to advise lawyers. *Jurimetrics*, 15:303–314.

Porter, B. W., Bareiss, E. R., and Holte, R. C. (1990). Concept learning and heuristic classification in weak-theory domains. *Artificial Intelligence*, 45(1–2).

Prakken, H. and Sartor, G. (1998). *Judicial Applications fo Artificial Intelligence*, chapter Reasoning with Precedents in a Formal Dialogue Game. Kluwer Academic Publishers.

Rau, L. (1988). Exploiting the semantics of conceptual graphs for efficient graph matching. In Esch, J., editor, *Proceedings of the Third Annual Workshop on Conceptual Graphs.*

Raz, J. (1979). *The Authority of Law.* Clarendon Press, Oxford.

Redmond, M. (1990). Distributed cases for case-based reasoning; facilitating use of multiple cases. In *Proceedings of AAAI-90*, Boston. American Association for Artificial Intelligence.

Rissland, E. and Soloway, E. (1981). Constrained example generation: A testbed for studying issues in learning. In *Proceedings of the Seventh International Joint Conference on Artificial Intelligence*, pages 162–164.

Rissland, E. L. (1988). Artificial intelligence and legal reasoning. *AI Magazine*, pages 45–55.

Rissland, E. L. (1990). Artificial intelligence and law: Stepping stones to a model of legal reasoning. *Yale Law Review*, 99:1957–1981.

Rissland, E. L. and Skalak, D. B. (1989a). Case-based reasoning in a rule-governed domain. In *Proceedings of the Fifth IEEE Conference on Artificial Intelligence Applications*. Institute of Electrical and Electronic Engineers, Inc.

Rissland, E. L. and Skalak, D. B. (1989b). Combining case-based and rule-based reasoning: A heuristic approach. In *Eleventh International Joint Conference on Artificial Intelligence*, pages 524–530, Detroit, Michigan.

Rissland, E. L. and Skalak, D. B. (1989c). Interpreting statutory predicates. In *Proceedings of the Second International Conference on Artificial Intelligence and Law*, pages 46–53, Vancouver, B.C.

Rosch, E. and Mervis, C. B. (1975). Family resemblance: Studies in the internal structure of categories. *Cognitive Psychology*, 7:573–605.

Russell, S. and Norvig, P. (1995). *Artificial Intelligence: A Modern Approach*. Prentice Hall, Englewood Cliffs, New Jersey.

Russell, S. J. (1986). *Analogical and Inductive Reasoning*. PhD thesis, Stanford University.

Salmond, J. (1900). The theory of judicial precedent. *L. Q. Rev.*, 16.

Sanders, K. (1994). *CHIRON: Planning in an Open-Textured Domain*. PhD thesis, Brown University.

Schaaf, J. (1995). Fish and sink: An anytime-algorithm to retrieve adequate cases. In *Case-Based Reasoning Research and Development: First International Conference on Case-Based Reasoning (ICCBR-95), Lecture Notes in Artificial Intelligence 1010*, pages 538–547, Sesimbra, Portugal. Springer.

Schank, R. C. (1982). *Dynamic Memory, A Theory of Reminding and Learning in Computers and People*. Cambridge University Press, Cambridge, England.

Schauer, F. (1987). Precedent. *Stanford Law Review*, 39:571.

Sergot, M. J., Sadre, F., Kowalski, R. A., Kriwaczek, F., Hammond, P., and Cory, H. T. (1986). The british nationality act as a logic program. *Communications of the ACM*, 29:370–386.

Sherman, D. (1991). Reasoning in income tax through logic programming. In Narayanan, A. and Bennun, M., editors, *Law, Computer Science, and Artificial Intelligence*, pages 233–258. Ablex Publishing Corporation, Norwood, NJ.

Simpson, R. L. (1985). *A Computer Model of Case-based Reasoning in Problem Solving: An Investigation in the Domain of Dispute Mediation*. PhD thesis, Georgia Institute of Technology.

Skalak, D. and Rissland, E. (1992). Arguments and cases: An inevitable intertwining. *Law and Artificial Intelligence*, 1(1).

Smith, I. and Faltings, B., editors (1996). *Advances in Case-Based Reasoning: Third European Workshop on Case-Based Reasoning (EWCBR-96), Lecture Notes in Artificial Intelligence 1168.* Springer Verlag.

Smyth, B. and Cunningham, P., editors (1998). *Advances in case-based reasoning: 4th European Workshop on Case-Based Reasoning (EWCBR-98), Lecture Notes in Computer Science, 1488,* Dublin, Ireland. Springer Verlag.

Stanfill, C. and Waltz, D. (1986). Toward memory-based reasoning. *Communications of the ACM*, 29(12).

Stoljar, S. (1980). *Moral and Legal Reasoning.* The MacMillian press, Ltd.

Stone, J. (1947). *The Province and Function of Law.* Stanford University Press, Palo Alto.

Stone, J. (1959). The ratio of the ratio decidendi. *Modern Law Review*, 22:597,603–604.

Sycara, K. (1985). Arguments of persuasion in labour mediation. In *Proceedings of the Ninth International Joint Conference on Artificial Intelligence*, pages 294–296.

Thagard, P. (1989). Explanatory coherence. *Behavior and Brain Sciences*, 12(3):435-502.

Thagard P., Holyoak, K., Nelson, G., and Gochfeld, D. (1990). Analog retrieval by constraint satisfaction. *Artificial Intelligence*, 46:259–310.

Toulmin, S. E. (1958). *The Uses of Argument.* Cambridge University Press.

Tyree, A. (1989). *Expert Systems in Law.* Prentice Hall.

Veloso, M. (1992). *Learning by Analogical Reasoning in General Problem Solving.* PhD thesis, Carnegie Mellon University.

Veloso, M. and Aamodt, A., editors (1995). *Case-Based Reasoning Research and Development: First International Conference on Case-Based Reasoning (ICCBR-95), Lecture Notes in Artificial Intelligence 1010.* Springer Verlag, Sesimbra, Portugal.

Walker, R. (1992). *An Expert System Architecture for Heterogeneous Domains.* PhD thesis, Vrije University.

Wambaugh, E. (1894). *The Study of Cases.* Little, Brown, second edition.

Warner, R. (1989). Three theories of legal reasoning. *Southern California Law Review*, 62(5).

Wess, S., Althoff, K., and Richter, M., editors (1993). *Topics in Case-Based Reasoning: First European Workshop on Case-Based Reasoning (EWCBR-93), Lecture Notes in Artificial Intelligence 837.* Springer Verlag.

Wettschereck, D. and Aha, D. (1995). Weighting features. In *Lecture Notes in Artificial Intelligence*, pages 347–358, Sesimbra, Portugal. Springer.

Winston, P. H. (1980). Learning and reasoning by analogy. *Communications of the ACM*, 23(12).

Wittgenstein, L. (1958). *Remarks on the Foundations of Mathematics.* Oxford University. Edited by G. H. von Wright, R. Rhees, and G. E. M. Anscombe, and translated by G. E. M. Anscombe.

Appendix A
GREBE's Analysis of 7 Worker's Compensation Hypotheticals

This appendix sets forth examples of GREBE's analysis of 7 worker's compensation cases. These cases fall into two sets of related hypotheticals. For each case, an English paraphrase of the facts of the case is set forth first, followed by a verbatim transcript of GREBE's analysis. GREBE's output is in verbose mode for the first case in each group, *i.e.*, the complete explanation structure is set forth, and in comparison mode for the remaining cases, *i.e.*, only those portions of an analysis that differ from the preceding analysis are set forth.

Journey case number 1

Sally lived in the Austin area and was employed as a software engineer by a computer firm, Austin Research. Sally was asked by her supervisor to repair a technical problem in a system used by a Dallas customer of Austin Research requiring several days to fix. Sally drove to Dallas and checked into a Holiday Inn. While carrying her bags down a hallway that had just been mopped, Sally slipped and fell, injuring herself.

```
Query: Is Austin Research liable under worker compensation to
Sally for Sally's injury under the facts of Journey Case number
1?

Under Vernon's Ann.Tex.Civ.St. article 8309 section 1b, Austin
Research is liable under worker compensation to Sally for
Sally's injury if:

    Sally's injury was sustained by Sally while engaged in
    going through the hotel lobby in the course of employment
    by Austin Research.

    This conclusion follows from Vernon's Ann.Tex.Civ.St.
```

article 8309 section 1b if:

a. Sally was employed by Austin Research, as stated in the given facts.

b. Sally's injury occurred during going through the hotel lobby, as stated in the given facts.

c. Going through the hotel lobby was an activity in furtherance of Sally's employment.

Two conflicting arguments can be made concerning whether going through the hotel lobby was an activity in furtherance of Sally's employment.

The stronger argument is that:

Going through the hotel lobby was an activity in furtherance of Sally's employment.

This conclusion follows from the strong analogy between the given case and the facts of Aetna Cas. Ins. Co. v. Orgon, 721 S.W.2d 572 (1987) that were relevant to the conclusion that drinking water at the hotel was an activity in furtherance of Orgon's employment.

This analogy is supported by the following inferences:

A. That Sally had the need for rest, which is stated in the facts of the given case, is similar to the fact that Orgon had the need for water.

B. Sally being in Dallas entailed Sally staying at a hotel.

This conclusion follows from the very strong analogy between the given case and the facts of Aetna Cas. Ins. Co. v. Orgon, 721 S.W.2d 572 (1987) that were relevant to the conclusion that Orgon being in Bryan entailed Orgon staying at hotel.

This analogy is supported by the following inference:

The fact that the sum of the duration of the trip to Dallas, the duration of returning from Dallas, and the duration of fixing the software problem is greater than the duration of Sally's waking hours.

C. Going through the hotel lobby led to a decrease in the intensity of the need for rest.

I. Sally sleeping at hotel required Sally being in the hotel room which was achieved by going through the hotel lobby, as stated in the given facts.

II. Sally sleeping at hotel led to a decrease in the intensity of the need for rest, as stated in the given facts.

Relevant differences between the given case and Aetna Cas. Ins. Co. v. Orgon, 721 S.W.2d 572 (1987) with respect to the issue whether going through the hotel lobby was an activity in furtherance of Sally's employment are that:

- Sally was not engaged in consumption in going through the hotel lobby.

Whereas in the Orgon case:

- Orgon was engaged in consumption in drinking water at the hotel.

However, a weaker argument can be made that:

Going through the hotel lobby was not an activity in furtherance of Sally's employment.

This conclusion follows from the strong analogy between the given case and the facts of Liberty Mut. Ins. Co. v. Preston, 399 S.W.2d 367 (1966) that were relevant to the conclusion that the trip to Garner Park was not an activity in furtherance of Preston's employment.

This analogy is supported by the following inference:

> That Sally walked while going through the hotel lobby, which is stated in the facts of the given case, is similar to the fact that Preston was the driver during the trip to Garner Park.

Relevant differences between the given case and Liberty Mut. Ins. Co. v. Preston, 399 S.W.2d 367 (1966) with respect to the issue whether going through the hotel lobby was an activity in furtherance of Sally's employment are that:

- It was not the case that going through the hotel lobby was a deviation from the trip to Dallas.

Whereas in the Preston case:

- The trip to Garner Park was a deviation from the trip to Abilene.

d. Sally's injury originated in Sally's employment.

   i. Sally's injury was a hazard of going through the hotel lobby, as stated in the given facts.

   ii. The stronger argument is that going through the hotel lobby was an activity in furtherance of Sally's employment, as was shown above.

e. The rule barring compensation for accidents occurring during traveling is inapplicable to going through the hotel lobby.

   This conclusion follows from Vernon's Ann.Tex.Civ.St. article 8309 section 1b if:

   i. Going through the hotel lobby falls within a

statutory exception to the rule barring compensation for accidents occurring during traveling.

This conclusion follows from Vernon's Ann.Tex.Civ.St. article 8309 section 1b if:

Sally was directed in his employment by Austin Research to engage in going through the hotel lobby.

This conclusion follows from the rule of Jecker v. Western Alliance Ins. Co., 369 S.W.2d 776 (1963), that there is an implied direction to perform activities in furtherance of employment if:

The stronger argument is that going through the hotel lobby was an activity in furtherance of Sally's employment, as was shown above.

ii. The dual purpose rule is inapplicable to going through the hotel lobby.

This conclusion follows from the dual purpose rule of article 8309 section 1b if:

Going through the hotel lobby was not both in furtherance of the personal or private affairs of Sally and in furtherance of Sally's employment.

Under the facts of the given case, going through the hotel lobby was not an activity in furtherance of the personal or private affairs of Sally.

Journey case number 2

The same facts as Journey case number 1 except that during her stay in Dallas Sally decided to drive to the Fort Worth Science Museum. On the way, Sally had an automobile accident.

Query: Is Austin Research liable under worker compensation to

Sally for Sally's injury under the facts of Journey Case number 2?

The stronger argument in Journey Case number 2 is that Austin Research is not liable under worker compensation to Sally for Sally's injury. Moreover, this argument is stronger here than under the facts of Journey Case number 1.

The analysis in Journey Case number 2 is identical to the analysis in Journey Case number 1 except for the issue whether the trip to the museum was an activity in furtherance of Sally's employment.

Two conflicting arguments can be made concerning whether the trip to the museum was an activity in furtherance of Sally's employment.

The stronger argument is that:

> The trip to the museum was not an activity in furtherance of Sally's employment.
>
> This conclusion follows from the very strong analogy between the given case and the facts of Liberty Mut. Ins. Co. v. Preston, 399 S.W.2d 367 (1966) that were relevant to the conclusion that the trip to Garner Park was not an activity in furtherance of Preston's employment.

However, a weaker argument can be made that:

> The trip to the museum was an activity in furtherance of Sally's employment.
>
> This conclusion follows from the analogy between the given case and the facts of Aetna Cas. Ins. Co. v. Orgon, 721 S.W.2d 572 (1987) that were relevant to the conclusion that drinking water at the hotel was an activity in furtherance of Orgon's employment.
>
> This analogy is supported by the following inferences:
>
> a. That Sally had the need for rest, which is stated in the facts of the given case, is similar to the fact that Orgon had the need for water.

b. Sally being in Dallas entailed Sally staying at a hotel.

This conclusion follows from the very strong analogy between the given case and the facts of Aetna Cas. Ins. Co. v. Orgon, 721 S.W.2d 572 (1987) that were relevant to the conclusion that Orgon being in Bryan entailed Orgon staying at hotel.

This analogy is supported by the following inference:

> The fact that the sum of the duration of the trip to Dallas, the duration of returning from Dallas, and the duration of fixing the software problem is greater than the duration of Sally's waking hours.

Relevant differences between the given case and Aetna Cas. Ins Co. v. Orgon, 721 S.W.2d 572 (1987) with respect to the issue whether the trip to the museum was an activity in furtherance of Sally's employment are that:

- Sally was not engaged in consumption in the trip to the museum.

- It was not the case that the trip to the museum took place at the Holiday Inn.

- The trip to the museum was not a step of Sally staying at a hotel.

- It was not the case that the trip to the museum led to a decrease in the intensity of the need for rest.

Whereas in the Orgon case:

- Orgon was engaged in consumption in drinking water at the hotel.

- Drinking water at the hotel took place at the Ramada Inn.

- Drinking water at the hotel was a step of Orgon staying at hotel.

- Drinking water at the hotel led to a decrease in the intensity of the need for water.

Journey case number 3

Austin Research had a job of several months duration in San Antonio. To induce Sally, who lived in Round Rock, to accept this job given the lengthy commute, Austin Research agreed to provide free transportation (a van service) to San Antonio. Sally accepted the job, but was injured when the van had an accident midway between Austin and San Antonio.

Query: Is Austin Research liable under worker compensation to Sally for Sally's injury under the facts of Journey Case number 3?

The stronger argument in Journey Case number 3 is that Austin Research is liable under worker compensation to Sally for Sally's injury. Moreover, this argument is stronger here than under the facts of Journey Case number 2.

The analysis in Journey Case number 3 is identical to the analysis in Journey Case number 2 except for the issue whether the trip to San Antonio was an activity in furtherance of Sally's employment.

Two conflicting arguments can be made concerning whether the trip to San Antonio was an activity in furtherance of Sally's employment.

The stronger argument is that:

> The trip to San Antonio was an activity in furtherance of Sally's employment.
>
> This conclusion follows from the very strong analogy between the given case and the facts of Liberty Mut. Ins. Co. v. Chesnut, 539 S.W.2d 924 (1976) that were relevant to the conclusion that Branum's transporting Chesnut was an activity in furtherance of Chesnut's employment.
>
> This analogy is supported by the following inference:
>
>> Unusually long travel time made Sally travel pay a necessary inducement for Sally to engage in working in San Antonio.

> This conclusion follows from the very strong analogy between the given case and the facts of Liberty Mut. Ins. Co. v. Chesnut, 539 S.W.2d 924 (1976) that were relevant to the conclusion that unusually long travel time made providing transportation to the drill site a necessary inducement for Chesnut to engage in oil drilling.

However, a weaker argument can be made that:

The trip to San Antonio was not an activity in furtherance of Sally's employment.

This conclusion follows from the strong analogy between the given case and the facts that are relevant to the conclusion that ordinary commuting to work is not an activity in furtherance of a typical employee's employment as held in American General Ins. v. Coleman, 157 Tx. 377, 303 S.W.2d 370.

This analogy is supported by the following inference:

> That Sally was the passenger in the trip to San Antonio, which is stated in the facts of the given case, is similar to the fact that a typical employee was the driver during ordinary commuting to work.

Relevant differences between the given case and ordinary commuting to work with respect to the issue whether the trip to San Antonio was an activity in furtherance of Sally's employment are that:

- The San Antonio site was not under the direct control of Austin Research.

Whereas in the typical commute out case:

- A typical workplace is under the direct control of a typical employer.

Stanley case number 1

Stanley was employed by Tower Construction Company as the head of a surveying crew at a large construction site. Stanley took the surveying tools home with him every night and was responsible for bringing them to the construction site each morning. He was injured in an accident while driving to work on morning carrying the surveying tools in his car.

```
Query: Is Tower Construction Company liable under worker
compensation to Stanley for Stanley's injury under the facts of
Stanley Case number 1?

Under Vernon's Ann.Tex.Civ.St. article 8309 section 1b, Tower
Construction Company is liable under worker compensation to
Stanley for Stanley's injury if:

   Stanley's injury was sustained by Stanley while engaged in
   the trip to the construction site in the course of
   employment by Tower Construction Company.

   This conclusion follows from Vernon's Ann.Tex.Civ.St.
   article 8309 section 1b if:

    a.  Stanley was employed by Tower Construction Company, as
        stated in the given facts.

    b.  Stanley's injury occurred during the trip to the
        construction site, as stated in the given facts.

    c.  The trip to the construction site was an activity in
        furtherance of Stanley's employment.

        Two conflicting arguments can be made concerning
        whether the trip to the construction site was an
        activity in furtherance of Stanley's employment.

        The stronger argument is that:

            The trip to the construction site was not an
            activity in furtherance of Stanley's employment.

            This conclusion follows from the very strong
            analogy between the given case and the facts of
            Agricultural Ins. Co. v. Dryden, 398 S.W.2d 745
            (1966) that were relevant to the conclusion that
            the trip to Nederland was not an activity in
            furtherance of Dryden's employment.

        However, a weaker argument can be made that:
```

The trip to the construction site was an activity in furtherance of Stanley's employment.

This conclusion follows from the strong analogy between the given case and the facts of Liberty Mut. Ins. Co. v. Chesnut, 539 S.W.2d 924 (1976) that were relevant to the conclusion that Branum's transporting Chesnut was an activity in furtherance of Chesnut's employment.

This analogy is supported by the following inference:

> That Stanley was the driver during the trip to the construction site, which is stated in the facts of the given case, is similar to the fact that Chesnut was the passenger in Branum's transporting Chesnut.

Relevant differences between the given case and Liberty Mut. Ins. Co. v. Chesnut, 539 S.W.2d 924 (1976) with respect to the issue whether the trip to the construction site was an activity in furtherance of Stanley's employment are that:

- The benefit conferred by Stanley's wages was not the trip to the construction site.

- It was not the case that unusually long travel time made Stanley's wages a necessary inducement for Stanley to engage in surveying the construction site.

Whereas in the Chesnut case:

- The benefit conferred by Chesnut drilling wages was Branum's transporting Chesnut.

- Unusually long travel time made Chesnut drilling wages a necessary inducement for Chesnut to engage in oil drilling.

d. Stanley's injury originated in Stanley's employment.

i. Stanley's injury was a hazard of the trip to the construction site, as stated in the given facts.

ii. The stronger argument is that the trip to the construction site was not an activity in furtherance of Stanley's employment, as was shown above.

e. The rule barring compensation for accidents occurring during traveling is inapplicable to the trip to the construction site.

This conclusion follows from Vernon's Ann.Tex.Civ.St. article 8309 section 1b if:

i. The trip to the construction site falls within a statutory exception to the rule barring compensation for accidents occurring during traveling.

This conclusion follows from Vernon's Ann.Tex.Civ.St. article 8309 section 1b if:

Stanley was directed in his employment by Tower Construction Company to engage in the trip to the construction site.

This conclusion follows from the rule of Jecker v. Western Alliance Ins. Co., 369 S.W.2d 776 (1963), that there is an implied direction to perform activities in furtherance of employment if:

The stronger argument is that the trip to the construction site was not an activity in furtherance of Stanley's employment, as was shown above.

ii. The dual purpose rule is inapplicable to the trip to the construction site.

This conclusion follows from the dual purpose rule of article 8309 section 1b if:

The trip to the construction site was not

both in furtherance of the personal or private affairs of Stanley and in furtherance of Stanley's employment.

Under the facts of the given case, the trip to the construction site was not an activity in furtherance of the personal or private affairs of Stanley.

Stanley case number 2

The same facts as Stanley Case number 1 except that Stanley was paid a separate salary for bringing the surveying tools to the construction site.

Query: Is Tower Construction Company liable under worker compensation to Stanley for Stanley's injury under the facts of Stanley Case number 2?

The stronger argument in Stanley Case number 2 is that Tower Construction Company is liable under worker compensation to Stanley for Stanley's injury. Moreover, this argument is stronger here than under the facts of Stanley Case number 1.

The analysis in Stanley Case number 2 is identical to the analysis in Stanley Case number 1 except for the issue whether the trip to the construction site was an activity in furtherance of Stanley's employment.

Two conflicting arguments can be made concerning whether the trip to the construction site was an activity in furtherance of Stanley's employment.

The stronger argument is that:

The trip to the construction site was an activity in furtherance of Stanley's employment.

This conclusion follows from the very strong analogy between the given case and the facts that are relevant to the conclusion that conveying commodities is an activity in furtherance of a typical truck driver's employment as held in Jecker v. Western Alliance Ins. Co., 369 S.W.2d 776 (1963).

This analogy is supported by the following inference:

The surveying tools being at the construction site was the goal of Tower Construction Company.

i. The surveying tools being at the construction site was a prerequisite for surveying the construction site, as stated in the given facts.

ii. Construction site being surveyed was achieved by surveying the construction site, as stated in the given facts.

iii. Construction site being surveyed was the goal of Tower Construction Company, as stated in the given facts.

However, a weaker argument can be made that:

The trip to the construction site was not an activity in furtherance of Stanley's employment.

This conclusion follows from the very strong analogy between the given case and the facts of Agricultural Ins. Co. v. Dryden, 398 S.W.2d 745 (1966) that were relevant to the conclusion that the trip to Nederland was not an activity in furtherance of Dryden's employment.

Stanley case number 3

The same facts as 1 except that Stanley owned the tools, leased them to his employer, and was responsible for their maintenance as a condition of the lease agreement. Stanley was injured while driving to a shop to have the tools repaired.

Query: Is Tower Construction Company liable under worker compensation to Stanley for Stanley's injury under the facts of Stanley Case number 3?

The stronger argument in Stanley Case number 3 is that Tower Construction Company is not liable under worker compensation to Stanley for Stanley's injury. Moreover, this argument is stronger here than under the facts of Stanley Case number 2.

The analysis in Stanley Case number 3 is identical to the analysis in Stanley Case number 2 except for the issue whether the trip to the repair shop was an activity in furtherance of

Stanley's employment.

Two conflicting arguments can be made concerning whether the trip to the repair shop was an activity in furtherance of Stanley's employment.

The stronger argument is that:

> The trip to the repair shop was not an activity in furtherance of Stanley's employment.
>
> This conclusion follows from the very strong analogy between the given case and the facts of Texas Gen. Indem. Co. v. Bottom, 365 S.W.2d 350 (1963) that were relevant to the conclusion that the trip to Hillsboro was not an activity in furtherance of Bottom's employment.
>
> This analogy is supported by the following inference:
>
>> The trip to the repair shop was undertaken pursuant to a contractual obligation separate from Stanley's employment.
>>
>> This conclusion follows from the very strong analogy between the given case and the facts of Texas Gen. Indem. Co. v. Bottom, 365 S.W.2d 350 (1963) that were relevant to the conclusion that the trip to Hillsboro was undertaken pursuant to a contractual obligation separate from Bottom's employment.

However, a weaker argument can be made that:

> The trip to the repair shop was an activity in furtherance of Stanley's employment.
>
> This conclusion follows from the analogy between the given case and the facts of Liberty Mut. Ins. Co. v. Chesnut, 539 S.W.2d 924 (1976) that were relevant to the conclusion that Branum's transporting Chesnut was an activity in furtherance of Chesnut's employment.
>
> This analogy is supported by the following inference:
>
>> That Stanley was the driver during the trip to the repair shop, which is stated in the facts of the given

case, is similar to the fact that Chesnut was the passenger in Branum's transporting Chesnut.

Relevant differences between the given case and Liberty Mut. Ins. Co. v. Chesnut, 539 S.W.2d 924 (1976) with respect to the issue whether the trip to the repair shop was an activity in furtherance of Stanley's employment are that:

- The construction site was not the destination of the trip to the repair shop.

- The benefit conferred by Stanley's wages was not the trip to the repair shop.

- It was not the case that unusually long travel time made Stanley's wages a necessary inducement for Stanley to engage in surveying the construction site.

Whereas in the Chesnut case:

- The drill site was the destination of Branum's transporting Chesnut.

- The benefit conferred by providing transportation to the drill site was Branum's transporting Chesnut.

- Unusually long travel time made providing transportation to the drill site a necessary inducement for Chesnut to engage in oil drilling.

Stanley case number 4

The same facts as 1 except that Stanley performed some of his job duties—making architectural charts—at home. On the day of the accident, Stanley did some work at home and was driving to the construction site when he had an automobile accident.

Query: Is Tower Construction Company liable under worker compensation to Stanley for Stanley's injury under the facts of Stanley Case number 4?

The stronger argument in Stanley Case number 4 is that Tower Construction Company is liable under worker compensation to Stanley for Stanley's injury. Moreover, this argument is stronger here than under the facts of Stanley Case number 3.

The analysis in Stanley Case number 4 is identical to the analysis in Stanley Case number 3 except for the issue whether the trip to the construction site was an activity in furtherance of Stanley's employment.

Two conflicting arguments can be made concerning whether the trip to the construction site was an activity in furtherance of Stanley's employment.

The stronger argument is that:

> The trip to the construction site was an activity in furtherance of Stanley's employment.
>
> This conclusion follows from the very strong analogy between the given case and the facts of Meyer v. Western Fire Ins. Co., 425 S.W.2d 628 (1968) that were relevant to the conclusion that the trip to his office was an activity in furtherance of Meyer's employment.
>
> This analogy is supported by the following inference:
>
> > The duties of Stanley's employment included transporting surveying tools.
> >
> > i. That transporting surveying tools was accomplished by the trip to the construction site, which is stated in the facts of the given case, is similar to the fact that the trip to his office occurred in the process of inspecting houses.
> >
> > ii. The duties of Stanley's employment included the trip to the construction site.
> >
> > This conclusion follows from the very strong analogy between the given case and the facts of Jecker v. Western Alliance Ins. Co., 369 S.W.2d 776 (1963), that were relevant to the conclusion that the duties of Jecker's employment included the trip to the customer's home.

However, a weaker argument can be made that:

> The trip to the construction site was not an activity in

```
furtherance of Stanley's employment.

This conclusion follows from the very strong analogy
between the given case and the facts of Agricultural Ins.
Co. v. Dryden, 398 S.W.2d 745 (1966) that were relevant to
the conclusion that the trip to Nederland was not an
activity in furtherance of Dryden's employment.
```

Appendix B
Legal Precedents in the Worker's Compensation Knowledge Base

Published Judicial Opinions

- *Aetna Cas. Ins. Co. v. Orgon,* 721 S.W.2d 572 (1987).
- *Agricultural Ins. Co. v. Dryden,* 398 S.W.2d 745 (1966).
- *Carson v. Industrial Underwriters Ins. Co.,* 586 S.W.2d 943 (1979).
- *City of Dallas v. Bradford,* 646 S.W.2d 302 (1983).
- *Hackfield v. Pac. Employers Ins. Co.,* 393 S.W.2d 720 (1965).
- *Janak v. Texas Employer's Ins. Co.,* 381 S.W.2d 176 (1964).
- *Jecker v. Western Alliance Ins. Co.,* 369 S.W.2d 776 (1963).
- *Liberty Mut. Ins. Co. v. Chesnut,* 539 S.W.2d 924 (1976).
- *Liberty Mut. Ins. Co. v. Preston,* 399 S.W.2d 367 (1966).
- *Mapp v. Maryland Cas. Ins. Co.,* 726 S.W.2d 516 (1987).
- *Meyer v. Western Fire Ins. Co.,* 425 S.W.2d 628 (1968).
- *Smith v. Dallas County Hospital Dist.,* 687 S.W.2d 69 (1985).
- *Texas Gen. Indem. Co. v. Bottom,* 365 S.W.2d 350 (1963).
- *U.S. Fire Ins. Co. v. Brown,* 654 S.W.2d 566 (1983).
- *U.S. Fire Ins. Co. v. Eberstein,* 711 S.W.2d 355 (1986).
- *Vaughn v. Highlands Underwriters Ins. Co.,* 445 S.W.2d 234 (1969).

Paradigm Cases

- *Typical work activity*
- *Typical commuting to work*
- *Typical commuting from work*
- *Typical transportation of commodities for hire*

Summary of Selected Precedents

1. *Janak v. Texas Employer's Ins. Co.,* 381 S.W.2d 176 (1964). Janak was a member of a crew engaged in drilling an oil well near the town of Ecleto. Janak was injured in an accident while a passenger in a car driven by Draplia, another member of the drilling crew. The accident occurred during a deviation from the direct route to Ecleto. The purpose of the deviation was to get ice at the town of Runge to cool the crew's drinking water. Water was not available at the drillsite and was not furnished by the employer.

The Texas Supreme Court noted that injuries incurred while commuting are not ordinarily compensable under worker's compensation. However, the Court reasoned that a passenger in a business carpool is in the course of employment when traveling on a journey whose purpose is to perform a service in furtherance of the employer's business. Janak's right to recovery therefore hinges on whether Draplia was in the course of his employment at the time of the accident.

Vernon's Tex. Rev. Civ. Stat. Ann. art. 8309 §1b states that injuries occurring during traveling are compensable only if the transportation was "furnished as a part of the contract of employment, or ... paid for, ... or ... under the control of the employer" or if the worker was "directed in his employment to proceed from one place to another place." Since the transportation was not furnished or paid for by the employer and was not under its control, whether Draplia was in the course of his employment at the time of the accident depends on whether he was "directed in his employment to proceed from one place to another place."

The Court noted that *Jecker v. Western Alliance Ins. Co.*, 369 S.W.2d 776 (1963), held that the direction to proceed from one place to another place can be an implied direction provided that the purpose for the travel was in furtherance of the employer's business. The Court concluded that there was sufficient evidence to support the jury's finding that the deviation to Runge was in furtherance of the employer's business. The hot working conditions at Ecleto made ice "reasonably essential" to the continuance of drilling operations. The deviation to get ice was thus analogous to a deviation to get tools essential for the drilling operation, which is clearly impliedly directed, and distinct from a deviation to a "a particular kind of hamburger," which is "just as clearly not ... impliedly directed by the employer." The fact that it was customary in the drilling business for the employer to pay for ice was additional evidence that in hot weather ice in drinking water was reasonably necessary to furtherance of the business.

2. *Vaughn v. Highlands Underwriters Ins. Co.*, 445 S.W.2d 234 (1969). Vaughn worked as a truck driver hauling three loads of sulfur per night from a mine to a factory. Each round trip from the factory to the sulphur mine and back again took approximately 4 hours. Vaughn normally stopped to eat each night at a roadside restaurant during his second return trip to the factory. On the night of the accident, a technical problem at the factory delayed unloading the first load of sulfur. Vaughn's boss told him that to get back on schedule, he would not be able to stop to eat on his second trip, but should instead eat during the delay in unloading the truck. Vaughn therefore set out on his motorcycle toward a nearby restaurant, but was injured in an accident that occurred on the way to the restaurant.

The Court stated that normally "an injury received while using the public streets in going to or returning from the place of employment is not compensable because not incurred in the course of employment." However, the Court noted that exceptions exist when the traveling is "a special mission at the direction of the employer or is ... a service in furtherance of the employer's business." The Court identified the central issue as "whether the action of [Vaughn] in making what was to him an unnecessary trip to get food, at the direction of his employer, constituted the performance of a service in furtherance of the employer's business."

The Court analogized the facts of the case to *Janak v. Texas Employer's Ins. Assoc.*, 381 S.W.2d 176 (1964), in which an employee was injured during a deviation from a direct route to an oil-drilling site to buy ice. The Court in *Janak* had reasoned that given the torrid environment of a southern Texas drill site, ice water was "reasonably essential" for the continuation of the drilling operation. Buying ice was therefore more like "picking up tools essential to the drilling operation," an activity in furtherance of employment, than buying "a particular kind of hamburger," a clearly personal activity.

The Court in *Vaughn* reasoned that in view of Vaughn's lengthy shift, having food was reasonably essential for Vaughn to perform his employment duties, just as having ice was reasonably essential for the oil drilling activities in *Janak*. Driving to the restaurant was not a personal activity because it was only necessary because of APF Co.'s instructions not to stop at the roadside restaurant on the second load. These factors, together with the fact that APF Co. directed Vaughn to drive to the restaurant, support the conclusion that driving to the restaurant was an activity in furtherance of Vaughn's employment.

3. *Jecker v. Western Alliance Ins. Co.*, 369 S.W.2d 776 (1963). Jecker was in charge of sales, delivery, and servicing of appliances for his employer, Bay Chevrolet, Inc. He was killed when returning from a trip to repair a range purchased from Bay and still under warranty. The Court ruled that the rule that bars recovery for injuries sustained injuries incurred while traveling is inapplicable if "the workman is traveling on the public streets or highways pursuant to express or implied requirements of his employment contract." The Court concluded that there was sufficient evidence to sustain the jury's finding that Jecker's trip was "in the furtherance of his employer's business and in the performance of duties imposed by his contract of employment."

4. *U.S. Fire Ins. Co. v. Eberstein,* 711 S.W.2d 355 (1986). The decedent, Dr. Allan Eberstein, had left a golf course where he had participated in a golf tournament and was driving on an interstate highway on his was to visit a patient when he was involved in a fatal car accident. Eberstein was the sole employee of Dr. Allan Eberstein, P.A., which provided the car he drove at the time of the accident and paid all the expenses associated with the car.

The Texas Court of Appeals reversed a judgment in favor of the wife and children of Eberstein, ruling that as a matter of law Eberstein was not in the course of his employment when the accident occurred. The Court held that Eberstein drove to the golf course on a "purely personal mission and, as a result of that personal mission, he had to drive the car on a return trip from the golf course, whether he intended to return home or to visit a patient." The mere fact that transportation was furnished by the employer did not in itself establish that the injury "originated in his word" or "was received while he was engaged in or about the furtherance of the affairs or business of the employer."

Appendix C
Predicates Having Precedents as Warrants

- **in-furtherance-of-employment** (*e.g.*, an employee's working on an assembly line is ordinarily an activity in furtherance of his employment)
  - Precedents of predicate:

    Aetna Cas. Ins. Co. v. Orgon
    Carson v. Industrial Underwriters Ins. Co.
    Vaughn v. Highlands Underwriters Ins. Co.
    Meyer v. Western Fire Ins. Co.
    Jecker v. Western Alliance Ins. Co.
    Liberty Mut. Ins. Co. v. Chesnut
    U.S. Fire Ins. Co. v. Brown
    Janak v. Texas Employer's Ins. Co.
    Typical work activity
    Typical transportation of commodities for hire
  - Precedents of negation of predicate:

    Mapp v. Maryland Cas. Ins. Co.
    Liberty Mut. Ins. Co. v. Preston
    Agricultural Ins. Co. v. Dryden
    Smith v. Dallas County Hospital Dist.
    U.S. Fire Ins. Co. v. Eberstein
    City of Dallas v. Bradford
    Texas Gen. Indem. Co. v. Bottom
    Hackfield v. Pac. Employers Ins. Co.
    Typical commuting to work
    Typical commuting from work

- **reasonably-essential-for** (*e.g.*, having adequate air and light at a job site is reasonably essential for performing employment duties)
  - Precedents of predicate:

    Vaughn v. Highlands Underwriters Ins. Co.
    Janak v. Texas Employer's Ins. Co.

- **passenger-in-business-carpool** (*e.g.*, being a passenger in a car pursuant to a reciprocal agreement to provide transportation to a common work-site)
  - Precedents of predicate:

    Janak v. Texas Employer's Ins. Co.

- **duty** (*e.g.*, a repair person may have an implied duty to drive to the location where the repairs are to be performed)
  - Precedents of predicate:

    Jecker v. Western Alliance Ins. Co.

- **necessitation** (*e.g.*, directing an employee to work late may necessitate that the employee make a trip to a restaurant that would not have been necessary under the customary schedule)
  - Precedents of predicate:

    Vaughn v. Highlands Underwriters Ins. Co.

- **separate-contractual-obligation** (*e.g.*, having an obligation to perform an activity that arises from an agreement distinct from the employment agreement)
  - Precedents of predicate:

    Texas Gen. Indem. Co. v. Bottom

- **necessary-inducement** (*e.g.*, providing free transportation may be necessary to induce employees to accept a job several hours commuting time from their home)
  - Precedents of predicate:

    Liberty Mut. Ins. Co. v. Chesnut

- **overnight-stay-entailed** (*e.g.*, performing job duties at a place sufficiently distant work site may entail staying near the work site overnight)
  - Precedents of predicate:

    Carson v. Industrial Underwriters Ins. Co.

Appendix D
21 Hypothetical Cases

Car-pool Cases 1–3

1. Joan and Donald were employed by the school district as teachers at a middle school and car-pooled together. Each workday, the driver of the car-pool was responsible for picking up some sandwiches on the way to work for both teachers to eat because there was no cafeteria at the school. On the day of the accident, Donald picked up Joan at her house and drove toward the school. Donald then deviated from the direct route to the school on his way to the sandwich shop. Before reaching the sandwich shop, Donald had an automobile accident in which Joan was injured. Does Joan have a claim for worker's compensation against the school district?
2. The same facts as 1, but the accident occurred after Donald had purchased the sandwiches and was back on a direct route to the middle school. Does Joan have a claim for worker's compensation against the school district?
3. The same facts as 1 except that
   - The deviation was to buy magazines for the teachers to read during their lunch break, rather than to buy food, and
   - The teachers were compensated for their expenses in commuting to school.

   Does Joan have a claim for worker's compensation against the school district?

Car-pool Cases 4–6

4. Joan and Donald were employed by the school district as teachers at a middle school. Donald was paid a salary supplement by the school district for providing transportation for Joan to the middle school. Each day the teachers bought sandwiches on the way to work because there was no cafeteria at the school. On the day of the accident, Donald picked up Joan at her house and drove toward the school. Donald then deviated from the direct route to the school on his way to a sandwich shop. Before reaching the sandwich shop, Donald had an automobile accident in which he was injured. Does Donald have a claim for worker's compensation against the school district?
5. The same facts as 1 except that Donald and Joan car-pooled together (thus Donald was not paid a salary supplement for transporting Joan), and Donald decided that as long as he was in the shopping center buying sandwiches, he would pick up some magazines to read at lunch. Before reaching the sandwich shop, Donald had an automobile accident in which he was injured. Does Donald have a claim for worker's compensation against the school district?
6. The same facts as 2, except that
   - The deviation was to buy magazines for the teachers to read during their lunch break, rather than to buy food

- Donald decided that as long as he was in the shopping center buying magazines, he would pick up a sandwich for lunch.

Does Donald have a claim for worker's compensation against the school district?

Journey Cases 1–3

1. Sally lived in the Austin area and was employed as a software engineer by a computer firm, Austin Research. Sally was asked by her supervisor to repair a technical problem in a system used by a Dallas customer of Austin Research requiring several days to fix. Sally drove to Dallas and checked into a Holiday Inn. While carrying her bags down a hallway that had just been mopped, Sally slipped and fell, injuring herself. Does Sally have a claim for worker's compensation benefits against Austin Research for her injury?
2. The same facts as 1 except that during her stay in Dallas Sally decided to drive to the Fort Worth Science Museum. On the way, Sally had an automobile accident. Does Sally have a claim for worker's compensation benefits against Austin Research for her injury?
3. Austin Research had a job of several months duration in San Antonio. To induce Sally, who lived in Round Rock, to accept this job given the lengthy commute, Austin Research agreed to provide free transportation (a van service) to San Antonio. Sally accepted the job, but was injured when the van had an accident midway between Austin and San Antonio. Does Sally have a claim for worker's compensation benefits against Austin Research for her injury?

Jarek's Case

Jarek was employed as a railroad porter by the Denver and Rio Grande railroad. Jarek normally worked from 8:00 A.M. to 5:00 P.M. Because of an unusual workload, Jarek was asked by his employer to work late. Jarek requested and was given permission to walk several blocks home to tell his wife that he would be working late so that she wouldn't worry about him. He slipped and was seriously injured while walking home. Does Jarek have a claim for worker's compensation benefits for his injury?

Goodwrench Cases 1–3

1. Gary Goodwrench was employed to repair and maintain two oil pumping stations by the owner of the pumping stations. Goodwrench supplied his own transportation and set his own hours. Goodwrench was injured when he had an accident driving from the first pump station, on which he had just completed maintenance, to the second pump station. Does Goodwrench have a worker's compensation claim against the pump station owner?
2. The same facts as 1 except that accident occurred when Goodwrench was driving from home to the first pump station. Does Goodwrench have a worker's compensation claim against the pump station owner?

3. The same facts as 1 except that the accident occurred when Goodwrench was driving from the first pump station to a restaurant for a regular lunch break from his maintenance work on the first pump station. Does Goodwrench have a worker's compensation claim against the pump station owner?

Goodwrench Cases 4–7

Gary Goodwrench was employed to repair and maintain two oil pumping stations by the owner of the pumping stations. Goodwrench supplied his own transportation and set his own hours.

4. Goodwrench visited each of the two pump stations every work day. The pump station owner compensated Goodwrench for his traveling expenses. The accident occurred when Goodwrench was driving from home to the first pump station. Does Goodwrench have a worker's compensation claim against the pump station owner?
5. One night, the pump station owner asked Goodwrench to stay late to make emergency repairs at one of the pump stations. Instead of eating dinner at home after work, as he normally did, Goodwrench drove to a nearby fast-food restaurant to pick up some sandwiches to eat during his evening of repair work. Goodwrench was injured in an accident on the way to the restaurant. Does Goodwrench have a worker's compensation claim against the pump station owner?
6. Goodwrench repaired a different pump station every day. Each morning the pump station owner told Goodwrench which of several pump stations needed work, and Goodwrench would drive to that pump station to perform his work. Goodwrench was injured while driving from home to the pump station he had been told to repair that day. Does Goodwrench have a worker's compensation claim against the pump station owner?
7. The same facts as 3 except that there is only a single pump station and Goodwrench was "on call." That is, when a pump station was in need of repair, the pump station owner would call Goodwrench and ask him to travel out to the pump station to make the necessary repairs. Goodwrench was injured in an accident occurring while driving to the pump station in response to a call from the owner. Does Goodwrench have a worker's compensation claim against the pump station owner?

Stanley Cases 1–4

1. Stanley was employed by Tower Construction Company as the head of a surveying crew at a large construction site. Stanley took the surveying tools home with him every night and was responsible for bringing them to the construction site each morning. He was injured in an accident while driving to work on morning carrying the surveying tools in his car. Does Stanley have a claim for worker's compensation against Tower Construction Company for his injuries?
2. The same facts as 1 except that Stanley was paid a separate salary for bringing the surveying tools to the construction site. Does Stanley have a claim for worker's compensation against Tower Construction Company for his injuries?

3. The same facts as 1 except that Stanley owned the tools, leased them to his employer, and was responsible for their maintenance as a condition of the lease agreement. Stanley was injured while driving to a shop to have the tools repaired. Does Stanley have a claim for worker's compensation against Tower Construction Company for his injuries?

4. The same facts as 1 except that Stanley performed some of his job duties—making architectural charts—at home. On the day of the accident, Stanley did some work at home and was driving to the construction site when he had an automobile accident. Does Stanley have a claim for worker's compensation against Tower Construction Company for his injuries?

Appendix E
GREBE's Relation Vocabulary

GREBE's relational vocabulary includes inverses of all relations shown in the table below, e.g., the inverse of *had-duties*, which appears in the table, is *duty*, which does not appear in the table.

accrues	achieves	agent
amount	arises-from	attempt-to
benefit-promised	benefits	business
compensated-activity	compensated-interval	compensation
concurrent	concurrent-subprocess	contained-thing
container	controls	customer
decreases	destination	directed-activity
directee	director	distance
distance-between	driver	employee
employer	enhances	explained-by
facts	frequency	greater-than
had-deviation	had-duties	entailed
had-emotional-need	had-exception	had-family-need
had-fatigue	had-goal	had-home
had-hunger	had-physiological-need	had-recreation-need
had-step	had-thirst	had-thirst
hazard-of	hours	in-furtherance-of-employment
impedes	increases	induced-activity
induced-person	inducement	inducing-thing
industry	industry-custom	influencing-thing
information	information	informee
informer	instrument	intended-activities
intensity	interrupts	inverse
involves	is-greater-than	isa
lessee-obligation	lessor-obligation	listener
location	m-minus	m-plus
name	necessary-inducement	necessitated-activity

necessitated-by
necessitating-activity
necessitation
necessitation-goal
need-of
normal-activities
obligation
occurred-during
originated-in
overnight-stay-entailed
owns
paid-activity
passenger-in-business-carpool
pay
payee
payor
permitted-activity
permittee
permitter
person-directed
physical-demands
possessor
precedent
precedes
prerequisite
prototype-ebe
reasonably-essential-for
reduces
reimbursement
replaced-activity
replacement-activity
requested-activity
requestee
requester
return-trip
rule
source
speaker
specified-in
specifier
state-of
state-of-being-at
subprocess
substitution-goal
temperature
thing-consumed
thing-conveyed
thing-influenced
thing-known
thing-leased
thing-possessed
thing-purchased
thing-read
thing-repaired
thing-there
thing-transported
to-achieve
to-enable
took-place-at
traveler
typicality
uniquely-depends-on
unit
victim
knower

Appendix F
GREBE's Structure Matching Algorithm

GIVEN:

- a new case *NC*
- a proposition, *(Pred* $A_1 \ldots A_n$*)*, to be explained in *NC*, and
- a precedent constituent *PC* for predicate *Pred*, consisting of
  - a set of criterial facts, *T*, represented as tuples, and
  - the proposition *(Pred* $B_1 \ldots B_n$*)* which the precedent constituent explained

DO:

1. Initialize the search frontier *F* with a single node, N having the following fields:
   - N.*mapping*, an initial mapping consisting of the correspondence between the objects in the explained proposition and the objects in the proposition to be explained,
   - N.*tuples-remaining*, a heuristic reordering of the tuples in *T* by estimated importance
   - N.*unmatched-tuples* ← nil
   - N.*proportion-remaining* ← 1.0
   - N.*proportion-unmatched* ← 0.0
   - N.*increment* ← 1/(length *T*)
2. **Repeat** until a result is returned
   (a) Find the node O ϵ *F* for which the proportion-unmatched is least. If several nodes have the same proportion-unmatched, choose one for which the proportion-remaining is least.
   (b) **If** O.*proportion-remaining* = 0.0 **then** return O.*mapping* and O.*unmatched-tuples*
   else
      i. Let *(Pred* $C_1 \ldots C_k$*)* be the first tuple in O.*tuples-remaining*
      ii. Let *M* be the set of mappings from $C_1 \ldots C_k$ onto the objects of *NC* consistent with O.*mapping* under which for each $m \in M$ either
         - *(Pred* $m(C_1) \ldots m(C_k)$) is in *NC*, a *perfect* match, or
         - *(Pred′* $m(C_1) \ldots m(C_k)$) is in *NC*, where *Pred* and *Pred′* are semantically similar, a *partial* match
      iii. **If** $M = \emptyset$ **then**
         - remove *(Pred* $C_1 \ldots C_k$*)* from O.*tuples-remaining* and add it to O.*unmatched-tuples*

- increment O.*proportion-unmatched* by O.*increment*
- decrement O.*proportion.remaining* by O.*increment*

else remove O from F and for each $m \in M$, add a new node O_m to F with the following fields:

- O_m.*tuples-remaining* ← *O.tuples-remaining* − *(Pred* $C_1 \ldots C_k$*)*
- **If** there was a perfect match under m **then**
  - O_m.*unmatched-tuples* ← O.*unmatched-tuples*
  - O_m.*proportion-unmatched* ← O.*proportion-unmatched*

  else
  - O_m.*unmatched-tuples* ← O.*unmatched-tuples* + *(Pred* $C_1 \ldots C_k$*)*
  - O_m.*proportion-unmatched* ← (semantic distance between *Pred* and *Pred′*) ∗ O.*proportion-unmatched*
- O_m.*mapping* ← $m \cup$ *O.mapping*
- O_m.*proportion-remaining* ← O.*proportion.remaining* − O.*increment*

Optionally,[1] if some alternative consistent mapping involving objects $C_1 \ldots C_k$ might be precluded by mappings M, add a node O′ in which (*Pred* $C_1 \ldots C_k$) is unmatched, *i.e.*,

- O′.*unmatched-tuples* ← O.*unmatched-tuples* + *(Pred* $C_1 \ldots C_k$*)*
- O′.*mapping* ← *O.mapping*
- O′.*proportion-unmatched* ← O.*proportion-unmatched* + O.*increment*
- O′.*proportion-remaining* ← O.*proportion.remaining* − O.*increment*
- O′.*tuples-remaining* ← O.*tuples-remaining* − *(Pred* $C_1 \ldots C_k$*)*

The search frontier is stored in a 2–3 tree (Aho et al., 1974) to insure that the search cost of step 2(a) is no greater than the log of the length of the frontier.

[1]Omission of this step leads to a greedy algorithm. GREBE ordinarily operates in greedy mode because GREBE's ordering heuristics insure that the tuples of T are considered in the optimal order. However, these heuristics are specific to the current conventions for representing the facts of worker's compensation cases. In the general case, the greedy mode is not guaranteed to return the best mapping. However, the nongreedy algorithm is much slower. For example, in the mapping from the criterial facts of *Vaughn-ifo-pc* to *Jarek's Case*, the greedy algorithm generates 4 nodes in 37 iterations, whereas the nongreedy algorithm generates 91 nodes in 247 iterations.

Index

About the Author

Karl Branting is associate professor of computer science at the University of Wyoming. He received a B.A. in philosophy from the University of Colorado in 1975, a J.D. from Georgetown University Law Center in 1980, and a Ph.D. in computer science from the University of Texas at Austin in 1991. His research interests include case-based reasoning, machine learning, cognitive modeling, and applications of artificial intelligence to natural resources management, ecology, and law.